DATE DUE

DEMCO 38-296

Romances
with Schools
A Life of Education

John I. Goodlad

McGraw-Hill

New York   Chicago   San Francisco   Lisbon
London   Madrid   Mexico City   Milan   New Delhi
San Juan   Seoul   Singapore   Sydney   Toronto

the "Class of '57," written by Don Reid and
ie of Cash, Inc. (BMI) / administered by Bug
ission.

3 7 6 5 4

ISBN 0-07-143212-4

McGraw-Hill books are available at special quantity discounts to use as premiums and sales pro-
motions, or for use in corporate training programs. For more information, please write to the
Director of Special Sales, Professional Publishing, McGraw-Hill, Two Penn Plaza, New York,
NY 10121-2298. Or contact your local bookstore.

 This book is printed on recycled, acid-free paper containing a minimum of 50%
recycled, de-inked fiber.

Library of Congress Cataloging-in-Publication Data

Goodlad, John I.
  Romances with schools : a life of education / John I. Goodlad.
    p. cm.
Includes bibliographical references (p.   ).
ISBN 0-07-143212-4 (POB : alk. paper)
  1. Goodlad, John I.   2. Educators—United States—Biography.
3. Education—Philosophy   I. Title.
  LB885.G66   2004
  370'.92—dc22

                                                  2003024623

For
all those whose good work
has provided countless others
with warm memories of
a place called school

Contents

Part Three
As a Hybrid Educator

Our memory of experience, our individual pasts, are like trees fallen in a river. The current in the river is the passing of time. . . . But as the current of time keeps flowing, the aging log begins to break down. . . . There are hard, cross-grained whorls of memory that remain inexplicably lodged in us long after the straight-grained narrative material that housed them has washed away. . . . These are our "river teeth"—the time-defying knots of experience that remain in us after our autobiographies are gone.

David James Duncan
River Teeth (New York: Bantam, 1995), pp. 3–4.

Acknowledgments

Nearly a decade ago, Phyllis Edmundson gave me a little book of memoirs entitled *Inventing the Truth* and suggested I write one. Given the book's title, I decided that, should I do so, I need not worry about the vagaries of my memory. I had no interest in writing even a fanciful story about me, but the idea of a memoir about schools as I had experienced them over a long period of years appealed. Thank you, Phyllis, for getting me started.

I wrote three chapters and requested comments from colleagues— too many to name here. They recommended that I continue, but that was the only agreement among the group. The manuscript went into a file drawer where it remained for a couple of years. My thanks to them is genuine but muted. In part because of David Imig's nagging and Roger Soder's occasional queries as to how I was doing, I recommenced the work, producing three new chapters and, without further consultation, revised the initial three. I thank you both. And my appreciation goes to all of you for teaching me what I should have learned years ago: If you want to make progress with a book, sharply limit seeking input from others.

When I next picked up the manuscript after another long delay, my list of friendly critics consisted of just three: Corinne Mantle-Bromley, Stephen Goodlad, and Paula McMannon. The father-son relationship with Stephen and my somewhat higher titular authority (without commensurate power) in the democratic hierarchy of the Institute for Educational Inquiry assured smooth sailing to the finish line. Thank you for making the final lap of the journey less bumpy than the early ones. Special recognition goes to Paula for her keen sense of what I was trying to accomplish and sharp editorial eye. Timothy J. McMannon managed to find time to join her in a final reading and editing. Thanks very much, Tim, for your customary good work. I am indebted to Frank Charles Winstead for capping production of the book by contributing from his wonderful photos of bygone schools days the one that adorns the dustjacket.

I have dedicated several previous books to a person variously known to friends and relatives as Lynn, Len, and (to our children) Irving, whose given name is Evalene. This time, she is a major player in my story as irreplaceable partner and companion. There is no way to express in public my love and appreciation. Fortunately, as always, she did not ask to take a peek at what I was putting on paper, or this book would still be a work in progress awaiting our agreement on the truth.

Some names among the many people referred to in this manuscript are fictitious, largely because my memory failed to bring back those they were given, but some names remembered I changed for reasons not always rational.

John I. Goodlad

Part One

As a Pupil

North Star School
(Courtesy of North Vancouver Museum and Archives,
British Columbia, Canada)

Chapter 1

The Early Years

The interior life is in constant vertical motion; consciousness runs up and down the scales every hour like a slide trombone. It dreams down below; it notices up above; and it notices itself, too, and its own alertness.

ANNIE DILLARD[1]

The wooden sidewalk ended at the edge of the spacious playground. There before me was what I had only imagined before—North Star School. I turned and ran.

Anticipating this day, I had been curious and excited. Curious because I had never seen a school. Excited because of vignettes brought home by two older brothers. Andy's were of the extracurricular. Bill's were of in-school exploits and personalities.

For Andy, school had been peripheral. On reaching the legal leaving age of fourteen the year before, he had quit. By fibbing about his age, he had become the proud driver of the local grocer's delivery truck for the handsome weekly wage of ten dollars (roughly equal to our family's income at the time). The Andy who departed home and school early and whom I came to know best as an adult spoke seldom of school. I recall only his occasional bitter comments about the school's early and unsuccessful efforts to make of him a right-handed rather than a left-handed writer.

For Bill, school was a kind of cinematic adventure with himself as actor and cameraman—both in the parade and watching it, somewhat in the fashion of the then-contemporary writer F. Scott Fitzgerald. He whetted my anticipation of his favorite teacher, Miss Frith, heroine of

3

the school drama: pretty, fair, strict, and fun. (Alas, she and I just missed coming together.)

Bill's challenges in moving through the grades were not those encountered on the paths of reading, writing, and arithmetic but were of the fences marking the boundaries. For him, fences were to be tested, climbed, and cleared. Not surprisingly, then, by the time he reached the eighth grade, taught by Principal Dobson, Bill and Mr. Dobson were quite well acquainted. The chief keeper of the fences and one of the school's most experienced and skilled fence challengers could now keep close watch on one another.

For the first few years of my life, then, North Star School was a story, not a place: a story created out of bits and pieces of information and my imagination. It shimmered, along with other fantasies, among the realities of a happy daily existence. Meal and bed times varied little; nor did bedtime prayers and Sunday school. Beyond these regularities, I ran free, spanked only once, I think, and gently. By now, repeating the much stricter child-rearing regimen experienced by my brothers had no appeal for my parents.

The richness of my life on a rural mountainside connected hardly at all with the economic poverty that was our lot (I learned only later). Nor did it connect meaningfully and appreciatively with how my father managed to earn a few dollars with his skilled hands of carpenter-cabinetmaker, given his damaged lungs (from the post–World War I flu epidemic that had preceded my birth). Nor with what he and my mother did to put food on the table by tending to the chickens, a grievously misbehaving cow, and an extensive fruit and vegetable garden.

Lacking friends and knowledge of friendship, I missed neither. Whatever void there otherwise might have been was filled with the imaginary Bobby and Tommy in sunny "Calibefornia"—that far-off dreamland that so beckoned in later life. I wrote the script for our conversations, and so we never quarreled. I planned to visit them some day. Where my vision of a sunny place with orange trees came from I do not know.

William James must have had adults in mind when he spoke of our diurnal experience as "a big blooming buzzing confusion," as did Irwin Edman in describing life for most people as "a drowsy reverie, interrupted by nervous thrills." For me, those early years were rhapsodic. Yes, the pieces of music were disconnected, but each summer assured the continuity of raspberries, green transparent apples, yellow plums the size of chicken eggs, and small speckled trout slowly moving their tails in the cold water of a little stream. Winters, too, were predictable: the first snowflakes settling slowly on leaves about to fall, the magic of Christmas, and disastrous sleigh rides on the ten-inch tailgate of Bill's homemade toboggan. Should there ever have been any doubt in my mind about God's being in His Heaven and all being right with the world, it was dispelled night after night by the soothing rhythm of rain on a roof not insulated against the cacophony of the elements.

Images of North Star School, conjured up by Bill's ongoing narrative, had flickered in and out of my experience like the galaxies in the frequently cloudy skies of coastal British Columbia. As the summer of my sixth birthday approached September (it was, at that stage of life, a long, long time from June to September), these images entered more and more into the conversations with Bobby and Tommy. But I had little vocabulary for them; the images remained chimeric.

North Star School. The name had a romantic appeal. Do children everywhere look in awe for the North Star and then the Big Dipper? Or do these become commonplace and lose their luster when the skies commonly are clear? Summer fades early north of the forty-ninth parallel. With the coming of September, the blaze of light I had created around North Star School dimmed appreciably, too. Perhaps there were some things my brothers hadn't told me. An unease crept uninvited into my being. I became mildly claustrophobic.

YEAR ONE

Day One

The first day of school had arrived. With it came sensations of near terror. In retrospect, I believe it was less the pending near unknown that unnerved me than a sense of the known gone, perhaps forever. The days of my short life had been filled with little romances stirred mostly by the flora and fauna of my environment, romances that frequently led to intriguing fantasies. Nothing until this day had suggested the possibility that all this might end. I was fearful.

My first day of school had not the decency to dawn miserably. Being restrained inside school by driving rain might have eased the pain of being denied a day of paradise outside in my special place on earth. Instead, the morning was obscene in its physical loveliness.

Down the dirt road of the Timber Mountain foothills we went, Mother and I, to the paved Carisbrook Street, then through the park (where I would later often tarry on the way home from school) to the main artery, Lonsdale Avenue. A short walk southward brought us to the electric streetcar terminal and the tracks straight down the center of Lonsdale, with but one bend to the ferryboats that connected North Vancouver to the goods and delights of the metropolis, Vancouver. This was familiar territory.

But at the terminal, we turned abruptly westward into the unfamiliar. I took my mother's hand. Soon, we came to the end of the wooden sidewalk. There stood the source of my claustrophobia—a two-story prison just beyond the intervening ground. I fled.

Kenny took me in tow before I had run twenty yards. The two Moir boys were near neighbors, a quarter of a mile or more distant. Kenny was in age about halfway between me and our two older brothers, Norm and Bill. It was his frequent fate to be left behind with me on those precious Saturday afternoons when Norm and Bill ditched us both, after chores were done, to explore the hills. Kenny saw me safely placed among children grouped at the bottom of a long stairway leading to a schoolhouse doorway, from which there appeared a teacher clanging the five-minute warning bell—the kind that is now a collector's pride.

This was not the building I had first seen. It was the lower school of two, physically and academically housing the first six grades on the lowest of four plateaus. Above each of the two plateaus on which the school buildings were separately located were generous-sized playing fields with soccer (football to us) goals at the ends. The building I had first seen embraced the seventh and eighth grades, a manual arts shop, a tiny library, the principal's tinier office, and the "boiler room"—Mr. Smyth's sanctuary. As matters turned out, I never reached the upper classes of North Star School. I came to see just the inside of the library, and this only for the brief time it took to obtain and return books.

Officially, Mr. Smyth was the school's janitor (the designation "custodian" came much later). In the culture of North Star School, however, he was much more. Although Principal Dobson's physical presence beyond the upper school (where he and just one other teacher taught the two classes of seventh- and eighth-grade pupils) was relatively infrequent, and often dramatic, Mr. Smyth's was virtually ubiquitous. If he was not at the edge of the school grounds watching children arrive in the morning and leave in the afternoon, or in a hallway as children sought the bathrooms, or calming the clamor in the basement "pit" where dozens of us chased a small ball on rainy days, we anticipated his imminent arrival. Not a big man, he was, nonetheless, a formidable one. A long stare from those dark eyes or a twitch of his drooping black mustache was enough to get one's heart beating faster. Principal Dobson's authority and Mr. Smyth's presence went unquestioned.

That first day wasn't so bad after all. With the second ringing of the handheld bell, other teachers appeared at the top of the stairs. We were quickly sorted into groups and herded into our respective classrooms. For most of the children, since this was the only school they had attended, little direction was needed. For those of us embarking on our first romance, the carefully planned regimen left little room for creativity. We were soon seated, quiet, and attentive.

What followed is blurred; I remember few details. Miss Laing introduced herself, laid down some rules and expectations, handed out a textbook or two (with clear, firm instructions as to their use), and gave each of us a note to our parents regarding the pencil and notebook that were our responsibility to purchase and have in hand the following day. There may have been more; I don't recall. I joined Harvey, a somewhat more distant neighbor than Kenny and the only person known to me in the class, and we headed for home. Free once more and the day still young.

Day Two

Next day, after passage of about the same amount of time as the day before, we were dismissed at the ringing of a bell, presumably from the top of the now-familiar outside stairs. We were free; much of the day remained; Harvey and I reconnoitered. From Bill, I had heard of a stream somewhat further to the west where he and Norm Moir had fished. Harvey and I ventured forth toward this unexplored mecca.

The creek proved to be sturdy, its waters still moving briskly after two months of the near-rainless summer. Lacking hooks and line, we had no expectations of serious fishing. Rather, we worked at cornering minnows—tiny trout—among the rocks and scooping them into the rusty cans we had been farsighted enough to search out and pick up along the way. By early afternoon, we were headed home with our catch.

About to cut through the school grounds, we became victims of inspiration and fate. We would show our prizes to Miss Laing who might still be there. Indeed, she probably slept there. We burst into her classroom and stood transfixed. Class was still in session.

We were in deep trouble. Miss Laing's harangue slowly penetrated. It takes a little while for one's spirits to fall from buoyancy to the bottom of the pit. We were truants already. Further, we had broken the law in catching and keeping the baby trout. (There was at that time, I later learned, an eight-inch minimum.) We were not just bad boys. We were *stupid little boys*.

The bell that had sent us jubilantly on our way had been for the fifteen-minute midmorning recess. Weeks passed before Harvey and I were allowed the luxury of this daily break. I think our sentence was shortened because Miss Laing wanted out of the prison duty of watching over us. She, too, needed recess.

I never quite warmed to Miss Laing after that. I didn't think she was wrong, although I thought that the punishment did not seem to quite fit the crime because I had difficulty seeing the event as a crime. The loss of recess was an inconvenience. It was the humiliation that hurt—feeling naked during the overdone scolding before thirty pairs of unbelieving eyes. I didn't dislike Miss Laing; I only felt that she had made a mistake, just as Harvey and I had. But she knew the regularities of school; we did not.

A curious thought comes to me. In three quarters of a century of close association with schools, I have encountered little reference to what must be one of the most abrupt passages of life—that from home one day to school the next. From privacy to public space with no place to hide. From center stage one day to anonymity in the chorus the next. From relative freedom to considerable restraint. From personal possessions to shared group possessions. From the familiar to the unfamiliar; from known to unknown boundaries. Is there any greater potential culture shock?

Schools are an adult creation intended to shape adulthood. They perform a relatively inexpensive and safe custodial role with all taxpayers contributing to the public purse. What would the daily lives of adults be like without them? Our society without schools would be more restrictive on adult mobility than our society without automobiles. Children linked unsupervised to the Internet is no substitute for children linked to Sally Smith's classroom for six hours each day.

What is the interior life of each child on that critically important first day of school? Why is the setting of nursery school for the four-year-old so different from that of the first-grader in "school"? Why is the school setting not more like an ideal home setting as Jane Roland Martin proposes in her imaginative book, *The Schoolhome*?[2]

Most of us regard the way schools are as the way they ought to be. What would the passage from home to school be like if we designed it with the children in mind? Would all those who would reach their fifth or sixth birthdays before September 30 be the ones not having to wait another year to enter kindergarten or the first grade as is the case now? Or might those turning five or six in October, November, December, and so on enter on their birthdays? And why not a birthday party on that historic day of being allowed to go to the place called school? And then those who have been celebrated could participate in the birthdays of those to arrive later. Each child receives; each child gives. How novel and innovative it would be to design schools for and, in part, with children. In what ways would they be significantly different?

Mr. Partridge

I hated Mr. Partridge. There is a line in the musical play, *South Pacific,* about our having to be carefully taught to love and to hate, to hate all the people our relatives hate. Some hates come on full-blown. Mr. Partridge was one of these.

I had not known any hates at home, neither the ones that arise quickly nor those that are slow to build. There were people my parents didn't warm to. My father boiled over when our nearest neighbor spread the rumor that he faked bouts of being bedridden to avoid regular work—because, said Mr. Baker, he looks so well. But that didn't stop my father from going to Baker's aid when that need arose. The woman my mother viewed as an irresponsible mother never knew that her son, Harvey, lives to this day because of my mother's quick actions during still another absence of his mother. My parents took their Bible seriously, and I think they knew what "love thy neighbor" means.

I am awed to this day, then, by the suddenness and the voltage of the hate that coursed through my being that winter afternoon many, many years ago. And, from my adult perspective, by how little triggered it. Perhaps it was because hate and I had been such strangers to one another.

The school year was several weeks along when Miss Laing announced, with more than routine explanation, that a Mr. Partridge would be with us a couple of days each week to conduct us in singing. We were privileged, we were given to understand, that Mr. Partridge would give time to us younger children when he usually concentrated on choral groups in the upper grades. We were to grace his presence with our rapt attention and cooperation.

I didn't warm to Mr. Partridge, but, in the spirit of my parents, I attempted to give him respect. I don't think he liked children. I imagined that he always washed his hands after being with us—over a period of time that turned out, blessedly, to be short.

We memorized and sang, in inharmonious chorus, an assortment of old ditties Mr. Partridge exhumed from his childhood in England. Little of this connected in any way with our lives. But I must admit to still occasionally humming at times a sorrowful tune that went, more or less, like this:

Early one morning just as the sun was r-i-i-sing,
I heard a maiden singing in the valley below:
"Oh, never grieve me; oh, never leave me;
How could you u-u-se a poor maiden so?"

Mr. Partridge scowled, scolded, cajoled, threatened, all the time waving his flexing baton, but we never exuded gusto, let alone harmony. We did enjoy dragging out "r-i-i-sing" and "u-u-se" far beyond what was intended, which didn't help matters. I have been told that there is no such thing as a monotone, in the sense of inability to produce more than one note, but I came close to qualifying for Mr. Partridge. And Mr. Partridge had sniffed me out early on. He descended on me in the middle of a ditty. His thin baton flicked hard across the center of my head, front to back (or so it felt). Hate overwhelmed me, holding in the tears before they could fall (or so it seemed).

Mr. Partridge never again came close to me. Was he ashamed? Did he see in my eyes the resolve to climb like a monkey all over him if he ever did that again? Mr. Partridge never came to know the favor he did me in filling up so much of the space one might reserve for hate as to make me inhospitable to new entries. Nor did he come to know how much he stirred my later passion for the place called school to be a romantic rite of passage for all children. Some weeks later, North Star School closed for the afternoon out of respect for the announced funeral services of Mr. Sterling Partridge. I didn't attend; nor did I experience any sorrow. But I did think it would have been better for both of us if he had just moved on to someplace else on earth.

Learning of my connection with a school or university, people newly met over the years invariably have asked me what grade or what subject I taught. My answer almost always takes care of teaching as a subject of conversation. The door to further elucidation closes, much as the classroom door closes once the students are seated. I find it fascinating that almost everyone is almost as ready to talk about their school experiences as they are the weather and yet find so little to pursue when the perspective is *teaching* in schools. Is this because schoolteachers are not observed in their daily work as are salespeople, police officers, carpenters, and road repair workers? As Dan Lortie and Philip Jackson point out in their books, *Schoolteacher* and *Life in Classrooms*,[3] respectively, teachers are at center stage for a small group in isolation from the workaday world of other adults.

Miss Laing was never in the classroom with Mr. Partridge. Today, teachers' observing or teaming with other teachers in the classroom is still considered innovative. The process of teaching is rarely on display. It should not surprise us, then, that attention to schools is, to some degree, on inputs such as instructional materials and, to a much greater extent, on tangible outcomes such as musical performances, exhibitions of student work, interschool sports, test scores, and report cards. Proposals for school "reform" are primarily addressed to outputs. On the selection of teachers as inputs, people with subject majors in college but with no other preparation in teaching and retired military personnel rank high. For many people, discipline—the subject of instruction and the strict control implied—are what teachers and schools are all about.

It is rarely the pedagogy of our teachers we remember. Rather, it is their classroom personalities. Teachers teach who they are. Who they are is ubiquitous, influencing each of us more than we know, day after day, year after year during the portion of that fifth or sixth of the life span now spent in schools. The history or mathematics they taught or failed to teach us pales in comparison with what they taught us about being human. I learned little or nothing about music from Mr. Partridge but a good deal about who I am as a human being.

Most Days

It bothers me a bit that a few negative days at schools stand out in my mind. Perhaps it is because they so contrast with an overall benign image that has few specific markers. Rather than a big blooming buzzing confusion, my perception of school is more of a stroll through a garden, sometimes among flowers, berries, and fruit; sometimes among barren, leafless trees and shrubs. The walks home, which would not have occurred had school not existed, are more sharply etched in my mind than are the days in school from 9:00 to 3:15.

In the fall, there was crunching through maple leaves, inches high in the grass of the park, and picking a few richly patterned red, gold, yellow, and green leaves for the inevitable drawing and painting in class. In winter and early spring, there was the certain and invariably disastrous contest of testing water's surface tension. Ditches, often deep, ran along the sides of most roads to carry off the water that found its way down the mountainsides. On rainy days, we wore "gumboots" that rose to a few inches below the knees. The contest was to wade deeper and deeper into the clear-running ditches without going quite deep enough to bring the cold, cold liquid over the tops and around one's toes. There were no winners. After dumping out the overflow and wringing out the socks, the choice was going sockless or squashing the rest of the way home in the soggy wool. The cold interiors of the gumboots were no deterrents at all to participation in the next contest.

I was nervous throughout that first year and was absent quite often—not for long periods but for a day or two at a time—after my mother decided just before it was time for me to leave that my heaving stomach augured a bad day at school. She then suffered guilt when, after an hour or so, she yielded to my plea that I was well enough to go outside and play. I had to be careful to judge my timing and her mood to avoid the occasional decision to send me late with an explanatory note. Thanks to a sensitive stomach—*that* I did not fake—I enjoyed a somewhat shortened school year.

I was on the verge that first year of following in my brother Andy's footsteps. I had built no claque of admirers as Bill had for his courage.

There was no teacher I admired, as Bill did Miss Frith, even though she and her class only lived on in his memory. That was, I think, when I became aware of and made friends with Albert, whom I thought enough of to introduce to my mother when he and I chanced to encounter her on one of her rare long trips to the few shops scattered about the street-car terminal.

A kind of cloud hung around Albert. The conventional wisdom among his classmates was that we were to keep away lest we get rained on. And, sure enough, there was virtually a daily altercation around him, with someone crying out to Miss Laing and Albert remonstrating that he hadn't meant to do it or take it. Albert knew well the route to Principal Dobson's office.

Albert was at the periphery, physically as well as socially and academically. The trips to Mr. Dobson's office sometimes resulted in expulsion—a rare and dreaded phenomenon in those days. With little truancy or expulsion, there usually was no one out there for Albert to join. And so he came to the edge of the playgrounds on each day of suspension silently observing our play, forbidden by the rules to step over the assumed line or to speak to us. Mr. Smyth's ubiquitous presence assured observance of these rules.

My mother felt sorry for Albert. She explained the cloud as having something to do with his not having a proper family, poor boy. I, too, felt sorry for Albert, but somehow I found reasons for admiration. The feelings of admiration were mutual; perhaps it had something to do with our differences. I sometimes brought to the conversations that characterized our evening meal news of Albert's latest exploits, clearly with admiration in my words and tone. My father invariably pressed me a little on the nature of these exploits and particularly on their observed consequences. Then he would ask, "Do you really want to be like Albert?" I think it was questions like this and other school-directed suppertime conversations that kept me securely within the enveloping membrane of school and classroom culture. In those days, the evening meal was a major educator of the young.

The classroom contingencies of that first school year are blurred. But sometime quite far along—probably in late winter—I became aware that something about my niche in this culture was amiss. It had to do with reading.

Several weeks earlier, Mr. Dobson had introduced to us a teacher who would take Miss Laing's place for a week. School had been canceled for a day earlier in the year so that all the teachers could attend a meeting. This was something different. Mr. Dobson spoke with pride of a special opportunity for Miss Laing to bring back to us some of the new developments in teaching—at least that's what I recall.

I thought I had been managing satisfactorily the occasions of standing and reading sentences and paragraphs from the reader and the workbook assignments that followed. Finished, I was left alone with my thoughts. Now, however, with Miss Laing back, we were directed, several at a time, to the chalkboard. My mind is as confused now as I think it was then about what followed. After chalking a vertical line to demarcate my space from my neighbor's, I printed out bits and pieces of words, putting marks over some of the letters, in accordance with Miss Laing's instructions.

None of this made any sense to me; I couldn't connect it with anything. Miss Laing appeared to be as frustrated with this, each time she came by, as I was. Her frustration arose, I think, out of my not "getting" it, and her not knowing why and (with time passing by) not being able to help me. I tensed up when she approached this haphazard exercise from which I derived no line of potentially corrective attack. Then I became aware that I shared this dreaded daily experience of not getting it with only a few others. What I later came to know as the phonics approach to reading wasn't working. I was overcome one more time with naked exposure.

A surge in the joy of experiencing efficacy came late in the year from an unexpected source. Early each June there was an all-day, all-school track and field extravaganza. I had never run competitively. But I ran a lot for the sheer joy of it, rolling in the grass and gasping for air when ultimately winded. Often I ran downhill, sometimes nearly all the way to school. On many of these occasions, I reached that exhilarating state runners talk about when awareness of breathing and of the feet touching the ground disappears. Presumably, I reached that state of "flow" described by Mihaly Csikszentmihaly in which, performing at one's very best, one rises above worldly matters of time and space.[4] Ultimately, one stops, not winded but now conscious of breathing. I sometimes reached this state on level ground, especially with a breeze at my back. The euphoria and the sheer joy came back to me years later, when *Forrest Gump* ran right out of his boots and across the field to safety from the chasing automobile. I ran beside Forrest, my feet a few inches from the ground, laughing out loud in the theater.

That is the way I ran that bright day in June. I took first prize in several races. But it was Miss Laing who laughed in joy. The teachers helped out with the egg-and-spoon races. Miss Laing put the egg in the spoon for me.

Endings

Alas, Miss Laing did not transfer her admiration for my running to the academic domain. The report card I carried home with me on that last school day of the year announced that I would be with her for a repeat of the first grade. I had flunked.

I am not at all sure that the implications of this development sank in. Summer had arrived, and, with it, freedom once more. I cast no blame or anger on Miss Laing, then or now. What I learned about her later told me that she was a serious professional, striving to become better. Perhaps the runner she had observed convinced her that we could now run together in reading.

I don't know what my parents read into the decision. They didn't agree with it and requested a hearing with Principal Dobson. I believe that it was the only time they entered directly into the life of the school on my behalf. If I got into trouble at school, I endured an inquisition at home. They had not, however, said a word to me or to Miss Laing about the second-day fishing expedition and the subsequent curtailment of recess (news of which had been formally conveyed by North Star School). I think they disagreed with her judgment on that episode but chose to remain silent.

Not this time. Miss Laing joined Mr. Dobson for the hearing. By telephone (yes, it had been invented by now, but since we shared the ringing with other families, it offered little privacy), my parents had learned that my failure was one of not learning to read. Now my father wished that he had intervened sooner.

The story my parents later told me is that I was reading a little before I began school. Nothing much in sequence but a veritable handbag full of words: on the cereal boxes, bits of the newspaper comic strips, the billboards above the windows of the streetcars, miscellaneous signs, and so on. Then, sometime quite far along in the school year—probably in late winter—I began in the evenings to read out loud from the primer. Presumably, I wasn't reading to anyone in particular, but before beginning, I always established myself nearby at a time of relative silence when I was sure to be heard. My parents were very pleased for a while and then puzzled.

On one occasion, my father noticed that my turning of the pages didn't coincide with my reading of them, or vice versa. I had memorized the text. Perhaps the same was going on in my reading aloud when called upon in class. This may have contributed to Miss Laing's puzzlement on finding me not able to perform whatever word conjugations she had assigned for me and several others at the chalkboard and yet accurate in my repetition of the text. From considerable word recognition before school, I had regressed to illiteracy some months later.

My parents thought it best that I be given a fresh start in the second grade, assuring Mr. Dobson and Miss Laing that they would blame nobody but themselves if things failed to work out. Principal Dobson supported their recommendation. Perhaps Miss Laing saw a challenge slipping away from her. She was somewhat less than gracious in predicting that no good would come of it.

I knew little about the regularities of schooling and didn't feel very strongly one way or the other. And summer had arrived.

The primary grade classrooms of my time up to the near present were incredibly people-oriented and people-dependent. The artifacts were few and simple, completely lacking technological connections with the world beyond. There was no "Wendy House," as in the English Infant School (the primary years), in which to seek occasional sanctuary. There were teachers' lavatories but no teachers' room, and so the best in privacy Miss Laing could hope for was to move us out of the classroom at recess and lunchtime. On the many rainy days, we sought refuge in the basement "pit," or under the eaves, or just got wet.

In the classroom, the pupils connected or disconnected with one another through the muted language of eye and body movements. We were often amazed by Miss Laing's accurate interpretation of what we thought was covert. She set the tone for most of the interpersonal relationships and movements, like a mother mallard duck but with a much larger brood. The connections were far more personal than curricular. Unlike secondary and higher schooling, there were no textbooks, essays, and the like around which to spar. The family comes to mind as a parallel, but more in the abstract than in reality. Few families spend this much time together.

What strikes me most forcefully now about the primary classrooms and, indeed, the elementary school classrooms I have encountered since is the teacher's isolation in combination with relentless exposure to children in a small space. What must be the impact on a teacher's psyche over time, especially in small communities where private lives often are so public?

As a former teacher at all grade levels, I am now sharply aware of how alone Miss Laing was all day as an adult and as a teacher. She did not join colleagues for lunch in a nearby coffee shop as adult workers commonly do. She did not share any teaching activity or engage more than casually in conversation with fellow teachers about matters of consequence to those of us who were her only companions each school day. There was no one to help her with me.

And so, had my parents not intervened, I would have faced beginning a second year in the first grade—a situation comparable in stress to what I had faced on my first day at North Star School. Pernicious elements enter schooling to complicate the lonely decision making of teachers. What recourse do they have in seeking to deal with what often is patent nonsense? What schools might be like if designed for children boggles the mind. And schools would become infinitely more interesting places for adults and cause teaching to become one of our most appealing professions. Our concept of teaching in schools would be profoundly changed.

INTERLUDE

Saturdays lost their special preciousness in summer. Every day was precious, once chores were taken care of. With more hours spent around and near home, there was less to report at suppertime. Mealtime was shorter; evening prayers individualized; several hours of additional daylight beckoned; bedtime waited for darkness to come. Lying on our backs in the grass or on the roof of our chicken coop, we watched for the first stars and then, with the North Star growing brighter, traced the outline of the Big Dipper and then the little one. Some mornings, Bill would assist me out of the bedroom window for a barefoot run across the dew-laden grass to pick a few Italian plums or whatever was ripe. Oh, what a wonderful world!

Sometimes, even the trek to Sunday school was welcomed because of the occasional ferry trip to Vancouver and the picnic to follow in Stanley Park with my mother's brother's family. With his high school days now approaching, Bill's graduation from Sunday school was imminent, and he might have been excused earlier had he not been required to accompany me. I don't know how my mother managed to find a nickel for each of us so that we could buy a soft drink afterward.

I think it was during that August of my seventh birthday that Bill and I decided to challenge a basic principle of gravity. It was one of those Sundays with a pending visit from my father's two brothers and their wives from Vancouver. When they came, it was for dinner—quite thoughtless, I now think, about the burden they placed on my mother and our finances. They were the prosperous relatives. Uncle Andy and Aunt Mary (my, how parsimonious the list of names to choose from in those days) were members of that elite group of automobile owners, an asset that enabled them to bring ice cream from the store at the streetcar terminal—ice cream just beginning to melt by the time of their arrival.

Bill's option and mine was whether to change out of our Sunday school clothes for the uncertain hours of awaiting the arrival or to keep them on and stay out of messes. On this particular Sunday, we chose the latter. With boredom setting in, we decided on a walk, keeping in sight of the road that would bring the ice cream car into view. We walked up beside the deep water overflow ditch that paralleled the road, the stream still running moderately in late summer. We then crossed the wooden bridge of a logging road and began our return on the other bank. Arriving opposite the path that would lead us home, but on the other side of the ditch, we debated whether to go on to the next crossing or to return by the logging road bridge. Bill suggested a third alternative.

The bank on which we stood was slightly higher than the other. He was confident that he could jump the gulf between, which was deeper but narrower at this point. Clearly, I could not. But there was open running space back of the bank. By joining hands, coordinating our running speed, and perfectly timing our joint leap, we might make it. We practiced, the process of stopping in time upsetting our rhythm. We decided that our time had come.

I had grown quite a bit during the summer and had put a bit of flesh on my skinny frame. But surely my now-longer legs would compensate. One . . . two . . . three . . . go. We were off. Almost simultaneously with leaving the bank's edge, I dropped like a stone. Bill's effort to save me before letting go of my hand, taking but a fraction of a second, was sufficient to bring him down beside me. We were a mess in our Sunday best. I'm still not quite clear on why our experiment didn't work. Perhaps we didn't have a tailwind. The only flow we experienced was that of the cool ditch water coursing around our feet and legs. How different the ambience of our time and place from that of the young today. How different the ambience of the schools.

YEAR TWO

The Fresh Start

Harvey and I talked of the pending school year as if we were heading down into the valley of doom. But I found myself to be mildly excited. It was becoming a little difficult to find new and interesting things to do. Summer had recovered a bit after a sudden slippage, but the days had lost some of their warmth, and the evenings, sneaking up earlier each day, required a sweater or jacket. School was in the air.

During the summer, I had come to know the Stackhouse boys—Harold and Tommy—and had played with them several times, almost always on their own turf, which they were either reluctant or not allowed to leave. Although they lived closer than did Harvey, they were a little younger, didn't yet go to school, and were not precisely on my trajectory of travel. The discovery of the tangible Harold and Tommy probably hastened into the mists of the past the imagined Tommy and his brother, Bobby.

I was to be off to school on my own this year. But, a few days before, Mrs. Stackhouse asked my mother if I would pick up Harold on what would be his first day. I was pleased to do so. I was a big boy now—and a veteran. I would pass along to Harold all the inside stuff. Harvey joined us on the way, and we were three strong.

It was nice to rejoin so many old buddies at the bottom of the school steps. A mark of my confidence and knowledge was to escort Harold up the steps. But, over the summer, I apparently had forgotten Joy Dobson—not an easy slip of mind. Joy, Principal Dobson's daughter, had emerged the previous year as a chief protector of girldom. She and her female companions had taken over the top several steps as their castle and, most mornings, defied the boys to seize it. The first who tried were thrown down personally by Joy, unassisted. Rumor had it that a couple of the bigger boys in the lower school had been individually beaten up by Joy. They vigorously denied it but issued no challenges. To be beaten up by a girl—not a very big one at that—would be an embarrassment too great to bear. I backed Harold down the steps just in time.

Joy was strong and quick, no doubt about that. And gorgeous. Every boy in her age group probably was secretly in love with her at one time or another—and too vigorously denied it. Some admitted to lingering near her home from time to time; just out of curiosity, of course.

Joy was very much at the center of the rising boy-girl tension characterizing our age group, and in a positive way, I think. One had to be careful about one's teasing or answer to Joy. A slur upon another girl was a slur upon girlhood, sufficient to warrant a bloodied nose. We even had to be careful about where and how we recited the ditty we had forged from the names of two girls, with no words added: "Mary, Uno Marjorie Dunnitt." It was known that Joy could run you down to avenge. All this from such a pretty girl. Our respect for her spilled over, probably enough to instill in us some awe of and respect for the female species.

The established culture of North Star School spoke to more than reading, writing, and arithmetic. Boys especially were to be civilized. Developing respect for one another, our teachers, certain rules of behavior, and girls and women was part of the process. It was assumed, apparently, that savagery was more easily stirred in males than in females. This necessitated some special protection for women. We knew that discourtesy to one of our teachers—all women—brought the immediate attention of Principal Dobson. At the end of the day, we felt the eyes of Mr. Dobson or Mr. Smyth, unseen, upon our behavior until we passed from sight beyond the bushes framing the sidewalk.

Bill's descriptions of Mr. Dobson's sudden appearances on the playground were etched in my mind even before I saw several with my own eyes in my first year. One of these might be triggered by a bully running to trip a smaller boy and be gone. Within a few steps, he would be overtaken by Mr. Dobson who, reaching out with that steel hook Bill had described, caught the miscreant by the collar, jerking him sharply back onto his seat.

The hook had replaced the hand lost in the Great War—"the war to end all wars." His daughter would have been born just a couple of years after its end and named Joy—perhaps to symbolize her parents' feelings about the ending of that bloody conflict. I realize today how respected for his stewardship of North Star School Principal Dobson must have been at that time of still raw feelings toward "the enemy," given his known active participation in the postwar peace movement. He and Mr. Smyth virtually assured a peaceful, good citizenship-producing custodial role for the community's major guiding star, our school. Joy's contribution was best known to her schoolmates.

With summer over, the child-rearing role of parents was considerably lightened for five days each week, days that would quickly shorten, enveloping each domicile in early darkness. There was no television, let alone movie rating scales or parked automobiles; the church (I don't recall a non-Christian edifice) made its contributions on weekends—not only with religious services on Sunday mornings but often with Friday evening all-girl and all-boy games and social activities. Home, school, and church were quite closely linked in the delicate process of child rearing.

Where did the local movie house stand in the campaign to eradicate savagery in the young? The Saturday matinee was the big attraction, to be taken advantage of whenever one could come by the necessary fifteen cents. However, the manager was not about to bring in a picture that would jumpstart his telephone and even trigger a boycott. Besides, the cartoons were harmless nonsense in which the good characters always won out over villainy. Even in the main feature, the good guys were quickly demarcated from the bad guys—the good cowboys in white hats and the train robbers in black. What child would want to be identified with the bad? Parents rested easy when the movie featured Tom Mix who nobly rode the range a few years before the equally trusted Randolph Scott. There was little thought as to how the Indians were depicted, and they were now safely on the reservations anyway.

Miss Hamilton

I guess that Harold, herded as I had been the year before, found his way to the proper classroom. How would I have felt about being with him in the first grade, had my parents not intervened? The thought didn't cross my mind because that experience, thankfully, did not occur. Had

I found myself in the first grade once more, however, I might have sought out Albert, now in his third year of school but still in the second grade, and been cloned in his image.

Instead, I was in the warm cocoon of old friends—buddies cultivated over a year that had constituted a sixth of my life span. School had begun to matter. And I felt the wind at my back.

Miss Hamilton differed markedly from Miss Laing: older by perhaps a decade, brunette instead of blonde, slim and somewhat frail-looking rather than tall and athletic-looking, soft-voiced to the point of straining one's hearing in contrast to a voice of power and command. Her daily dress was what my mother might have worn to something quite special. Miss Laing had worn an off-white smock over her regular clothes. Miss Hamilton's dark eyes were behind heavy-rimmed glasses (with a few inches of small beads hanging from the frame close to the sides of her head) that became a feature of her face. Miss Laing's blue eyes had no such decoration. Children notice these things.

Miss Hamilton issued few rules and listed only very general expectations. She left the impression that you were to figure out how to help her teach you.

Miss Hamilton loved books. She didn't say anything when we began to fidget, disturbed the quiet by dropping more and more books and pencils, and raised the decibel level of our mumbling. Instead, she walked to the center of the front of the classroom, a book in her hand. Slowly and almost lovingly, she removed the dust jacket and laid it carefully on the desktop of the nearest pupil. In the hush obtained without a word spoken, she began to read. Her choices were impeccable. By the time she closed the book and said that it would be on her desk and available to anyone who wanted to finish the story, we were hooked.

There was always a new activity after the brief reading. Sometimes we would go quietly outside and walk quickly around the entire school building. I remember a few times when she closed the book abruptly and said that she would finish her reading outside. We would then cluster eagerly around her on the playground, anxious to get the rest of the story. There never was a problem with hearing her then. I remember that, on those occasions, there always was something on the outside to connect with what was inside the book, such as billowing clouds out of which might come the dragon to threaten the knight on the white horse (cloud). Miss Hamilton connected our consciousness with the surroundings.

I blossomed. I don't know when the wind for reading began to push at my back. Miss Hamilton introduced us to the little library in the upper school. On nice days, she sometimes took us to her home where we ate cookies, leafed through books of many pictures, and waited breathlessly for her cuckoo clock to perform. The sad days were when a substitute teacher took over, which was rather often. Miss Hamilton didn't just *look* frail. With the substitute, we usually behaved as we knew Miss Hamilton would wish us to behave.

That was my year to be a little more frail than usual: chicken pox, a severe cold or two, several dizzy spells. I gobbled up books most of the time and nearly all the time when ill in bed. Most nights my mother performed a ritual "lights out" check to end my reading by flashlight under the covers. "Bad for your eyes," she said. I realized only later the yeoman services she performed in keeping me supplied. Her monthly trip to Woodward's in Vancouver on "95¢ day"—three pounds of bulk butter for 95¢ and other bargains—brought home a book purchase she had managed. Her trips to the school library took her far out of her normal routes, necessitating very long walks. A book begun in the morning was finished in the evening. That was the Christmas my father gave me a pigskin bookmark with the words "Books are silent friends" burned into the leather.

An after-Christmas illness delayed my return to school for the first few days of January. I was shocked to find someone in my seat. Miss Hamilton directed me to one a couple of rows nearer the windows. The children close to me were not those who had come with me from Miss Laing's room and with whom I had been sitting all fall. That afternoon, I carried home a note to my parents informing them that I had been promoted to the third grade.

I guess that they had a better understanding of what this meant than I did. There was no great praise or special fuss over this midyear event that I recall. My parents, little schooled themselves, valued schooling very much but exerted no pressures beyond seeing to it that homework was completed before I had free time in the evening. In a household in which the cloud of my father's illness was always present, they worried more about my health than my academics. No doubt they took some satisfaction over their intervention the previous June and probably chuckled over Miss Laing's saying that no good would come of promoting me to grade two.

For me, the school day was much as it had been before the seat change. What counted was that I was with Miss Hamilton. I don't recall any learning strain in the transition. Yes, I was ill quite a lot that year, but I was less so in the second half than I had been in the first. We seemed to function as one class and one grade a good deal of the time. But separate groups for reading and arithmetic had been the pattern almost from the time I began school. I probably identified more with my third-grade classmates than I had previously. Strangely, I did not foresee the consternation yet to come as a result of the trajectory I was on that would carry me into the fourth grade and away from Miss Hamilton.

An upset stomach took me out of competition on the school's annual track and field day in June and out of Miss Hamilton's "graduating" party. On the following Sunday, Bill came home with a book. He had met Miss Hamilton down the road a piece, looking for our house—a long distance from hers. She had a book she said I had earned, which she would have given me on that last school day of the year. It was the full original version of *Robin Hood*. All went well in my reading of it until near the end. And then I was overcome by the failure of bloodletting to save his life. I wept at Robin's burial.

A few days later, I wept again. I was not to be in Miss Hamilton's class the next year. I was to be with Miss Burgess, I learned, while still recovering from the incomprehensible death of Robin Hood.

OUT OF SYNC WITH THE SYSTEM

I've had trouble piecing together in my mind the class-and-grade structure of North Star School. There were six classrooms, six teachers (including Mr. Dobson), and eight grades. There were, in addition, Mr. Mathews, a part-time manual arts teacher (who taught the boys while the girls took home-making—not yet "home economics"—elsewhere) and, for a short time the year before and not replaced, Mr. Partridge. There had to be some split grades that varied from year to year according to the grade distribution of pupil enrollment. Given the stability of the student population, this distribution probably was quite predictable.

During my time, the separation of the lower and upper schools was clear, with two teachers in the latter and four in the former. There may have been times when the two were merged. Miss Laing had only the first grade; Miss Hamilton, Miss Burgess, and Miss Frith shared combinations of grades two through six. My conclusion is that, at the time, Miss Hamilton had grade two and half of grade three; Miss Burgess had the other half of three and all of four; Miss Frith had five and six. Presumably, the structure was reviewed at the end of each year and assignments for the following year confirmed.

Years later, I think I've figured out what occurred. I felt ready for whatever it was that school required or, perhaps better, what Miss Hamilton valued in teaching and learning. Books must have played a big part, given my bouts of confined illnesses and reading combined. Before the teachers' meetings at the end of the year where, presumably, pupil placements for the following year would take place, Miss Hamilton must have decided that I was not about to drop suddenly from the trajectory I was on. Why not take full advantage of the wind at my back? Her arguments must have prevailed.

Miss Hamilton probably looked ahead to envision what might trigger my fall. I do not know how common it was for midyear grade shifts such as mine to be carried out. Once it was done, however, Miss Hamilton was confronted by two alternatives in considering my placement for the following year. I could stay with her in the third grade—which I would have chosen without further thought. This would result in spending my third year of school in the third grade with the classmates with whom I had begun the second—and I would be back on the normal schedule. My present third-grade companions would have moved on to Miss Burgess without me, on their normal schedule, and would be in her fourth grade.

The other alternative, the one Miss Hamilton recommended and that was approved, sent me to Miss Burgess. But I do not recall the grade designation on whatever communication was sent to my parents. Was I to join Miss Burgess's segment of the third grade for my third year in school? Or was I to be with my present third-grade classmates and become, with them, a fourth-grader? And suppose the fourth grade was too much for me, what then?

Are you still with me? How incredibly complicated what appears to be simple can be. And I've dealt with only one child—me. What about the Alberts, required to repeat a grade? Was the decision to have Albert held back made as carefully as the decision that took place for me? What was done with children such as Albert, retained to repeat a grade, should they suddenly spurt to perform like their promoted classmates? Do such children ever spurt?

THE WIND AT MY BACK

My initial image of Miss Burgess was not favorable. The four teachers patrolled the hallways during the daily ingresses and egresses of the classes. Miss Frith had scolded me a couple of times the previous year. (She didn't seem to know that I was the brother of one of her most enthusiastic admirers.) Miss Burgess also had once scolded me quite sharply. She was reported to have a quick temper.

Inside her classroom, however, I experienced a softer demeanor, albeit with flashes of impatience and rising temper. Miss Burgess was a veteran teacher, perhaps ten years older than Miss Hamilton. Red-haired and on the bulky side, she displayed great energy, creating a kind of protective aura around the entire class. One did not need to be told that she was in charge of her business and her class. She sensed trouble before it surfaced. Writing on the chalkboard, with her back to the class and not turning, she saw the spitball well before it reached its mark. Punishment was swift.

Miss Burgess's emphasis was on arithmetic and spelling, whereas Miss Hamilton had focused on books and reading. We added and subtracted numbers in our heads. There were weekly spelling bees, half the grade against the other half, that went on until, one by one, we were out of the contest and in our seats, with only the winning side remaining. I thrived.

There was a family card game at the time in which even churchgoers indulged. Dancing and card playing (no gambling) were not sins in the lexicon of my parents' religion. The game was whist, played with the same fifty-two cards but without the complications of bridge. Victory depended on a lucky deal (a necessity) and a sharp memory for all the cards already played and now hidden from view (the difference between winners and losers with hands of approximately equal value). There was an adding-up process at the end of each round and totals to be compared when "enough" was called. I was a whiz. My parents feared, I think, that I might become addicted.

I usually was the one to plead an evening game. My parents had other things on their minds, as did Bill. Although they enjoyed the game, they were more likely to be distracted—my mother to fix a pot of tea, for example. Success made me passionate for the game, assuring concentration that closed out distractions. And I was eager enough to ring out the concluding totals because I usually added up the figures. Miss Burgess's thing with arithmetic was, at the time, my thing too. The wind was at my back one more time.

And that wind continued to blow open the pages of book after book. I had the good fortune that year to meet and make friends with Ted Margetts. He had been attending, I believe, one of the two private schools for boys in the area, where his mother had placed him after her separation from Ted's father, a prosperous car dealer in another town. The circumstances had caused his mother to be very solicitous of Ted; he got most things he wanted. I was a beneficiary.

Books were high among Ted's wants: the Tom Swift series, the Motor Boat Boys series, the Zane Grey output, the adventures of Hopalong Cassidy. He read them; I read them. With all of the Tarzan books back on the shelves, we eagerly awaited the next one. The companionship was to go on for years, with the mutual interest in books never flagging. We lost contact with one another at about the time Ted entered medical school, just as Harvey and I entered graduate school, all of us many miles and two countries apart.

In retrospect, I think Miss Burgess hedged her bets in regard to my grade placement. Her fourth-grade group occupied the two rows closest to the windows and about half of another. The third-graders occupied the other half and the remaining two rows closest to the wall. I was in the middle of the middle row. One of her practices has bothered me over the years. She ranked her pupils each month and then rearranged the seating plan so that the child ranking first in each grade sat in a front seat of his or her grade's allotted territory.

The first reshuffling occurred early in the fall—probably at the end of September. I found myself in the front seat of the middle row. Presumably, I was now firmly ensconced in the fourth grade, but near the periphery.

A few months later, I was moved to the second row inward from the windows and, soon after, to the front desk in the first. I felt pretty good about this, of course. But I didn't feel completely comfortable with it, either, and found ways to hush up my mother when she talked about my ranking first again. What about the boys (always boys, I recall) in the back seats? Albert probably chose one of these even before seats were assigned. Also, I felt uneasy; it might not last. The climb to grace is exhilarating; the fall is not.

Schooling has become a massive enterprise. Massive enterprises call out for order and control. Massive immigration into Canada and the United States late in the nineteenth century and early in the twentieth century overran the rather casual conduct of schooling that had preceded it. With little else known about school attendees, their age became a defining feature and the age-graded school we have was born. The sheer convenience of it has provided a near-impenetrable rationale.

Today, there probably is no greater body of knowledge relevant to schooling than that of the individual differences among children and, indeed, among the various characteristics of individual children. The combination of environmental and biological phenomena that form individuality go far beyond the orderly character of the rainbow in creating a kaleidoscope of diversity. Not only do the trajectories of development among children differ widely, the trajectory for each child is erratic. The maturation of a specific trait eludes the packaging of equal amounts into equal periods of time. But not in the lexicon of schooling. Benjamin Bloom's thorough debunking of concept and practice decades ago caught our attention for a time but changed what we have grown accustomed to not at all.[5]

Miss Hamilton and her colleagues were caught up in the age-graded school—a year of aging time for a year of school time. Their daily experience called out for "hard" knowledge—to which we pay only rhetorical respect—to support their belief that this longstanding structure did not fit their students' variability. We have had such knowledge for decades. But misbegotten conventional wisdom still prevails in schooling and is massaged, often for political purpose, by those who determine its policies, with presidents and governors in the lead. "Leave no child behind," they say, while advocating practices that do. Our sensibilities and sensitivities are not yet attuned to the way in which schools are savaged on the inside by the entry of pernicious intrusions from the outside. Accountability and efficiency continue to be the burden of those called upon to maneuver on the inside.

MORE ENDINGS

I was soon to experience a fall—in a domain of previous success. Illness had deprived me the year before of assumed success in the races of the school's annual track and field day. I eagerly anticipated its coming once again. I recall winning some early race. It might have been the egg-and-spoon, which required careful balancing more than speed. Then I lost out in the two major events, in one of them quite miserably. Harold, younger than I but in my age grouping, finished ahead of me in both. He was astonished and embarrassed. He valued running and had admired mine, and generously endeavored to ease my embarrassment

by explaining that it was a fluke. Later that summer, he encouraged me
to accept his family's invitation to the bricklayer's picnic (his father was
a bricklayer). There would be races and I would win some of the very good
prizes. The only prize I won was that handed out to all the attending
children. My running prowess had gone with the wind. The trajectories
of children's traits rise and stall only to rise and stall again.

I was soon to be gone from North Star School. I was promoted by
Miss Burgess and, in September, would be in Miss Frith's fifth-grade
group. But even if my family had not moved from the little plateau on the
lower slopes of Timber Mountain and, necessarily, taken me from North
Star School, I would not have been able to check out Bill's admiration
of Miss Frith. She married that summer and, we were told, didn't teach
school in her new community. I, too, would be in a new community and
a new school.

I merely transferred from one school to another in the same school
district, but in my mind, the move was to a faraway place. At Ridgeway,
the academic winds were not to blow as strongly at my back as they
had at North Star School. Nor did they pick my feet up from the
ground in flow experiences at North Vancouver High School four years
later. Not all romances with schools are academic. Regardless of geographic place, however, school was now part of my being.

Chapter 2

The Middle Years

We grow and become both by letting go and holding on, leaving and staying, journeying and abiding. A good life is a balance of home and pilgrimage.

LAURENT A. PARKS DALOZ, CHERYL H. KEEN,
JAMES P. KEEN, AND SHARON DALOZ PARKS[1]

The move had been exceedingly painful and remains etched in my mind. I don't recall the factors involved and probably was not privy to all of them. My father had obtained an indoor job, better suited to his declining health. With car ownership never ours and still out of reach, the logistics of daily travel were formidable. And, no doubt, the demands of our minifarm had become a burden. Interest in it by a potential purchaser motivated my parents to look for a house in the southeast section of North Vancouver, several miles from our present home in the extreme north. The travel distance to my father's new work would be cut by at least two-thirds.

The move took place just a few days into the new school year. There was no point in my beginning the fifth grade at North Star School. With only our venerable wood- and coal-burning stove left to be loaded on the moving truck, my cat disappeared. The stove was lifted and she was found cowering and trembling below. Our dog wouldn't leave our sides, my cat the house. I scooped her into the cardboard box that I had prepared with an ample number of breathing holes. She promptly bit through, burying a long tooth into the thumb of my holding hand. I think that the pain and the stemming of blood kept my eyes and mind away from what we were leaving. I wept most of the way to what I perceived to be "the city."

No acreage surrounded our house this time. But the fifty-foot lot was deep enough for a front lawn, a backyard garden and fruit trees, even a chicken coop and run, and it would be much easier to maintain. Ridgeway School, just a few blocks away, was one of the largest of North Vancouver's six small elementary schools. I had merely transferred from one school to another in the same district, but for me, the move was to a foreign land.

For children, time and space are narrowly conceived—probably more in my childhood than in today's electronically connected world. For most days of the previous three years, my life and, indeed, my conception of the world had been defined primarily by two places: home and school. These provided continuity. All else was the stuff of adventure and anecdote. The daily trip between home and school, extending over fall, winter, and spring, brought awareness of terrain, seasons, and, to a lesser degree, community—assumed by me to be much the same everywhere. Movies and books brought glimpses of people in other places, but these were in the not-quite-real domain of my imagined Bobby and Tommy in the California of preschool fantasy. There had been neither radio nor television to become entwined with my real world of home, school, and weekend adventures. I still recall the expectant hush, one New Year's Eve, before my brother Andy was successful in bringing to our ears on his crystal set the surging noise of ongoing celebrations in New York City's Times Square. But this was virtual, not real.

I was not, then, entering only a different house and school, I was entering a new habitat not more than six miles from my previous one. There was not, fortunately, a new language to be learned. And I was not of a different color from the people I encountered. Yet, the move was traumatic. How traumatic moves to other places and schools must be for children who differ in language and color. I was abruptly separated from my inner circle of friends—Ken, Harvey, Harold, Tommy, Ted—with whom I would soon reestablish communication, and from classmates not to be encountered again until the high school years, when they would be near-strangers. The four intervening years would root me in time and space once more without destroying what I thought I had lost at the age of nine. Life is much more a transcending of experiences than a shedding of them.

MAPPING NEW TERRAIN

I suffered an infection from my cat's bite that justified a few days at home, days that I managed to extend with no accompanying diminution in my apprehension. I used them to explore my immediate environment.

In retrospect, I realize that this was not city. Nor was it suburban in today's sense: it was where families went, if possible, usually from lesser abodes, after the children became school age. Not to a development of architect-designed homes and manicured lawns but to an assortment of individual houses clustered in clumps like the products of poorly scattered seeds: a row of houses followed by a field of scrubby second-growth woods. The main roads were paved, the asphalt running haphazardly into the dirt at the sides. The power and telephone poles were of wood; the sidewalks were of gravel or concrete and usually fronted a block of houses, skipped a clump of woods, and reappeared to front the next block of houses. I could walk to school via the precise geometry of sidewalks or follow the winding path through intervening woods to come out across the street from the school.

I went by sidewalk on that first day (alone this time), a mid-September Monday, some two weeks after school had begun. Ridgeway was not a big school by today's standards, but housed entirely in one building, it looked huge to me. There were at least ten classes spread over eight grades. No auditorium, no gymnasium, no science laboratory, no lunchroom; these were nowhere in our lexicon of schooling. Pupils hurried home for lunch or carried one in a paper sack. No yellow buses lined the spacious playgrounds. They, too, were yet to come.

Like Principal Dobson, Principal Bennett was the supreme authority—a large, formidable figure with a heavy black moustache and bald pate surrounded by dark hair. Outside, I usually saw him early in the day, always wearing a hat: walking to school (if one arrived early enough to see him) or, occasionally, circling the building, stopping on each side to observe playground activity. He was aloof but very much a presence. Principals don't always teach school in the conventional sense, but they do educate.

Much more tangibly present were the white-bearded Mr. Hogarth, the janitor, and Rolf, his huge sheep dog—the kind whose eyes appear obscured behind a thick fringe of overhanging hair. They frequently were apart, Mr. Hogarth at one end of the bottom floor, perhaps, and Rolf at the other end of the top floor. The tales of Rolf's incredible feats were part of the culture of Ridgeway School, told far and wide. Whereas almost everyone had seen Mr. Dobson run down a miscreant at North Star School, Rolf's stare slowed one's running in the hallway to a walk. One walked carefully around Rolf, sitting solemnly where Mr. Hogarth had instructed him to stay. But, then, at intervals, he moved to new locations, as a watchman or policeman might do. Rolf was impeccably trained and performed his work with stoic efficiency, barking only when he thought the presence of his master to be necessary.

I believed these tales because I had seen Rolf in action before. Our family and the Hogarth family already were years into a friendship that endured through two generations. My parents, both raised close to the church, had become disillusioned with organized religion during World War I and, soon after my birth, sought to pursue the divine idiom through religious affiliation perceived by them to stay close to the teachings of the Bible. They thought they had found what they were looking for where the Hogarths thought they had found it. That's where they had attended church for several years and sent me to Sunday school from the time I was a toddler until their disillusionment set in once more—a few years before that of the Hogarths. They had found in too many of the parishioners the meanness, the bigotry, and the same hawk-like proclivities that had driven them from the mainstream houses of worship some years before. Not all teachings of the Bible are peace seeking, and not all churchgoers heed those that are.

And so I had friends at Ridgeway School in Mr. Hogarth and Rolf, although they and I were careful to suppress our relationship in the school's environs. The only other person known to me was Harcus, who bore my mother's family name and was distantly related. He and his brothers were, I assume, what are known as forty-second cousins. Our two families visited from time to time, usually at the occasional gatherings of those immigrants from northern Scotland who came together to celebrate and reminisce about their Orkney or Shetland Island heritage.

Harcus, a gentle sort, had a strong, tough buddy. I don't recall his name; Mike seems to fit. Harcus could not have been better protected by a paid bodyguard. Just as Joy had protected girldom at North Star School, Mike created a buffer zone around himself and Harcus at Ridgeway. From time to time, early after my arrival, they brought me inside of it, but clearly as a guest.

Ridgeway, too, had a lower-level pit. The girls had their basement, as well, and perhaps mayhem akin to that of the boys went on there, but I never saw it. Mike and Harcus introduced me to the boys' dungeon. The few times afterward that I ventured on my own were occasions when they were close by. Two conditions probably were significantly causal in regard to the differences between the North Star and Ridgeway pits: the latter served all the grades, and so the discrepancy in the age and size of the participants was considerably greater; the ratio of cubic inches of space to the pupil population was much less. At North Star, one could occasionally see and catch up with the fast-moving ball. At Ridgeway, the ball was only an excuse for being in the pit; inflicting and avoiding bodily pain was the real name of the game. I soon decided that Mike's buffer was insufficient protection.

The first few weeks of my initiation into the culture of Ridgeway School were uncommonly and blessedly free of sustained rain. I was to learn that the football (soccer ball) would be thrown out at recess every day, wet or dry. And I was to learn to my later advantage as a teacher the incredible therapeutic, custodial role of a soccer ball in the midst of several dozen boys on a large playing field, each boy arbitrarily picking the side to be on and then charging up after a kicked ball and charging back after a returning kick and a new trajectory. No teams, no positions, few rules—just kick it hard toward one's choice of goal posts, if one were lucky enough to get to the ball during the fifteen minutes of play. By November, the mud would thin the number of participants and prevent the ball from going far in any direction.

By October, I was settling into the routines and regularities—probably more comfortable in this new setting than were my parents. The reverberations from the stock market crash of that October 1929 reached them too, even though Wall Street was far away in "The States." From time to time, we heard of a suddenly bankrupt tycoon jumping from a window to the streets of New York. Loss of property acquired some years earlier (an event I learned about years later) did not change our modest lifestyle, but it did eliminate the prospect of our becoming well off.

Few people anticipated the impoverishment that would embrace most families and stretch for more than a decade into the Second World War. I don't know whether it was this depression or my father's failing health that terminated his new job. But I know now that it was inability to pay the taxes that lost us the expanse of undeveloped land between Vancouver and New Westminster in which my father and his two brothers had invested. Today, Burnaby is part of the thriving metropolitan corridor that joins these two cities in the delta of the mighty Fraser River—and there is a very busy Goodlad Street.

I was preoccupied otherwise with seeking a niche in my school's culture and making friends in the next block, especially with Jimmy and his dog. Most Saturdays, however, I walked the several miles, accompanied by an eager Lindy (our dog), to be with Harvey, the Stackhouse boys, or Ted. I liked Mr. Terry, my first full-time male teacher. Indeed, I liked Mr. Terry very much, so much that I began to think seriously about becoming a teacher.

A Painful Favor

The tackle would have drawn the admiration of a football coach. Coming from behind, at the knees, it threw me face-forward to the hard turf of the school ground. Knees and palms of my hands bleeding, I rose slowly to my feet. My adversary pranced around me in a circle, some ten feet distant, fists raised in a posture reminiscent of the famed, bare-knuckle boxer, Jack Sullivan. I waited, fists down but at the ready.

My attacker continued his slow, menacing walk around the perimeter of the circular space now occupied only by me. Ten feet or so separated us; the gathering crowd of boys watched silently a couple of yards farther out; some girls looked on curiously from a still greater distance. Our eyes were fixed on one another, my heart pounding and my ears still ringing from the impact that had crashed me to the ground. Strangely, my tackler seemed to be breathing more heavily and noisily than I. What he was saying came to me as through a fog.

Halloween had been celebrated the preceding Saturday evening. There had been a bonfire on the school grounds. Returning, Jimmy, a couple of other new friends, and I had passed by the row of houses immediately across from the school, a hundred yards or so from where I now stood. Most houses of the time shared some similarities: set back perhaps twenty feet from the street with a centered flight of a dozen or so steps leading to a stoop and the front door. The barrage of jeers directed at us by a clutch of boys on the porch and steps of one such house could not be ignored. The dried peas we shot from mouth-blown shooters were missiles very short of being lethal. Stones came flying in return. We fled.

My adversary was now telling me that I had hit his little brother with a pea. My cowardly attack was to be avenged. Having grown up with two brothers, fighting was not unknown to me. I had learned to pummel Harvey with my fists and not let him close for wrestling; with Ted, who took boxing lessons, my strategy was precisely the opposite. Fighting was something one did with friends and brothers (and, I suppose, with sisters); it stopped before anyone was seriously hurt. Basil (whose name I did not then know) continued in his menacing pose, breathing heavily, but came no closer. I waited. And I waited.

I'm sure that the whole thing was over in a couple of minutes, but even today I perceive it to have lasted a long time. I waited. Then Basil scooped up his bag from the ground, flung it over his shoulder, and, muttering, barged his way rudely and roughly through the ring of spectators.

Six weeks after my arrival, Basil had stirred the favoring wind I so badly needed. Schools have cultures. One must find a niche in each that surrounds one's passage from childhood to adulthood or remain alien to and alienated from its ethos.

Basil was in the eighth grade at Ridgeway School. On the short side for his age, he was, nonetheless, sturdy and stocky and considerably larger than I. Since moving into the neighborhood two or three years before, Basil's father had made it clear that the family was just passing through, living below its status, until a suitable location was found, closer to the private secondary school Basil would soon attend. The most prestigious private schools of the time were secondary, in the tradition of the early academies attended after tutoring. From there, one went on to a private college and a career in the family business, law, medicine, or perhaps the diplomatic service. Such a path was preordained.

Basil had come to Ridgeway with a formidable reputation, perhaps spread through the neighborhood by his father: trained in boxing, his games were rugby and cricket (in groups of boys coached privately on Saturdays). He had been seen leaving his house dressed in the proper sports attire; he was destined for leadership and privilege. Nobody had seen Basil fight. He became threatening when his name was pronounced with a long "a" as in the herb. But, most of the time, this was probably the result of our ignorance; I doubt that more than a very few of us had ever seen the name. And basil and other herbs did not have the popularity they enjoy today. Most gardens were of the potatoes, leeks, carrots, and cabbages variety.

I soon discovered that my stock had gone up markedly. I had done nothing other than stand my ground—mostly out of fear that giving in to my urge to run would result in being once more tackled to the ground. I had not known of Basil's existence; very few of Ridgeway School's pupil population had known of mine. But, suddenly, I was the David who had stood up to Goliath and blown away the myth of his superiority—and I was just a skinny little fifth-grader at that.

Basil had done me an enormous favor. It's a shame that so many things in life—power, expertise, affluence, even wisdom—are viewed as if on a balance scale. Getting more means someone else gets less. It was early in the school year; Basil and his family were gone by the time the year was half over. I heard that Basil entered a private school that had grades below as well as above the ninth and where, presumably, he played rugby and cricket. It was rumored that his father later became unhappy with his school of choice and that his unhappiness was over the school's failure to get Basil chosen a Rhodes Scholar. Poor Basil. I wonder if he ever found out who he was, given the masks created for him, just as I wonder whether his father's ambitions ever were realized.

Something had to give for either of their futures to be satisfying. Or, perhaps, just playing the game of "holier than thou" is satisfaction enough.

COMING TO TERMS WITH SCHOOL

In many ways, my year in the fourth grade with Miss Burgess at North Star School was a kind of prep course for my four years at Ridgeway. It was in the fourth grade that school as a place became predictable, without my knowing it at the time. Looking back, Miss Laing and Miss Hamilton dominate the first two years. I see them both quite clearly. Miss Hamilton I see vividly; Miss Burgess I see more as a redheaded stick figure. But I remember the mental manipulation of numbers, the spelling bees, her use of a pointer at the chalkboard and globe of the world, the changing seating arrangements. The regularities that cause critical observers to say that a school is a school is a school are what come most to mind. I wonder how Albert fared with these. Is one's fate in school virtually determined by or in the fourth grade? By then, most children have either made their peace with the regimen or are well on the way to a dubious relationship.

The regularities were in place in Mr. Terry's fifth-grade classroom. Yet, it is Mr. Terry and not those regularities that come mostly to mind now. Is it possible, then, for a teacher to transcend them—at least for most pupils? I wonder if any teacher transcended these regularities to reach out to Albert.

I think I associated with Miss Burgess those things that I came later to connect with school: grade levels, ranking of pupils, report cards, winners and losers, social status based on academic performance. I saw Mr. Terry, the first male teacher I had encountered, as apart from these things as a person and yet connected with these regularities as a teacher who had to deal with them. Perhaps I give him too much credit when I perceive him as being somewhat angry over what his role as a teacher required, seeing his occasional displays of anger with us as anger over some of the circumstances of teaching. My recollection is that we all, boys and girls, liked him.

As with Miss Burgess, the big things for Mr. Terry were arithmetic and spelling. I do not know why having everyone learn to spell all twenty-five words each week was so important to him. And I do not know what level of failure brought about a strapping on the hands. I experienced no other teacher who tied this form of punishment to the shortcoming. At least the execution took place out of sight in the cloakroom. Perhaps Mr. Terry believed the yells and ouches to be sufficient warning. I had the experience only once. It wasn't much, but it was humiliating. I thought no less of Mr. Terry for it. Indeed, I perceived Mr. Terry as "ours," superior to all other teachers in the school. Surely we were envied. His being ours and our being his was confirmed by his moving up with us into the sixth grade.

Two years of security and stability with a loved and respected teacher expanded my universe of schooling and beyond. My passion for reading had waned very little; spelling and arithmetic presented few setbacks. I had a safe haven from which to look and expand outward.

My recollection is that there was little in-class variation during those two years. The routine I remember from the year with Miss Burgess and the routine followed by Mr. Terry were very similar: a hefty chunk of arithmetic first thing each morning (when the mind presumably was fresh and quick); a Monday-morning introduction to the week's twenty-five words, with special attention to the first seven that included their use in sentences; six new words in the second class period of the day on Tuesday through Thursday and a test on all twenty-five on Friday; and then recess (for all classes in the school at precisely the same time). Usually, Rolf sounded the warning bell, held firmly in his teeth, on the west side of the building and then scampered through the corridor, bell clanging, to ring it a few seconds later on the east side. By the time Mr. Hogarth rang it again, we were close to settling down once more in our seats.

During the first of these two years, I had given up on the aimless chase after the soccer ball, and I avoided the pit virtually from the beginning. The fifteen-minute break was barely enough for a visit to the lavatory and a little conversation with friends. The tension and bursts of restrained anger I had perceived in Mr. Terry that first year almost vanished in the second. More and more of us took advantage of the fact that he permitted us to stay in the classroom at recess. Usually, he was there preparing for the next session, but he seemed to trust us during the times he was not. He managed to adroitly sidestep the probing questions into his personal life that came mostly from the girls. The boys were more inclined to talk about their out-of-class exploits and aspirations. He was a good listener.

Most days, we moved from the informality of recess into a formal check on attendance, homework delinquencies, pending events (such as inoculations and class pictures), and so on. Then, usually, the schedule called for history or geography. For both, there were textbooks: dull, factual, with each topic followed by a list of questions. Canada was at that time still part of the British Empire and not yet of Commonwealth status. Consequently, our flag was the Union Jack, and our primary patriotic song was "God Save the King" (not then the "Queen"), our secondary, "Oh, Canada." Magna Carta, the Crusades, the misfortunes of the wives of King Henry VIII, the triumph of the little British ships over the Spanish Armada—these and other historical events stood out over the dullness of memorizing dates now long forgotten. Canada's history also was geographically remote and was mostly about struggles between the immigrants and the Indians and the English and the French in the provinces east of Manitoba. Similar themes dominated in the little we learned about the history of the United States. The Boston Tea Party emerged as one of the most memorable events. In geography, we concentrated so hard on the maps of our province, British Columbia, and the British Isles that I learned to draw them quite accurately without benefit of our atlases and the outlines, which lacked particulars such as cities and rivers, that were in our workbooks and worksheets. I do not recall any of us complaining in or out of class about what appears now to be somewhat sterile and irrelevant (given the absence of connection with the great themes and cycles of human history). But the competition for our attention was not then what it is now: no television, no personal computers, no electronic information highway, no web sites. Out of school, we were largely on our own for creating recreation and entertainment.

An hourlong lunch break provided just enough time for me to walk home, eat lunch, spend a little time with Lindy and Fuzzy (my cat), check the bantams, and get back to school. I hadn't yet found anything more interesting to do at school during this time.

Afternoons in class were less consistently scheduled than were the mornings. Composition, grammar, and reading dominated, with much of the reading directed to lessons to be derived for our own writing. Handwriting—the MacLean Method—was thrown into the mix. Perhaps I was experiencing "the language arts," but I think the major thrust to integrate the lot into what critics characterized later as an abomination was yet to come. I recall the subjects as separately taught but with efforts to make connections. Grammar and composition were standard fare then and for years to come. Definitions of nouns and verbs, subject and predicate, were built firmly into my understanding of the English language.

Mr. Terry taught lessons in science two or three times each week. I recall the developmental progressions that led to full-scale frogs and butterflies. The 24-hour and 365¼-day orbits that effected daylight, darkness, and the weather were fascinating. The two huge Australian passenger ships that steamed into Vancouver harbor a few times a year provided a source of speculation regarding the contrasting seasons north and south of the equator. Mr. Terry illustrated the moon's eclipse with three different-sized globes and a flashlight. Given heavy dependence on the printed page in history, geography, science, and the rest, limited proficiency in reading would have been a serious handicap and, I'm sure, a major factor in one's sense of efficacy and, in all probability, one's liking of school.

The arts were peripheral. Mr. Terry's approach to the visual arts reflected his neat, orderly nature. We drew quite a bit. Our still-life drawings were cubes, pyramids, buildings, and other fixed objects. I learned quite a bit about shading with a pencil and the perspective required for drawing such things as highways fading into the distance. There was none of the slopping around with watercolors of previous years and no seasonal drawing and coloring of maple leaves, daffodils, and the like. Simon's incredible drawings apparently had gone unappreciated by his earlier teachers, probably because he sketched most of the time and did little else. Mr. Terry noticed. One day, Simon told us, with great excitement, that he was leaving Ridgeway School to attend a special arts school in Vancouver—with all expenses paid.

Our forays into the domain of music were less than inspiring. Mr. Terry did lead us, occasionally, in singing the lyrics from songs in a book that included the notes for the piano accompaniment he was unable to provide. He apologized, correctly, for the limitations of his voice; this admission put us at ease, and we rather enjoyed the break from other subjects. In the sixth grade, however, another teacher who was a specialist in music took over. She sought recruits for the school's Christmas concert and took on the daunting task of teaching us to recognize and sound the notes of the musical scale. They were about as meaningful to me as had been my encounters with phonetic analysis in the first grade. I don't think my singing voice had improved much, but I didn't get cracked across the head as a reminder of my deficiencies.

Although the mornings and afternoons were quite precisely organized into subjects and time slots, there were memorable exceptions. These were almost always connected to domains of human endeavor in our larger environment. Most history and geography classes had a mythical unreality to them: faraway times of kings and wars long gone with only dates as the fingerposts of recall; faraway places such as countries, cities, rivers, and mountains now became only map configurations. But the study of British Columbia's chief industries—logging, mining, fishing, and shipping—connected with our daily lives and was real.

Our fifth-grade "unit" on salmon fishing will always be with me. I taught it later; it is as fresh in my mind as it was then, largely because of the textbook's story that recounted four years in the life of a chinook salmon from an egg in the sand of a stream to a full-grown fish scooping a place for its own eggs in the sand of that same stream. We were with her on the long journey downstream to the Pacific Ocean, in her evasion of predators and avoidance of nets and hooks, and then on the journey back to the home stream and, finally, the exhausting struggle upstream to lay her eggs in the sand and die. For most of us, it was a highly emotional identification. We talked about it, read about it, marveled at it without any awareness of learning to read, spell, and think better. And, best of all, we learned something about our own human adventure in time and place.

The orderly efficiency of the fifth and sixth grades was tempered by Mr. Terry's efforts to inject some novel catch-hold point into at least one lesson each day. These were sharply restricted by the confines of a crowded classroom. There simply was no room for science displays or tables suited to special projects. We probably took a few field trips, but I remember only the one to a sawmill. I do not think we lost more than twenty or thirty minutes of instructional and learning time to organizational routines during a school day. Out of a thirty-hour week—five days from nine to noon, with a fifteen-minute recess, and from one to a quarter after three in the afternoon—Mr. Terry spent twenty-seven or twenty-eight hours in making it difficult to escape what he was trying to teach us. His classes were well above the norm in the efficient use of time—and probably would rank equally high today.

He had an adversary, however, that grew stronger and stronger in his sixth-grade class—the emerging onslaught of pubescence. Boys and girls were becoming a distraction for one another. Girls being somewhat more advanced than boys in this regard might have explained why boys were now closing in on girls in regard to academic performance.

The late Bruno Bettelheim is not the only student of human development to urge separate schools for boys and girls of about the age of my classmates and me. Bettelheim maintained that, together, you cannot teach them anything once puberty begins. Some of the irritation Mr. Terry had exhibited during our first year with him began to surface once more. He was well aware of the classroom dynamic that was increasingly eroding the attention to academics he sought to maintain.

Perhaps it was this awareness that caused him to blush and stumble a little in his search for words in telling us, a few days before the school year ended, that he was about to be married. He went on to say, more coherently, that he would not be back at Ridgeway the following year. He had accepted a teaching position in the high school of a town in the interior of British Columbia. We knew that he had been attending the University of British Columbia during summer sessions and, sometimes, in the evenings. Occasionally, the demands there had necessitated our having a substitute teacher. Now that he had completed the requirements for a bachelor's degree, he was qualified to teach at the high school level—and, given his pending marriage, the higher salary would have been most welcome. Our ownership of Mr. Terry increased; no other class in Ridgeway School would get him. It appeared to me that he had the near-perfect life.

Years of Hazy Definition

The first two of my four years at Ridgeway School loom large in my memory, as do the first three at North Star School. My memories of the three years with Miss Burgess and Mr. Terry are at the very core of what school is presumed to be—an immersion in the subjects traditionally attached to schooling. Strangely, although my years in the seventh and eighth grades were more dominated by the ethos of school than before, it is not the traditional image of school that dominates in my mind. Rather, it is what was outside of the academic core. The rest is murky. Not the regularities but the peripherals come to mind.

Of course, there was a full regimen of arithmetic (still not often referred to as mathematics), spelling, grammar, composition, geography and history, literature (British authors and what are now sometimes referred to as the Schoolroom Poets of the United States), some science (combined at times with health), and physical education. Some casual attention to the arts left no impression. I recall there being three teachers: our regular classroom teacher in the seventh grade whose name I do not recall; Mr. Edwards, who taught science, health, and physical education in both the seventh and eighth grades and was the responsible classroom teacher in the eighth; and Mr. Bennett, who taught, sometimes in the seventh and much more in the eighth, arithmetic, literature, and spelling, but not consistently. It was identification with mathematics, not athletics, that characterized the principals I encountered in elementary and secondary school. And, unlike all the female teachers I had encountered, my seventh-grade teacher (I will name her Mrs. Thompson) was married.

There was much attention to our handwriting. If "bad" in our compositions, we were marked down. Mrs. Thompson continued the formal lessons in the MacLean Method—a full-arm, sweeping movement that was supposed to produce rounded letters, fully open loops above and below each line, carefully crossed *t*'s, and an *a* differentiated clearly from *o*. One inserted formidable nibs into equally formidable long, wooden nib-holders and dipped into inkwell or ink bottle. There was a hierarchy of MacLean Method certificates, at the top of which was one for teachers.

There was a sort of kinesthetic ceremony to the whole: dipping the pen carefully to secure just the right amount of ink, transporting pen to paper without slopping ink onto the page, engaging in a few trial circles of arm and hand as a baseball pitcher might do, and then, rhythmically sweeping seamless word after word across the page before dipping once more. I was to encounter *the* Mr. MacLean later in normal school where, in the flesh, he taught *the* Method. Those who have had to read my handwriting will be astounded to learn that, in normal school, I was one of the few aspirants to secure the Teaching Certificate. Clearly, it has not served me well. It was at some time during my concluding years at Ridgeway School that the fountain pen was given reluctant approval. Those who could afford one were allowed to use it, but not for the lessons in the MacLean Method.

The year in the seventh grade at Ridgeway brought my second close encounter with Mr. Bennett. The first had been soon after my arrival, at recess, shortly after my decision to stay away from the pit. It was a dreary, rainy day. I sought my usual place of refuge: a nonfunctioning drinking fountain partially obscured by bushes in a corner near one of the school's entry doors. By standing in the bowl and leaning back against the wall, I just barely escaped the rain. Principal Bennett rounded the corner and I froze in place. His dark, disapproving scowl was enough to deny me this refuge forevermore.

From time to time, Mr. Bennett took over the seventh-grade class in arithmetic and, once weekly, spelling. He may have been checking on Mrs. Thompson through us. His spelling session was in two parts. The first was the usual listening to and writing that day's words; the second was listening to and writing Mr. Bennett's reading of a section of prose, the emphasis this time on both spelling and punctuation. Mr. Bennett had said that we should be able to determine the proper punctuation from his changing voice patterns and the length of his pauses.

It was a cinch: a period when his voice dropped and was followed by a relatively long pause, a comma for the short pause, a semicolon for a longer pause and usually a kind of break in the sentence, a colon for a still longer pause followed commonly by a list of things, a new paragraph for a very long pause and quite distinct shift in the narrative. We passed our papers forward to the front desk. Mr. Bennett gathered them up carefully, left, and returned them the following week with errors noted and sometimes with comments.

On one occasion, he said that he had a real challenge for us. We went through the same routine but with a much more complex narrative. I was called to his office the following day. It would not have been logical to accuse me of cheating because I was the only one to turn in a paper precisely conforming to the passages read. But he appeared to be some-what suspicious. Or, perhaps it was pride that he didn't want to reveal. He asked if I had read the piece before. He seemed satisfied when I told him that I merely followed the cues his reading provided. The experience caused me to relax a bit with Mr. Bennett the following year when he was close to being our full-time teacher for mathematics and literature.

I do not know whether Mrs. Thompson recognized that the girl-boy relationship was her adversary or just chose to ignore it. By now, it was the undercurrent that pulled the academic surface of the classroom down into it. Most of us possessed a combustible combination of enormous sexual ignorance and curiosity. Left subliminal so far as school was con-cerned, this duality produced silly innuendo and almost constant dis-traction. Perhaps Mrs. Thompson should have been teaching in a lower grade. She imposed a kind of infantilism on us that served both to keep the undercurrent precisely as such and to strengthen it. With some of the boys in particular, her denial was a kind of challenge. How close to precise allusion might they bring innuendo without bringing on a visit to Principal Bennett? I am reminded of those earlier contests to see how close to the top of our gumboots we could bring the water of the ditch without getting wet feet. But the spillover rarely occurred. Nobody wanted a command appearance with Mr. Bennett.

As the year progressed, evidence mounted to support the rumor that several of our classmates had advanced (or regressed) from fantasy to reality. Rumor had it that two boys and a girl in our class had been skinny-dipping in the cold waters of Lynn Creek and then warmed themselves buck-naked by a roaring campfire. Then there were later reports of this being seen. The undercurrent intensified. There were wide variations in the stories passed around—from the whole thing being fantasy dreamed up by the two boys as testimony to their vast experience to much exercise of imagination regarding what else was going on fireside. What the girl was saying to her friends, if anything, we boys never learned.

Mr. Edwards's class on health included a little human anatomy. He startled us one day by bringing to class the extraordinarily real-looking likeness of the skeleton marketed by the Denoyer-Geppert Company. But we never got around to putting flesh on the frame, and so were left to the excesses of our imagination. Teaching the eighth grade most of the time, he undoubtedly sensed the undercurrent in the seventh. But, not responsible day in and day out for our behavior, he cut short whispered innuendos with a sharp "knock it off."

In retrospect, I have some doubts about the power of separate schools for boys and girls to counteract the electric surge accompanying the onset of puberty. If one views academic achievement as the dominant or perhaps the sole measure of schooling, my guess is that separate schools win out—as some research suggests. But human development is accompanied by a time clock that clangs at times like a ship's bell. There is, I think, no reasonable way to muffle it. And today, the electronic surround experienced by adolescents and preadolescents will set the bells to clanging regardless of how our schools are organized. Schools today are up against a more powerful adversary than the time clock of emerging pubescence alone.

The educational philosopher Harry Broudy gave considerable credence to the role of serendipity in human affairs. I tend to share his view. The serendipity that steered me through the always-dangerous undercurrent of the seventh grade stemmed, in large part, from my being a year younger than virtually all of my classmates and the fact that I was not advanced physiologically for my age. The undercurrent was titillating but not as pervasive as it appeared to be for some of my male classmates. Also, I was fortunate in having an array of interests that caused school to be a competitor for my time. I wanted to get the school day and my homework out of the way as quickly as possible so I could get on with other things.

For example, I had not yet outgrown my interest in raising and caring for bantams—an interest some people sustain for a lifetime. I do not know how it originated, but my father sensed, fostered, and sustained it. He had a knack for and attachment to all living things, whether flora or fauna. He shared my grief when a stray cat wiped out several recently hatched fluff-ball chicks of my favorite hen and shored up the pen so that this could not happen again. At the in-between time in life when one has identity as neither child nor adult, perhaps it is important to establish some identity in being needed. I had Lindy, Fuzzy, and the bantams to take care of. A colorful rooster presiding over a small covey of hens is a sight to see! They needed me, and at the time, I needed them.

Probably more important, this sense of mutual need was beginning to manifest itself in a community sphere embracing more than home, school, and friends from childhood that seemed to have sufficed so far. I was becoming part of a neighborhood group that expected some things of me and I of it. Again I benefited serendipitously. This was not a gang whose members sought out one another for the approval they perceived denied at home or school or both. And yet, it was clearly led and dominated by one person, the oldest of a group that encompassed a very wide range in age, both male and female.

Walter was in charge. My friend, Jimmy, connected with the group through his sister Emma, a frail girl for whom this membership consumed her varying levels of energy. During the sixth grade, Jimmy and I had been on the periphery, participating from time to time in the games Walter was forever organizing. I think it was because of Walter's younger sister, Dottie, that I became more interested and involved the following year. About half the group was made up of Walter's siblings. There must have been half a dozen of them. We played by their rules or not at all, while still seeking to expand group membership.

I always felt a little alien. Yet, the timing of this association was propitious—indeed, serendipitous. I was never in the family home and never saw the father. It was not at all uncommon in those days for men who worked in the fishing, lumbering, and mining industries to establish their families in a community and then be absent much of the time. Wives stayed with their husbands in the camps until children came along. In the areas of heaviest coastal logging, there was an occasional floating school, built on logs and rafted to the shore. But in time, wives usually came to seek a more stable community settlement.

I think Walter was charged with the role of surrogate for his father. He took it seriously, presiding over and participating with his brothers and sisters as few fathers could have. As a result, I was never alone with Dottie or any of the others. On being accepted into the group, one became virtually a member of the family. As the youngest in my own family, I had no responsibility for younger siblings. But Walter made it clear that I had such responsibility now. The protective aura that he established over his brothers and sisters reminds me of the protective role over the female teachers and girls played by Mr. Smyth and Principal Dobson at North Star School. As a result, I too was having a protective, expanding, socializing experience during a critical stage of the transition from childhood to adolescence when the guiding power of both home and school commonly are in decline. My final year at Ridgeway brought me back into the school's orbit one more time.

THE EXTRACURRICULUM

What we think of as the school curriculum was for me, through the sixth grade, of sufficient interest to keep what happened in the classroom each day near the center of my existence. What happened in the rest of the school was relatively peripheral. There were few surprises after the fourth grade, but Mr. Terry transcended what might otherwise have been boring in the fifth and sixth. I had plenty to occupy my time at home and in the weekend and summer forays outward for which home was the fulcrum: warm summer days in the wretchedly cold water of a favorite swimming hole in Lynn Creek; trout fishing with line, hook, and worm in the creek that paralleled and then fed into the rushing Lynn (which would have been classified as a river in most parts of the country); going to the slopes of Timber Mountain on many Saturdays to visit with still steadfast friends from my earlier life.

In the seventh grade, however, the supporting pillars of school were crumbling. And the interests that had joined my father and me were becoming less engrossing. His health virtually forbade participation in the forays that took me beyond house and garden. My entry into Walter's "family" picked up a good deal of the slack. My, how critical in an uncertain time the circumstances of one's environmental surround can be. And how little control over the nature of those one has during that dangerous period of being neither child nor adult.

The bonds of connection with Walter and his group began to weaken significantly when the summer between the seventh and eighth grades faded into fall. School became a major fulcrum once more. But it was the extracurricular activities that most engaged my attention now.

There was, of course, some heightened tension with the curriculum. After all, this was the year of intended graduation. There would be exams to take in all subjects for which one was not recommended by the teachers and approved by Principal Bennett. However, with the deepening of the Great Depression, now into its gloomiest years, the specter of sitting for the eighth-grade graduation examinations once required of all had mellowed. Adolescents were not wanted in the long lines of job seekers. Attendance at high school offered relatively low-cost custodial care that would keep a good many of us off the streets and away from the likely gathering places. It was during these years that the age of fourteen (coinciding with the most common age of elementary school graduation) was increased to sixteen for compulsory school attendance. Presumably, the principals and teachers of elementary schools would rather move the oldest students along to the high school than have them languishing discontentedly for a year of repeating the eighth grade. Consequently, the percentage of students recommended, given passing grades on the exams, and advanced conditionally to the secondary schools increased steadily during the years. Today, critics would be grimly noting a decline in standards and complaining that graduation from school did not mean anything anymore. Of course, there were those who charged that it didn't then, either.

I doubt that principals and teachers had any sense of potency in regard to what was happening in the larger social surround and to the changing demographics of the school population. Yet, their pedagogical lives were being profoundly affected. The elementary schools had grown accustomed to their terminal, selective role. The eighth-grade graduation exams had been at least a stimulant for those pupils who wanted a choice of going on to high school or a certificate to carry away with them. The secondary school was geared to the expectation of receiving the best students. Those of least academic promise were unlikely to be in the classroom mix. The Great Depression radically changed this mix over a period of years, but it did not change the curricular menu. This disconnect between schools and those students of modest academic qualifications and, often, little motivation was to characterize schooling for years to come.

Just how aware school personnel were of this incongruence is difficult to determine. One gets the impression that there is, in schooling, a policy arena that has a life of its own, which exists quite apart from school practice even as it seeks to influence schooling. On the practice side, much is determined by what has gone before. What changed rapidly in my time was how long one was required to attend school. What changed much more slowly was how one would spend one's time there.

When I entered the eighth grade at Ridgeway School, Canada and the United States were three years into the Great Depression. My classmates and I were in that uncertain developmental period of being neither child nor adult, of becoming increasingly aware of the past, present, and future of the human race, without any accompanying sense of present or potential efficacy in some useful domain of human endeavor. It was difficult to feel rooted. Few parents were modeling what they had aspired to do. Neither they nor school could augur what the future might bring. This brought about, I think, a certain immediacy of the present that contrasts sharply with the racing to the future that has so captured and so captivates many of us today.

School for most of us was not preparatory for some later life but very much a present given, to be coped with and, to the extent possible, enjoyed for some 180 days a year from early September through most of June, at least until the age of sixteen. Some of us drew satisfaction from the curricular menu, some from the human narrative accompanying and surrounding it, some from the extracurricular, and some from all three. For this last group, life was especially rich, despite the prevailing economic poverty. For those finding only thin gruel in the daily curricular diet, however, there was no fulcrum to support and guide levers of action in the informal domains of school life. In the formal, one curriculum was to fit all. School, then as now, did not merely reflect inequities, it generated them.

The curriculum of the eighth grade resembled curricula experienced before. If one had done well before, as acknowledged by one's teachers, one was likely to continue to do so. Consequently, for me, the daily tension was that of ensuring, or at least of coming very close to ensuring, no sitting for matriculation examinations at the end of the year. Now, with there being no surprises (since the fourth grade) regarding the criteria and evidence of acceptable, if not commendable, performance, one could come to terms with the eighth grade. It warranted a balanced but not all-consuming perspective. There was much more to composing a life than the daily encounters in the classroom with mathematics (now transcending arithmetic), grammar, composition, literature, science, history, geography, and the rest. There was nothing in the daily regimen of class work that warranted the classification of extracurriculum. There was a curriculum and there was the discretionary time of recess and lunch breaks. During my first two years at Ridgeway, in the fifth and sixth grades, my out-of-class orientation was to the west-side playground where nothing of a planned and orderly nature took place. I hurried home for the noon hour. I continued to do so through most of the seventh grade, but as the year progressed, I more frequently brought a sack lunch and even tarried after school more and more often.

When my primary space beyond the classroom focus at Ridgeway School turned at the beginning of the seventh grade from the west-side to the east-side playground, I believe that Mr. Edwards was quite new to the school. He soon became the most visible teacher on the east side of the building, leaving the west to the more occasional scrutiny of Principal Bennett.

Mr. Edwards quickly put noon-hour order into our soccer playing. He taught us, while more or less joining in, a lot about dribbling, passing, kicking, and even heading the ball. Boys no longer just hung around for a short time and then drifted away after the 3:15 p.m. bell. By 3:30, most already were in roughly divided teams around the north goal posts. When Mr. Edwards was with us, there usually were two competing teams using both the north and the south goals. The dominant sound was the smack of a shoe on the ball.

It was in early spring, however, that Mr. Edwards became an even greater presence. His thing was the softball diamond and its use. When I had begun North Star School, brother Bill and his buddies in the upper school were addicted to football (soccer) from fall to spring, and then baseball took over. The Great Depression had not then taken away the necessary bats, balls, and gloves (no catcher's pads and mask; the catcher just crouched twice today's distance from the batter; bloody noses and broken fingers were common). We little guys in the lower school required only bat and ball. The ball was a placebo version— softer and a smidgen larger than a baseball. It suffered a lesser stitching too. With string and stuffing hanging loose, it often wove a deceptive course from pitcher to batter. Mr. Smyth diligently sewed it up until there no longer was fabric for the needle. We often waited a week or so for a replacement to appear. That is why the soccer ball frequently reappeared as summer approached.

Hardball baseball had disappeared at Ridgeway School (and presumably at North Star)—a victim of the Depression—by the time I reached the upper grades. The ball, both the real thing and the placebo, had been replaced by the softball—not soft but considerably larger than a "baseball." Mr. Edwards taught us the game, moving us around to play each of the positions. I found myself in the outfield most of the time but increasingly on the pitcher's rubber. Ridgeway played a game or two each spring with another school (there were no leagues). I watched during the seventh grade, played during the eighth. The big treat was when Mr. Edwards brought in (both springs) a team from North Vancouver's men's league—once to play another such team and once to play the pick of our school's players. I watched the first year; played the second.

What I remember most is the men's team's pitcher, Tino. Tino was not yet over the hill, but he was aged (at least twenty-five, I would guess)—and wise. He could whip a ball over the plate with great speed when he wished. But it was the other things he did that most entranced me. You could never tell what was about to come. Sometimes the ball came in at moderate speed and then veered beyond the outside edge of the plate; sometimes it came in very slowly, wobbled, and dropped; sometimes it maintained such an upward trajectory that the catcher (wearing a mitt) had to reach up sharply for it. Batters fell over swinging or hit little pop flies to the infield. Wonderful! Tino took it easy with us and fooled us mostly with tantalizing, slow pitches.

I practiced whenever and wherever I could. On long summer evenings, several of us would gather at the end of a sort of storage building at the edge of the west-side school grounds. There was always a bat and ball. By using the building's windowless wall as catcher/backstop, three or four of us could be in the outfield while someone pitched and another batted. I pitched a lot but enjoyed batting, too, since one then faced downhill and could get a good carry. It was nice to have and feel the wind at my back again.

I know that my parents worried at times about my late afternoon tarries at school and the short shrift I appeared to be giving to homework in the early evening. They were not aware, I think, of how much the whole of school, anchored by my having come to terms with what they perceived to be schools, ensured that I would not join those unfortunates who were serving the sentences that would come to an end with the celebration of their sixteenth birthdays.

Most of my classmates and I graduated and headed for North Vancouver High School, joining there that next September the graduates of the district's other elementary schools, some of them comprising very small cohorts. There were, I think, not many more than a hundred freshmen from which the class of '37 would emerge four years later. "North Van" could not have been a very big high school, especially given the dropout rate. Only about half of us were answering the roll call when our class graduated in 1937. Making school mandatory is not a very complex policy decision. Making school educationally compelling is quite another matter.

By the time I left North Star School at the age of nine to enter the fifth grade at Ridgeway, I had settled into the routines of schooling. I do not know of anything quite like them elsewhere. The troubling question pertains to the nature of the fit between these regularities and each developing self. There are many Alberts who find themselves out of sync. The ground rule is that they are at odds with the system, not the other way around.

In those early years, school expectations and the paths to them were quite clear: one was to learn to read, write, spell, and figure. A sense of success translated into a sense of personal worth. If one felt worthy outside and inside of school, the chances were good that the two quite different domains would be complementary and, at times, even enriching. This was very much the case with my reading—once beyond the first-grade debacle—and to a considerable degree, what the rest of school was about.

There was for many of us another joining, aided by the smallness of the lower school and its separateness from the even smaller upper school. The values that largely governed my life before school were the values that governed my life in school and even between home and school. It was rare for me to have transgressed in or on the way home from school without my mother knowing before I entered the doorway. The pieces of my life meshed.

My recollection of the Alberts and Annes for whom the pieces did not mesh is that dislocations in the external world exacerbated dislocations in the internal world of schooling and vice versa. In others words, there was negative rather than positive complementarity in the school-home relationship if daily experience in one or the other was dysfunctional. The comfort of a child in a supportive home too often changes to discomfort when he or she lags or meanders on the paths of schooling. The child loses out in both places.

There are, of course, children from dysfunctional homes for whom school is a sanctuary, and they do well there. The challenge for schools is to be good places for children regardless of the home and parental context. But with some parents believing that they are owners rather than caring stewards responsible for the nurturing of their children, this is an exceedingly daunting challenge.

The challenges increase with the advancing age of the students, commonly accompanied by the increasing size of the schools. How one looks to peers becomes more compelling than how one looks to teachers and, often, even to parents. At the upper grade levels of Ridgeway School (today part of the middle or junior high school), academic prowess was dropping in status for students below the social and athletic. But there was little in the curriculum to suggest accommodation and steps toward educational intervention.

The whorls of memory that remain in my mind from North Star School are of teachers' personalities—with that of the gentle Miss Hamilton dominant—and the three Rs that are virtually synonymous with schooling. From Ridgeway, I remember Mr. Terry fondly, but little of the academics commonly attached to the central purpose of schools—although, presumably, I was learning them. Clearly, Mr. Edwards and the playground became my bridge to the larger world and, in many ways, to the secondary phase of school that followed.

Neil Postman wrote powerfully and convincingly a few years ago about a special place called school for the young, a place that does not yet exist.[2] In a book written thirty years earlier, he and Charles Weingartner refer to a long line of contrary thinkers—different drummers—whose ideas envision such a place. Many more names could now be added to that list and a large body of knowledge cited in support of their reasons. Interestingly, the authors refer to these deviant thinkers as "romantics," which is to say, "they believe that the human situation is improvable through intelligent innovation. They are all courageous and imaginative thinkers, which means they are beyond the constricting intimidation of conventional assumptions."[3]

There is an irony in referring to these thinkers as romantics, "beyond the constricting intimidation of conventional assumptions." Their ideas have stimulated and sustained innovative practices at times, before what Barbara Benham Tye refers to as the deep structure of schooling takes over once more.[4] To transcend longstanding conventions is to enter domains of perceived unreality where romance and fantasy become one. As with romance novels, the contemplation of schooling as sketched by the romantics is to enjoy for a time the gratifying sanctuary of vicarious experience.

The impact of the romantics has been almost solely on the early years of schooling: the primary grades into the intermediate, but little beyond the sixth grade. The earlier years are what Alfred North Whitehead referred to in the development of children as the stage of romance—presumably congenial to romantic ideas for schools. "Romantic emotion is essentially the excitement consequent on the transition from the bare facts to the first realisations of the import of their unexplored relationships."[5]

Most children appear to be attuned to a readiness for the yet-unexplored, even in circumstances of dull monotony. In a study conducted more than three decades ago, colleagues and I assumed that the subject matter of elementary schools would evidence considerable intrinsic appeal for pupils. We were disappointed in the extent of its dull monotony but gratified by the general readiness of the children to respond to those occasional nuggets that aroused curiosity.[6]

One might well conclude from the above that the recommendations of the romantics for schools, since they are geared primarily to the developmental stages of children and knowledge of the learning process, can be implemented by imaginative, well-prepared teachers and some modest structural changes to accommodate individual differences. Although both are necessary for inspiring the later years, they are insufficient. With the intrinsic romance of childhood behind them, adolescents are driven by the biological within and the social-technological without.

It will take more than better teachers and modest structural changes to turn our secondary schools into the places for learning, places for joy envisioned by Theodore Sizer.[7] More fundamental interventions are required. Indeed, what is necessary educationally for the older adolescents who are now in school may be something quite different from the place presently called school.

The Statler Brothers, wondering what happened to their high school class of 1957, sang of life getting complicated when you get past eighteen. Today, they might well change the age to sixteen and still be off the mark. The one-size-fits-all school that took its present shape in the 1930s was a poor fit with reality even then. In the twenty-first century, it belongs in our romantic memories of once upon a time.

Chapter 3

The High School Years and a Little Beyond

Tommy's sellin' used cars
Nancy's fixin' hair
Harvey runs a grocery store
And Margaret doesn't care
Jerry drives a truck for Sears
And Charlotte's on the make
And Paul sells life insurance
And part time real estate

Helen is a hostess
Frank works at the mill
Janet teaches grade school
And prob'ly always will
Bob works for the city
And Jack's in lab research
And Peggy plays organ at the Presbyterian church

And the class of '57 had its dreams
We all thought we'd change the world
By our great works and deeds
Or maybe we just thought the world would change to fit our needs
The class of '57 had its dreams

Betty runs a trailer park
Jan sells Tupperware
Randy's on an insane ward
Mary's on welfare
Charlie took a job with Ford

Joe took Freddie's wife
Charlotte took a millionaire
And Freddie took his life

Johnny's big in cattle
Ray is deep in debt
Where Mavis finally wound up
Is anybody's bet
Linda married Sonny
Brenda married me
And the class of all of us
Is just part of history

And the class of '57 had its dreams
But livin' life day to day is never like it seems
Things get complicated
When you get past eighteen
But the class of '57 had its dreams
Ah, the class of '57 had its dreams.

THE STATLER BROTHERS[1]

My beginnings at North Vancouver High School were much less marked by tension than my first school beginnings had been. No trauma marred my expectations. The long walk was shorter than it seemed to be later. The two of us who came together first were soon joined by former Ridgeway schoolmates. We were a good-sized chattering covey by the time we crossed the southeast corner of the playing fields. Individuals and groups streamed in from all points of the compass.

Not only did I have friends this time, but there was the exciting prospect of rejoining former classmates from North Star School. But, after our initial greetings, they faded into the general student culture. I had added friends from Ridgeway to the continuing friendship with Harvey, Ted, and the Stackhouse brothers from North Star, but the two clusters remained apart in two different spheres of our respective lives. The pattern for one of life's passages already was setting in.

North Van High appeared to me to be a very large school. Surrounded by a concrete walk (part driveway and part teachers' parking area), the rectangular building stretched most of the distance from one street to the next. Once more, it was a school on sloping ground, and once more, the open playing space was generous: two basketball courts on the first plateau immediately to the west, a large field on the plateau below with the usual goal posts, and this time, a baseball (softball) diamond on its own space. A sort of running track circled the lower field. Beyond the steep bank on the east side, where we had entered, was another soccer field with ample surrounding space. This was the field I would cross a couple of times each school day for several years to come.

North Van High turned out to be a rather simple structure: an egg-crate of quite large classrooms on the upper floor, another on the lower. Each floor had a wide hallway all the way down the middle, with rows of metal lockers on the lower. This time, there was a small, multipurpose gymnasium with a lunchroom that served modest meals at noontime, but most of us commonly carried lunch in a paper sack. Mr. Shaw had his chem lab; we came to know where he was in his never-varying schedule when the rotten egg smell came drifting through the hallways. Even the jokes were written into his notes. You could see them coming when his lips pursed a little and short wrinkles appeared around his mouth. The beginnings of his chuckle sounded like the clearing of his throat. He was a great fan of his own jokes.

There was a classroom-sized library and a typing room presided over by a young female teacher, the smiling Miss Andruss. Adjacent to it was a small room for such things as mimeographing, where the student council met and the student newspaper was produced. An awkwardly sliding wall separated two of the largest classrooms on the top floor; with the wall slid back, accordion-like, we had our auditorium. There was a full-fledged principal's office with a small waiting area outside. Between the two basements was a kind of storage room where bats and balls were kept. It also housed an atrocious piece of equipment through which those students assigned the task passed the dirty chalk erasers each day that rain prevented their being clapped noisily together outside.

There were no pits this time; I guess we had outgrown that form of letting off steam. Students lounged around in their respective basements on rainy days, but most preferred seeking sanctuary at recess and noontimes wherever they could find it outside, in the library, or in a classroom. The lavatories were not conducive to lounging nearby. North Van High had been there for quite some time; the camphor crystals in the latrines did not accomplish all that was intended. The teachers had their own lounge and restroom facilities. The school packed quite a lot into its rectangular dimensions.

Large though North Van High appeared to me, it must not have been. By today's standards, it was small. Sifting through my memories of it again and again, I have been able to come up with the names and images of only nine teachers, one of them Principal William Gray. I vaguely recall three more; I don't think there were slots in the curriculum for a larger faculty. There was, of course, a janitor, with a sometime assistant, who was kept too busy to pay much attention to individual students.

THE NARRATIVES OF ADOLESCENCE

In retrospect, the adolescent years emerge as very scary: like sailing a small boat through the reefs and innumerable fjords of the rugged British Columbia coast without charts or other navigational aids, with eyes most of the time on the scenery rather than the rocks and tide rips. Such innocence as is retained keeps things looking much less scary than they really are. It often is said that God takes care of fools and drunkards. Adolescents should be added to this list and guided carefully through their loss of innocence.

Four interacting narratives made up our lives, the first three largely school-based: the academic, the extracurricular (mostly student-initiated sports in my time), the social, and everything else. Separating these out, one from the other, as though each was independent is impossible. Most parents are blissfully unaware of how all four narratives are playing out together at any given time. This ignorance mutes much of the fear of imminent danger. For policymakers to believe that they can guide the adolescent's boat by monkeying around with the academic tiller is sheer folly. But they keep trying.

Only a few very insightful adults—mostly writers rather than researchers—have even come close to connecting the three school-based narratives, let alone all four. The rare few who have managed a credible life narrative through integrating the four subnarratives have had to do so in retrospect. This probably involved a good deal of inventing what comes across as the truth. The enlightenment we get from the insightful is tempered by our realization that the "everything else" has markedly changed over the intervening years—by the rapidly increasing diversity in the citizenry, for example.

What would later become common in the daily lives of high school students outside of school was nonexistent or scarcely begun: automobiles, drugs and alcohol, television, guns, "the pill," shopping malls, easily available pornography. My, we were innocent! I have little doubt that the combination of home, church, and school played a cautionary role in several temptations and that fear of pregnancy played a greater role. How some things have changed! I am unaware of the statistics of the time regarding teen pregnancy, but only one instance came to the attention—all too visibly—of the high school group with which I associated. The girl in question was one that none of us seemed to know. She rode her bicycle determinedly to and from the school door each day well into her pregnancy before she disappeared. The story most believed was that her father was the causal agent. Our conversations combined wonderment and believing disbelief.

Clearly, the environmental context of my high school, reinvented today, would be far more anachronistic and antiquarian than the school I attended. The deep structure of that school is firmly anchored in today's shopping mall high school.[2] Mine provided very few elective subjects; no sweat or tee shirts; no interschool baseball, basketball, or football; no marching bands; and no counselors. And yet, thanks to its surroundings, for most of us it competed quite successfully for our attention.

My narrative here is of schools. In romancing the school of adolescence, there is likely to be more inventing of the truth than was the case with the two schools of childhood. This is because what the innocent perceives to be "school"—that is, the academic narrative overwhelming the other three—is more accurately descriptive of the lower schools. This comment may appear a little strange, given the conventional image of secondary school as primarily a series of encounters to gain some precision with the subject matters of organized knowledge. This is one of our most cherished, widely inaccurate, and pernicious myths. It leads to the misdirection of countless dollars and human lives.

Despite having spent a large part of my life in and near schools, my narrative is marred by the inescapable intrusion of conventional wisdom regarding their nature, inventions of memory, and the difficulties of describing just one school, which, like the schools of all our pasts, was only minimally a place and maximally an adventure in making a life. My school was not anybody else's school. Nor was it, even for me, the school I remember. Better to view my memories of North Vancouver High School and the other two as romances, with three chunks of acreage as their terrestrial grounding.

The Academic Narrative

The academic narrative was conventional, perceptions of its nature creating in most minds, year after year, images of what school was, is, and should be. It was the trunk of the tree from which the other school-based narratives branched out. The constituency of that trunk changes somewhat over the years, but the descriptive rubrics do not.

We went to Mr. Shaw in his chemistry lab. We learned that there were ninety-two chemical elements—no more, no less—and that the smallest pieces of matter harnessed for scientific understanding were molecules. Atoms were still smaller, but there was little known or about to be learned about these little guys. Chemistry, it appeared, encompassed a pretty "fixed" body of knowledge. We had our turn at producing the rotten egg smell. We liked the laboratory sessions best: we learned how to handle test tubes and the Bunsen burner, and we wandered about quite a lot on the pretense of observing what others were doing.

Somewhere down the road, we were introduced to the rudiments of physics, but I don't remember when or who taught it. In fact, I don't remember very much of the sequence of most of my courses or who taught them when. It seems to me that each comprised half of a school year and six or seven the whole of the academic curriculum in each half.

There was mathematics (we had graduated from arithmetic): a lot of algebra and, in the later years, some geometry. I was rather intrigued with the idea of using letters of the alphabet as placeholders for other things, but the more complicated the symbolism became, the less I saw algebra as having much to do with my "everything else" narrative. I liked geometry more, using the formula pertaining to the hypotenuse of a right triangle to help both a cousin and my father figure out the dimensions of flights of steps they were separately designing.

I do recall that several teachers taught mathematics. Like the sciences, English, and social studies, it was required throughout most or all of the four years. Entrance to the university required such, but not many of us were heading there. Competence in mathematics appeared to be quite common among the teachers and especially among principals. It had been the specialty of both Principal Dobson and Principal Bennett. It is assumed to be near the core of advancing civilizations. The reserved, respected William Gray, principal at the time of my arrival, taught math, but he had gone by the time I reached the upper grades where he commonly taught. He held a master of arts degree from the prestigious University of Edinburgh. That put him a cut above all educators known to us; he had both designated and earned authority. The more prestige and power one had, the greater the likelihood of teaching the highest grades and most essential subjects, apparently.

The several other teachers who sought to teach us mathematics included Principal MacDougal, the former vice-principal who had replaced Mr. Gray by the time I encountered him in class. Although he was quite approachable—he sometimes tossed the basketball with us at recess, picking up quickly on our nicknames—few felt comfortable with him. It was said that his temper was due to his having been gassed in The War. A whispered remark to a nearby classmate often brought a piece of chalk flying through the air, sometimes with stinging results.

There was some kind of brouhaha during my time with the parents of a girl who had been the victim of a misguided missile. Today, he would be sued.

"Willie" Stewart taught some of the classes in history, as did Mr. Chamberlain, who also introduced us to civics and government. Willie was the common name in the family for William; Will or Bill came with participation in the larger world. I think we called Mr. Stewart "Willie" behind his back to take him down a little. He was somewhat pompous and prone to sarcastic wit in the classroom. He was bitter about the war that had caught him up before its end and, as it turned out, unerringly accurate in predicting when and why the next would commence. Although a quite cheerful soul most of the time, he managed to add another cloud to those of the economic depression that hovered over us unrelentingly, with no signs of their opening up soon to let some sunshine through. Indeed, Willie's pending war, the longstanding depression, and the bands of low atmospheric pressure that sometimes induced dull day after dull day for weeks on end in the winters assured the presence of melancholy in that narrative of "everything else" as well as the ongoing school-based narratives.

Mr. Chamberlain's niche in the school's narratives was less sharply etched than for most teachers. His classes were never dull. Teachers' lives out of school were virtually unknown to us. They came and went as we did, slipping inconspicuously into and out of their respective neighborhoods. It was clear that Mr. and Mrs. Chamberlain had a rather rich life elsewhere. We were awed that they owned a boat—a cabin cruiser—and fished and canned salmon during the many weeks they lived aboard her in the summer. Pleasure boats were sufficiently rare in those days that some people could name a boat unseen just from listening to the rhythm of its engine.

I do recall that geography was slipped into the social studies curriculum, but it might have been part of our study of Britain's history, for example. Just as Mr. Stewart and Mr. Chamberlain took care of my historical introduction into a small piece of Western civilization (the closest we got to Eastern civilization was Admiral Perry's entry into Tokyo harbor), Mr. Chamberlain and Mr. Siddons introduced us to a small slice of its poetry and prose. Bill had prepared me a little for Don Siddons—always *Mr.* Siddons—praising his teaching, but mostly, I think, reflecting the praise Bill received for his "compositions," as we called our required written papers in those days.

That first year of English was mostly repetitive of what we were supposed to have learned in the lower grades: rules of grammar and composition with very little embellishment. With so much to see and do and learn in the world, why so much retracing of where we had been? Do teachers know and students learn that those laying out the curriculum assume that the fundamentals will be approached so casually the first time around that the same meals must reappear on the menu? Mr. Chamberlain introduced us to Herrick. One of the poet's lines has profound implications for all teaching and learning: "Look thy last on all things lovely every hour."

Mr. Siddons was a perfectionist in all things—dress, speech, writing, manners, field hockey, tennis (we were told)—and expected perfection from us. His scrutiny of our compositions was meticulous: spelling, grammar, sentence structure, organization, style—all caught his eye. The blue-back speller and its lists of twenty-five words for each week had gone with our childhood, thank goodness, but Mr. Siddons enjoyed the occasional impromptu spelling exercise, nonetheless. I recall his triumph in downing us with "syzygy," a word I didn't encounter again for at least forty years. Growing interest in outer space and such events as solar eclipses now brings it occasionally under the media's telescopic eye.

Two years of French was another requirement; I took it for four. The subject injected something new into the academic narrative. The first year was easy and fun. French and English had been Bill's best subjects; writing that encouraged some creativity boosting his marks in the latter. All of his French, I recall, had been with Willie Stewart, whom Bill had liked. He even resonated with Mr. Stewart's sometimes caustic wit, much of it directed at the students. It had been fun during Bill's high school years to read, under his tutelage, the French on the cereal boxes with the English version covered. Canada had not then the bilingual customs and expectations of today, but French was the highly approved second language—earning status above Latin in the curriculum.

I came into my freshman year, then, with a little reading and (more primitive) speaking familiarity with French, as I had with reading English entering the first grade. This time, however, I didn't nosedive. I gradually adjusted to Mr. Stewart. Some comment regarding having a long way to go to reach my brother had set me back a little early on. In thinking of Bill's academic likes and dislikes, as well as my own, I wonder if liking the teacher leads to liking the subject or vice versa.

My progress with French sagged a little in the second year but was to soar later with Mr. McIntyre, who, in the short time he had been at North Van High, had become the girls' heartthrob. The young Mr. McIntyre, yet a bachelor, spun his little roadster deftly each morning into a parking space beside the school building—one of only a couple of teachers who arrived each day in their own automobiles. There were neither student cars nor buses in the school's ecosystem.

With an armful of books, Mr. McIntyre came out of his car on a near-run and maintained that pace most of the day—a tall, lean combination of Fred MacMurray and Jimmy Stewart. He appeared almost immune to distractions that would have brought most teachers to a boil. When the decibel level demanded too much of his own voice, he appealed for less noise and got near-normal quiet.

Mr. Crute alternated classes in health and physical education for the boys. He had a rather tough time of it, obviously wanting to reach us but not quite able to do so. Presumably he was German (he spoke excellent English) since he was married to a German woman and had been (went the rumor) an officer in the Kaiser's army. He had a military bearing and appeared to live very much according to military regimen. One summer, I went with new friends for a couple of weeks to the camp he directed. We learned the proper way to set a tent and roll two wool blankets together to create a cocoon that was as cozy and warm as a padded sleeping bag. Unless one was ill, one took a mandatory jump or dive into the cold waters of the cove, followed by a cold shower, before breakfast each morning. The songs around the campfire in the evening were a bit corny, but bits and pieces still come drifting back. We did learn in one of the games, to our amazement, the degree to which messages passed orally from messenger to messenger came out quite differently from their beginnings. The message Mr. Crute whispered to the first of us carried scarcely a vestige of its origins even by the time it had moved just a small distance from person to person around the circle. And we had tried very hard to retain what was whispered just once in the ear.

Teaching us didn't get any easier for Ed Crute. A decade and a half in the past, the war was not forgotten. In 1933, Adolf Hitler came into near-absolute power and, in 1934, proclaimed himself *Führer*. Although Hitler was regarded as a comic figure early on, this perception was soon to change. Mr. Stewart had good reason to bring down upon us the gloom of another major war in the offing. Mr. Crute was to prove himself a Canadian asset in that war, I was later told, but the distant rumblings were no asset in his present life.

I recall there being only three female teachers in the faculty of a dozen or so that my memory tells me staffed the school. There was a counterpart to Mr. Crute: the attractive, quick-tempered young woman who took care of health and physical education for the girls. I think she rather enjoyed being perceived as doing a better job than Mr. Crute did. I only vaguely recall an older woman who carried considerable authority; she might have been Mr. MacDougal's vice-principal. She would have taught, too, but I don't know what. I would be embarrassed to learn now that I had been in one of her classes.

Then there was Miss Andruss. If Mr. McIntyre had a counterpart who was the heartthrob for the boys, it was she. Not a beauty, perhaps, but a charmer for sure. Her smile could warm a gloomy day. She was, to us, sophisticated. A little on the plump side, she knew how to dress and use makeup to best advantage and was much sought after by the girls for advice not shared with boys. And Miss Andruss lived in Vancouver, the big city, taking the long trip by ferry and streetcar each day.

Miss Andruss taught the secretarial arts and skills of commerce, almost exclusively the domain of girls: typing, shorthand, and bookkeeping. Most of the much smaller contingents of boys who took typing had Miss Andruss and utilitarianism on their minds, commonly in that order. She taught the "tiger method" of attacking the keys. The sloppily typed versions of salacious "literature" that circulated underground from time to time had their origins with these successive groups of male typists. Perhaps the girls had their own subterranean network. One of my occasional school chums told several of us that his heart practically stopped beating when Miss Andruss quietly picked up his palpitating pulp piece into which he was inserting captions for his illustrative drawings. He anticipated expulsion. Miss Andruss told him that such was shamefully inappropriate for her class. He was in love with her for months.

Planning one's academic schedule for each successive year presented few decisions. The sole elective I recall in mine was typing (for purely utilitarian reasons, of course). If there were home economics for the girls and some form of industrial arts for the boys, I missed them. The rising U.S. interest in vocational education had not yet reached British Columbia. Friends and I at Ridgeway School had envied (although I knew I was not suited) our slightly older buddy, Jack Scott, when he was selected for the much-respected Vancouver Technical High School that opened its doors to those in the region who met its admission requirements. That took care of the technical and hands-oriented students, who were more valued in the marketplace than the academic.

I doubt that the curriculum of North Vancouver High School changed much during the decade prior to my coming or for years afterward, despite significant changes in the student population to be served. My brother Andy and large numbers of his peers had not gone on to high school (Andy not even pausing to take the eighth-grade matriculating exams). Bill, two years younger than Andy, took many of the same courses with many of the same teachers I experienced six or seven years later.

With success in all but one of his courses, Bill passed the high school graduation exams and entered the job market. After a short stint (boring to him) in the local pharmacy, he chose the tough but adventurous life of a deckhand on a Yukon River sternwheeler, ferrying mostly freight to the upper reaches of the river, a job that supported our eating and my going to school. He then passed all of the exams that, combined with the necessary experience, certified him to be mate and then captain of riverboats in the Yukon and Northwest Territories. I graduated from North Van High under a less nerve-wracking policy: on the recommendation of the teachers who had taught me. One thing that did change radically over this span of years was the increasing significance of teachers' ratings over examinations in students' progress from rung to rung of the stepladder of schooling. Today, of course, it is the tests that count.

Meanwhile, the proportion of youths continuing in school accelerated over the proportion leaving early and entering the near-jobless employment market. This kept friends together and produced a student population paralleling in heterogeneity the resident population as a whole. This heterogeneity was not today's. The ancestral roots were English, Scottish, Irish, Welsh, Scandinavian, German, French, Italian, Dutch, Spanish, Polish, Asian. Ties to the various homelands remained close but geographically removed. The get-togethers back in the various homelands were parents' memories; the depression had seen to that. Somehow, these groups managed ethnic gatherings, many in their own or rented community halls. Their offspring rarely joined in once they reached adolescence.

There was some public assistance, entered into reluctantly by most families in need, with the expectation that such would be short lived. There were "pension" plans, mostly for the disabled, scaled to estimated need; there were newspaper-driven funds for the needy, a thermometer on the front pages showing the target figures, present attainments, and the gaps between. The ethnic organizations quietly took care of their own to the limits of their capabilities. Families with employed fathers rarely achieved financial stability. Nearly everyone was poor, about to become poor, or recently poor. There were, we knew, some wealthy families with children, whom we didn't know, in one or another of the two or three private schools. The few relatively well-off families we did know were careful to keep a very low profile and an unpublicized record of local philanthropy. North Van High School was an incredible social melting pot. There simply were few racial and ethnic differences to melt down. School was to provide, apparently, a common academic narrative to accompany our common financial impoverishment. Our high school was a place apart, connected very loosely to everything else while largely sharing the values of its surroundings.

The Extracurricular-Social Narrative

The academic curriculum that was put in place when only a small percentage of youths went to secondary school remained the academic curriculum when there was not much else for youths to do but go to school. This circumstance, then, might have driven as compensation a rich and varied narrative of the extracurricular and social. Such was virtually nonexistent. What did exist was flattened by the ubiquitous mantle of everything else the depression had so penetrated.

In my memory, the subject matters of the academic narrative are inseparable from those who taught them. Although North Van High was parsimonious in the social and extracurricular, the teachers were part of what existed, even as they played their robust role in the academic. Most of them seemed to be aware that they had some responsibility for civilizing us, and parents respected them for it. Indeed, teachers—especially high school teachers—were among the most respected people in their communities.

Today, descriptions of schooling would put the extracurricular and the social into separate categories and add a third, athletics, even though they intermingle in the currents of a school's culture. In my day at North Van High, however, there was little of an organized nature to bring one's nonacademic attributes to the forefront as I have mentioned above: no interschool athletics (beyond one annual event), no cheerleaders, no marching band, no popularity contests, no designer clothes. Some loosely organized, unpredictable activities, for which someone might or might not take continuing responsibility, arose from time to time, might or might not find a place in the culture for a few years, and disappeared. There was a social tide of modest flood levels in which the extracurricular, some intramural sports, and some school-wide events were occasional floating logs.

There were youths—more male than female—who arrived and departed with the opening and closing bells, attended classes but stood on the sidelines for almost everything else. The legal age for leaving school had risen to sixteen by then, but there was not a sudden exodus when this age was reached; there was a jobless vacuum beyond. Many of these bystanders would have been long gone otherwise. Instead, there was a steady erosion of seventeen- and eighteen-year-olds. Absent the depression, most probably would not have been there in the first place. Male and female clusters remained almost separate during recess and noon hour but usually merged on departing the grounds at each day's end.

Grouped on the concrete driveway during recess, the males on the periphery remind me in retrospect of turkey buzzards solemnly watching for the infirmities of a potential victim. I recall the young teacher of girls' physical education turning sharply and slapping the face of the startled tormentor who had not meant to be heard. There is something to be said for dealing with harassment directly.

Smoking was becoming more and more popular as I progressed through high school. Cigarettes were an integral part of movie romances; "a cigarette for two" was the theme of a popular song. The cheapest form of smoking, rolling your own (from a pouch of tobacco and a pack of cigarette papers), especially with just one hand, brought respect that a good grade in algebra couldn't match.

I wonder how Mr. MacDougal's stance on the rise of smoking among students would go over today now that smoking is connected with cancer. Concern began with the janitor's report to him of cigarette butts and odors in the boys' basement. The response was a written notice to us all that smoking on the grounds was not permitted. Several of the male group of bystanders came up with the creative idea of sneaking into adjacent woods for a smoke. The company grew until smoke equivalent to a wet-wood campfire drifted up through the trees. The renegades were no longer smoking on the school grounds, but they were violating another rule—leaving the grounds at recess. Principal MacDougal, a pipe smoker, addressed the matter head on by joining the group. It was legal to be off campus with a teacher.

I was in his math class at the time. Sensing our intense interest in this development, Mr. MacDougal explained that banning smoking wouldn't stop it, yet he could neither ignore it in school nor condone the forbidden departures. By joining the group—many of its members on the fringes of schooling—he could talk man-to-man, so to speak, and perhaps entice a few out of their alienation. He did. And he gained the respect of the alienated. But, of course, there was a downside. He made more beckoning to the rest of us those smoke signals drifting out of the woods. Although I had as yet no interest in smoking, I was tempted to join the group. I'm sure that some previous nonsmokers did. Had there been no unwritten admission requirement of smoking, there would have been more boys in the expanding circle of beaten-down brush than within the school's boundaries. No doubt, Mr. MacDougal's bold initiative was being much discussed in students' homes. Could there have been any consensus? I don't recall any formal termination of the council in the woods, but it ultimately faded away.

That's the way it was with most of the sparse extracurriculum: little fires were kindled, blazed for a while, and died almost unnoticed. The kindler was usually a teacher, sometimes a student. Mr. MacDougal, in particular, seemed frequently to be opening a door here, a door there, and inviting us in—sometimes by singling us out individually. I recall two such occasions—one that I passed through quickly, the other that settled my career destiny.

The sports in which I engaged with growing passion came with me from Ridgeway School; my games were soccer and fast-pitch softball. Mr. MacDougal liked rugby and announced the potential formation of teams. I shrugged when he asked me why I hadn't turned out, but I finally gave in. On the field, I had only the faintest notion of what the game was all about, but Coach MacDougal stressed taking care of one's counterpart on the other team. The ball was put in play. I had never tackled, but once I had been perfectly downed, and so I caught my man at the knees. Coach MacDougal's praise brought me out a second time, but then the season was over. By the time school reopened in September, I had grown from 108 to 127 pounds. I had jumped from the bantam weight limit (110) over the next weight category and was now at the bottom of a higher one. That ended my career in rugby.

Not so with Mr. MacDougal's inauguration of a Future Teachers' Club—an organization beginning to catch on. I don't recall what we did that first year; I think it was mostly talk. But I do remember two days of teaching the following year when I had become a senior. Mr. MacDougal had let it be known among the elementary schools that seniors in the club were available as occasional unpaid assistants. Several of the principals and teachers had joined with us on occasion to tell us about the joys and tribulations of teaching.

Principal Dempsey of Lonsdale School, the district's largest elementary school, had called regarding a lower-grade teacher's need for a helping hand and I had gone. I didn't like it. The teacher didn't know how to use me, and I felt like a fifth wheel. Principal Dobson's request was quite different, and he was delighted with the prospect of getting a former North Star pupil. I jumped at the chance, and North Star School was briefly back in my life once more. But my old awe of Mr. Dobson returned to make me almost as nervous as I had been on that first day of school.

Mr. Dobson had to attend a meeting. He wanted me to take over his class for the day—not his principal's role, thank goodness. The skipping of two half-grades at North Star School had resulted in my beginning North Van High just a couple of weeks after my thirteenth birthday. I was now several months beyond the sixteenth. The common age of graduating from elementary schools was fourteen. It was not uncommon for pupils, usually boys, to flunk a couple of grades along the way. There would quite likely be in Mr. Dobson's class several boys my own age. I was terrified—virtually at the level of first sighting North Star School.

I need not have been. For one thing, I was fortunate in not having in that class a clone of my brother Bill. Mr. Dobson had mellowed, I had heard. Perhaps the emotional and physical scars of war had healed a bit. He provided me in advance with a meticulously planned schedule for the day. I was programmed; the day moved along smoothly and surprisingly quickly. I doubt anyone knew I had age-peers in the room. The teaching mantle adds some years. Mr. Dobson called Mr. MacDougal the following day to express his appreciation and the hope that I would become a teacher. Whereas earlier I had swum around the bait, I now was hooked.

Teaching as a career was not necessarily my choice above all others. Medicine and law had passed through my mind, but quickly. They were out of the question, given the costs involved. Had costs not been a barrier, however, I might have made the same choice. Indeed, the thought of not doing so has only fleetingly crossed my mind. The road not taken was one of the best accidents of my life.

Traditions are an important part of school culture. The depression was ending most of those traditions at North Van High; photographs in the lobby area at one end of the top floor reminded us of what had been. There were, of course, the uniformed sports teams—reminders of days when teams crossed the harbor to Vancouver for interschool games. There had once been, it appeared, a faculty-student baseball game. I tried unsuccessfully to resurrect it for softball. The annual faculty-female student field hockey game remained and gave us a view of surprisingly burly male legs in shorts—and an equally surprising image of several men competing not only to beat the girls but also to excel over one another. After all, North Van High was a male-dominated compound.

Another tradition still remaining was the day of interhigh track and field events that brought us into competition with much larger high schools in Vancouver. We nearly always came off well, piling up second- and third-place points, but rarely first-place points. We excelled in the relays where smooth baton handling could compensate for having mostly smaller runners. The event of the day for us this time was the 880. The long-legged Burnett was a head taller than everyone else in his senior class. We had watched Mr. Siddons quietly coaching him each late afternoon on the lower field's track. Again and again they had gone over the timing of Burnett's final spurt.

The runners were bunched up on precisely the opposite side from our space in the stands when Burnett's opportunity came. Suddenly, he was out in front, his long legs appearing to rise so as to be parallel with the ground, his spikes surely grabbing air since we didn't seem to see them touch the ground. Burnett had the wind at his back, cutting the finish tape at least six yards ahead of his nearest competitor.

We went wild. We had jumped on the scoreboard to within a few points of the leading Strathcona High. The sighs of relief from Strathcona's benches in the stands were palpable when an overanxious North Van girl fumbled the baton in the relay race that concluded the day's events. After all our yelling and screaming, we could speak only in grunts and whispers on the returning ferryboat. Next day's sports pages described us as "that gutsy little school on the other side of Burrard Inlet."

The female teachers tried admirably to put some civility and social efficacy into our lives. The tensions of sexual interests and differences had surfaced in the pre-pubescent years of the fourth to sixth grades and surged with puberty. For my closest friends and me—and, I think, for many other boys—the interest expressed itself largely in observation and imagination. The girls were more discretely observational and overtly invitational. We were clumsy, more inclined to strut than approach on an awareness of being observed.

Consequently, the occasional school dances were disasters. The boys lined the walls; the frustrated girls ultimately took to dancing with one another, bringing frowns from the attendant teachers. Luring a red-faced recalcitrant boy into dancing only compounded embarrassment. It was Miss Andruss who recommended that "mixers" were the answer.

Mixers were the remedy tried in many high schools, I later learned. The intent of mixers was to mix everyone together in a party atmosphere. There was a ballroom dance or two, a little square-dancing (which legitimated clustering to listen to the caller without having to dance), some easily learned rhythmic routines (put your right foot in, take your right foot out, etc.), some march-around-the-perimeter interludes, and various games. Miss Andruss introduced us to the increasingly popular "Doing the Lambeth Walk"—a total group dance that required little in skill.

The Leap Year effort to give wallflower girls a chance to invite a date backfired. The boys they most wanted to take were already spoken for. These girls were forced to turn to second, third, or no choices. Many stayed home. I doubt the event became a tradition. At one of the last mixers I ever attended, friends and I found ourselves regarding Harcus with near awe: he showed up with Joy—yes, *the* Joy Dobson. They had been dating. The rather shy and quiet Harcus had moved in where others feared to tread. No tomboy now, Joy plucked a bit of lint from his jacket—a domestic touch. We looked on in envy. What would it be like to have a girlfriend like that? And how would one get over a falling-out?

I don't know how long Joy and Harcus dated after high school. The class of '37 had its dreams, and new complications set in after eighteen. The last I heard of Joy, she was pursuing a dancing career in London;

Harcus was a dentist married to someone else. Whatever happened to the others?

In their various ways, the teachers of North Van High did a lot to civilize us, much of it through example. They didn't have many tools to work with. Had they been given some discretionary money, I think they would have significantly enriched our school-based narratives. Since a core of the student body remained quite stable, with a steady drip of dropouts from the upper years and the rare replacement by new-comers, the teachers and students came to know each other rather well in our small school, despite the usual teacher-student barrier. Peel off the public-created shroud and many teachers emerge as sensitive, involved, concerned human beings. For as long as any of us can recall, including from the literature of bygone eras, teachers have been por-trayed as silly, stuffy, and naive. In recent years, movies and television have maligned them in spades. Even the Statler Brothers—nostalgic of their high school days—got in the little slur: "Janet teaches grade school and prob'ly always will." It is folly to believe that we can have both good schools and unappreciated teachers.

But had there been additional money, it would have been because more was flowing into the hands of the citizenry, too, and so there would have been hosts of interests to serve: classes for the "gifted" (most quite ordinary), a marching band, interschool athletics for the few, sports uniforms, buses serving the far corners of the district (putting greater burdens on taxpayers to sustain the already extended streetcar service), politicians' ambitions, standards and tests throughout that "would mean something," and one would hope, services and programs that would bring cerebral-palsied children out of the closet. A manage-ment system with an organizational chart and people to run it would have been required. As it was, the buck stopped with each school prin-cipal. When Mr. Gray was invited to leave the principalship of North Van High, it wasn't to go to the superintendency of the district. There was none. He became attached to the low-profile board of education in some way, probably, in the pattern of districts elsewhere, becoming its secretary-treasurer. He showed up occasionally in our school and, I under-stand, became increasingly involved in matters of finance and personnel.

Had there been more money available, I'm confident that its flow would have benefited us quite equitably, given the fact that most of us were in a boat of common financial deprivation.

The Narrative of Everything Else

Our common disadvantage blocked out some of today's "everything else." There were no parked cars or automobile joyrides to worry about. Although a few fathers dropped off students some mornings on their way to work, only one student (a newcomer arriving midway in the four years) owned his own automobile, a sleek, black, Ford coupe. Because of shipping interests in Vancouver, apparently, Douglas Dollar of the Dollar Steamship Company family found himself in North Vancouver High for a time.

Many families had a phonograph (gramophone) and a few records, with the listening dog on the RCA Victor label. Radios were becoming significant items of furniture in some homes; there were no boom boxes. Television was yet to replace the evening family conversation and the card games with guests. You still could easily tell the good guys from the bad guys in the movies and needed no rating system or a psychiatrist to tell you it was okay to watch Randolph Scott, Tom Mix, Roy and Dale, Nelson and Jeanette, and the singing cowboy, Gene Autry. The school-based narratives were not, then, fighting for attention in a context of the powerfully educative technological distractions, diversions, and excursions into a larger virtual world yet to come.

At the core of the narrative of everything else was the neighborhood. The absence of self-controlled transportation made getting out of one's neighborhood a deliberate act: to walk to the school serving all neighborhoods, to board streetcar or both streetcar and ferry to go to work or to shop. There was no pull of a mall magnet. In its various subtle ways, the neighborhood shaped the transition into adulthood, sharing this transition with the school to the degree that the two linked in some way. This linkage was highly individual and quite fragile, its nature significantly determining just how scary adolescence might turn out to be.

The boundaries of neighborhoods were very loosely determined, with each tending to be centered on the porches and in the yards of a cluster of houses. In each, the young found a gathering space or two. One learned to pass on the perimeter of some of these spaces if heading for the other side, especially on summer evenings. The youth groups of the neighborhoods I knew were more like clans. One would not be shot or knifed on passing through but might be roughed up. The boys were very protective of "their" girls, especially if the girls made overtures to other boys passing by. These overtures probably were motivated both by boredom with the now-familiar neighborhood boys and provocative interest in creating a diversion.

The narratives of schooling were, for most of us, the most powerful alternatives to the relentless shaping of neighborhood propinquity: If the passage through high school did not provide some appealing glimpses into the romantic possibilities of a world beyond one's neighborhood, the future regarding virtually all the major elements of making a life narrowed into several self-fulfilling prophecies regarding whom one would marry, how one would earn a living, and what values one would cling to. Adolescence is, indeed, a perilous journey; life can be very difficult even before one reaches eighteen. With so much in the surroundings dangerously educative, school must be more than a race for good grades. Most parents agree, today's policymakers should note.

With higher education not part of the future for most of us, visions of the future sharply restricted by the neighborhood ethos and the continuing economic depression, and the high school years just a period of marking time for some of us, the fortunate were those who connected with the larger adult world in some self-fulfilling way during these years. But, once again, the scope of possibilities was narrow, the successful finding of a bridge serendipitous. A richer extracurriculum at North Van High would have helped immensely, especially if it could have focused on developing individual talents.

The larger world did reach most neighborhoods to some degree. The big band jazz era was burgeoning, finding its way into radio broadcasts and movies. Harvey went to see every movie featuring Nelson Eddy serenading Jeanette MacDonald in his Canadian Mounted Police uniform somewhere in the Rocky Mountains—several times to each. Most of us favored the Bing Crosby style of crooning. (Frank Sinatra probably was practicing the rhythm of his breathing somewhere in Hoboken, New Jersey.) But Harvey took to Nelson Eddy sufficiently to imitate him recognizably in the local amateur contests then beginning to precede the scheduled movie. A young man in a neighborhood I avoided took diffidently to school, but may have been one of the lucky ones anyway. For hours on end each evening, the notes of his clarinet playing drifted through the air. Bennie Goodman and Artie Shaw no doubt were two of his role models.

I was one of the lucky ones, thanks in large part to serendipity. It helped enormously to be both of one's neighborhood and legitimately out of it—to live as a neighbor while avoiding the perils of being too much caught up in neighborliness during those scary adolescent years. By the time of my entering North Van High, I was addicted to soccer and softball. In the latter, I had apprenticed myself to my memory of Tino's pitching. The coming of spring brought pickup games at school every noon hour. Sandwich in one hand and the ball in the other, I got plenty of practice. Then came our new neighbors.

Douglas Renhoff was unique. In a series of operations, one of his legs had been reduced to a stub encased by ten inches of pant leg. But this didn't slow him down. With one leg and one crutch, he entered two-legged races and often won. He had swum Burrard Inlet—several miles through waves and tides. One of his present hobbies was managing a team in the men's softball league, made up of several North Vancouver teams and one from neighboring West Vancouver. Doug Renhoff sometimes pitched—not spectacularly, but quite satisfactorily.

Learning of my interest, Doug initiated our pitching and catching in his backyard. He was impressed. Spinning the ball from a low start so that it was rising at home plate had come quite easily to me, as had the straight fastball. I had my own versions of Tino's pitch that curved away from the batter, dropping just before he swung—one finger paralleling the ball's seams for the very slow, tantalizing one, and two fingers for the pitch with a little more "swift." By the age of fifteen, I was on Doug's team, pitching a couple of times a week and playing in the outfield the rest of the time. Also pitching at school nearly every day, I was on my way to a wrecked right shoulder.

What a way to avoid getting into trouble close to home and to expedite the transition into adulthood. There came a sense of grown-up responsibility on reading about each of our games in the local newspaper. It was nice to have a girlfriend (from another neighborhood) rooting for me in the stands and to begin to learn that there were choices of many kinds outside of one's own neighborhood. The complications that arise when you get past sixteen are not just what you get into; they have a lot to do with what you come with and encounter there.

Do we need today's high-profile, interschool sports teams and events for a small proportion of the student body (and the entertainment of the public), an enterprise that cultivates and sustains huge high schools? Do these provide sufficient reason for prolonging the adolescence and delaying the adulthood of seventeen- and eighteen-year-olds in an environment that is ill-suited for them and in which they probably are not the best role models? The answers to both questions range from probably not to definitely not. However, as the prestigious former presidential candidate Ross Perot learned to his chagrin, the recommendation of his governor-appointed commission to curtail these in Texas was both ignored and maligned. There is, nonetheless, a growing parental interest in small schools where the personal, social, vocational, and academic goals can be well served, absent such teams and events.

WHATEVER HAPPENED TO THE CLASS OF '37?

I was two months shy of my seventeenth birthday when my life as a secondary school student became nothing more than a series of snapshots on the walls of memory. The final snapshot found its place quietly and unobtrusively. I was soon to come back to North Van High, but in a capacity best described as on the periphery of its culture and not at all romantic.

Graduation was a slipping away, not an event: no valedictorian, no athletes honored, no speeches made, no caps and gowns—indeed, no schoolwide graduation ceremony. Those of us who matriculated without examinations were released a week early, leaving the others to sweat through one or several exams. Then we came back to pick up our diplomas. I vaguely recall teachers' congratulations as we passed in a hallway, and my homeroom teacher, Mr. McIntyre, saying a few words of goodbye and good luck.

On the way out, I lingered in the lobby area of the near-empty upper hallway, slowly moving from photograph to photograph. I was waiting, I think, for something to happen. I don't know what, but something quite momentous—like the best of those futures in one's horoscope, like having the wind at your back. It didn't happen.

I was alone, looking intensely at the photos on the wall as though I had never seen them before: well-arranged clusters of graduating seniors of bygone years, dressed in their very best. I wondered what had happened to the classes of '36, '35, and '34. My thoughts must have connected me with the sense of mortality we humans share. I was suddenly over-whelmed with the reality of my father's death the previous February. When the tears began to come, I hurried down the familiar well-worn stairs into the bright sunlight of a beautiful June day and set out for home across the corner of the upper soccer field. I wonder whatever happened to the class of '37.

Chapter 4

Becoming a Teacher

The purpose of life is learning. When one ceases to learn, one ceases to live life to the fullest. . . . Teaching is a complex process that requires continuous learning.

Before going to sleep I always ask myself three things: one, what did I learn today; two, what did it mean; and three, how can I use it?

RALPH W. TYLER[1]

NORTH VAN HIGH REDUX

There is a peculiar parallelism in entering school and leaving it. The life of security and contentment I had known for my first six years had been suddenly jarred by insecurity and apprehension on beginning school. Eleven years later, the certainty of most of my daylight hours was again suddenly replaced by uncertainty and unease.

Are these transitions now eased for the young by the entry of many to nursery school or kindergarten before the first grade and by the ceremonies and celebrations of graduation? My guess is that the beginnings and endings are, for most, still fraught with trauma. This is largely because of the enormous ecological differences between schools and everything else. But surely we need better bridges. Surely these will come when our schools are more places for the young and less the instruments of adult purpose.

During concluding weeks of the twelfth grade, classmates and I talked about what was next to come. For the very few planning to enter university—almost exclusively the province's only one, the University of British Columbia—there was little speculation. They were headed for at least four years of tertiary schooling; the major uncertainties lay beyond. They conveyed a degree of understandable smugness, accompanied by considerable curiosity about the plans of those who were to venture forth into the world of adult responsibility. After all, although of the same age, their full entry into that world was to be delayed by a period somewhat akin to extended adolescence. We were intuitively aware of the differences, differences that remained for decades a source of tension between "town and gown." It would take a second world war to advance higher education a few notches higher in the lexicon of public support and a few lower in special privilege.

For most, expectations were a combination of uncertainty and hope. In a few weeks, we would walk across the playgrounds for the last time and abruptly become adults. Canada and most of the rest of the world were not yet out of the Great Depression, but there were employment stirrings, especially in the longstanding bread-and-butter industries of mining, logging, and fishing. Hope springs eternal, especially in the young. "We harvest the fruit of hope in order to begin again to hope"— these words accompany the colorful images in one of Sister Mary Corita's serigraphs. Still, most of us were acutely aware that there are complications out there where one becomes an adult. We thought little about those past eighteen who had once been with us at North Van High but were no longer.

As things turned out, my transition into adulthood was to be more gradual than I had anticipated. I had decided years before that I would like to be a schoolteacher. This meant elementary school teacher, since the requirement for secondary teaching was a college degree—out of the question for me, as were such other occupations as lawyer and physician. I would go to normal school for a year after graduating from high school. But the rules had changed. Completion of the first year at a university was now required. The bridge to teaching was now two years long and probably closed to me.

But then a glimmer of hope had appeared. The gates into teaching tend to open wide when there is a shortage of teachers and remain loosely latched even when there is a surplus—a strange contradiction of economic principles. Perhaps it was the presence of a ministry of education in British Columbia that produced an uncommonly sensitive weighing of quantity, quality, and even equity. The long depression had produced a bulging surplus of would-be elementary school teachers. The requirement of one year of successful university attendance had markedly slowed the stream. But it also had dried it up for the most economically disadvantaged. Some wise person or group in the policy arena authorized the offering of the first year of higher education in selected, qualified high schools. Thankfully, North Vancouver High School was one of these. It would open its doors also to graduates of West Vancouver High School in our neighboring, smaller municipality—but perhaps not to me.

The additional amount of money for what was called Senior Matriculation was not enough; a small tuition fee was required. I recall it being ten dollars per month, although perhaps that was what could be negotiated for special cases of financial hardship. But it was more than my mother could set aside out of her limited resources. My Uncle Andy stepped into the breach, and in September, I would be back for a fifth year at North Van High.

SCHOOL AS EDUCATIONAL INSTRUMENT

Nearly two dozen of us showed up to comprise the class of '38. We were all graduates of the high school class of '37—seven or eight from West Van High, the rest from North Van, half of us headed for elementary school teaching. Most of the rest hoped to be sophomores the following year at the University of British Columbia. This new educational route accommodated more than future teachers.

The school ambience for us was quite unlike what it had been during the preceding four years. For me, it lacked romance; perhaps that is why the experience was not memorable. We were not part of the school culture but houseguests, temporarily residing there. We were not part of the youth culture either, but more adults in waiting. Our relationship with teachers was strangely different, too. We were not peers but not exactly pupils either. We did not defy their authority, but we were not part of it, although we may have sought to be. When we occasionally lapsed into childlike silliness, it took only a stare to stop us in embarrassment. We just didn't know who we were.

We followed the regular school calendar and schedule but kept largely to ourselves. I do not recall kicking a soccer ball around or pitching a softball at noon, although I did both during the year in leagues completely separated from school. There were no stores nearby to attract us during the noon hour, and we had little money to spend anyway. We spent most of this time in our classroom, the girls knitting or crocheting, the boys playing checkers, cribbage, chess, or card games. Mostly we talked, with a teacher sometimes joining us.

We talked of serious things: whether there would be jobs for those of us heading for elementary school teaching, about what the others of us planned to do, and about war. The threat of Hitler was becoming more palpable. We were still in the high school, but our heads and expectations were much of the time someplace else. The class work was something we had long been accustomed to.

The curriculum was rigorous: trigonometry, biology, physics, French, Latin, history, and literature. Our teachers were not going to have Senior Matriculation looked down upon by the university as second-rate. Their teaching was different from what we had experienced previously; they invited questioning and invoked discussion. They were trying to give us something more than and different from what had grown familiar. When I learned later about the large freshman lecture classes of the university, I began to realize how favored we had been. I am sure my own later teaching was affected positively by the experience. Something else was very different in the student-teacher relationship. Perhaps because we were serious and not at all diffident about the learning, the teachers sought diligently to help us. They wanted us to succeed, and we knew it. I remember that Mr. McIntyre's French class (he was our homeroom teacher, too) was heavily devoted to writing. He read everything we wrote, carrying home our papers nearly every night and returning them very much blue-penciled the next day. And he also devoted extra time to individual tutoring.

There was a subtle shift in our orientation to the work. We were no longer picking and choosing among what interested us and what did not. There were no peaks and valleys; the whole flattened out before us as of equal value and interest. We did not know what among it all was most valued by our teachers and, therefore, most likely to be tested. One could not afford to take off on a tangent with something of special appeal, to the extent even of pursuing it beyond school. I do not recall reaching out from what I was trying to comprehend for something else of relevance to read or do. What we were doing was a necessary step to where we thought we were going.

An irritation began to nag at me. I knew I was on my way to becoming a teacher, but little of what I was doing each day seemed to connect. I was too often an irritant in a class, asking the teacher for practical implications and applications—not to teaching but to anything beyond school. The answers were no more satisfying than those to questions of usefulness students at all levels ask of their teachers and get the same response, "You will find it useful later on."

In retrospect, I think I was after connections to the big themes of the human conversation. This expectation had been fulfilled only occasionally during my previous four years of high school. I was now endeavoring to integrate the ongoing pieces of my total surround and make some sense out of my life. But this fifth year was isolated from it. I was expecting a lot of my teachers to have my classes in school connect. But shouldn't what one does in school each day help one deal with that larger part of life outside of school?

School and the education it was providing had become an instrument, a tool with which to gain entry into another part of life's passage. My orientation to the curricular demands was anything but the orientation—often romantic—one attaches to the liberal studies. Their lure had been obliterated by the lure of a vocational credential for which this year of Senior Matriculation was a requirement, not learning for its own sake.

Nonetheless, I think I got the hang of that year several months into it. Clearly, what was necessary was to get through it with reasonable comfort, just as it had been with Miss Burgess in the fourth grade.

Don't long for Miss Hamilton's reading and her cuckoo clock. Just do it. After all, the teachers were giving more support than I had received during the preceding four years, and I had plenty of things to keep me satisfyingly involved outside of school. But it was a strange year of being in some ill-defined place in life between dependent, nearly useless late adolescence and independent, useful adulthood.

A passage in Wendell Berry's *Jayber Crow* brings that year vividly to mind. Orphaned early on, Jayber was sent away to a church orphanage called The Good Shepherd where he was well taken care of. There he became fond of reading and of words. At about the age of fourteen, he began to suspect that he might be called upon to preach. Although he actually heard no voice, he decided that he had better accept the call that had not come in case it had come and he had missed it. And so he became a preministerial student at Pigeonville College. He had a pretty good life there, studying for classes, reading, waiting on tables, and even earning a little money doing odd jobs in Pigeonville: "My life just filled out into all the freedom it was allowed." Then those big questions for which he had no answers began to catch up with him, such as "If we are to understand the Bible as literally true, why were we permitted to hate our enemies?" As the questions piled up, he decided that he could not preach when he did not have any answers.[2]

The air around us senior matriculants at noon often was heavy with our discussion of questions we could not answer. The teachers who sometimes joined us were short on answers, too. But at one o'clock, we went back to classes and had better luck answering questions we had not asked—and would not have addressed had we not been in school.

Several of us had gotten into heavy-duty wrestling with troublesome questions the year before. A classmate, Conn Templeton, was one of the finest human beings I ever met. He struggled a lot with weighty questions rarely discussed in school, such as why war would bring peace. He convened several of us to talk about his frustration and what we might do about the big human problems. We formed a club—with a corny name, Saturday Knights Club—and decided to meet one Saturday evening each month. We scheduled questions for discussion over several months, selected common readings in advance, passing around the chore of making all necessary arrangements and of hosting the sessions. We devoted about half the time to the heavy stuff, the rest to assorted games and entertainment. There were budding musicians among us. Indeed, that year we even sponsored noon-hour concerts of student performers at school.

We continued somewhat more sporadically the following year, spending more time just socializing with knights who were elsewhere than attending Senior Matriculation with the rest of us. To bolster attendance, we decided to include girlfriends. We covered most of the questions I had earlier heard my parents and relatives arguing about long into the evenings. Time, age, and place did not much change the contents of this perennial human conversation.

In this second year, we were drawn more and more into the European scene and the stirrings of Hitler's Germany. Why were listeners so mesmerized by the cadence and words of Hitler's speeches? Why did so many believe, with Rudolf Hess (in a speech, June 1934), that the Führer was obeying a higher calling and surrender silently to his orders? Surely fear did not account for the whole of it. Were we inevitably slipping into wide-scale war? Were we too young for the agenda of the Saturday Knights Club to be part of the agenda of school? Conn Templeton was the first class associate of my youth to be killed in World War II. He was blown to pieces by a bomb as he sought to make his way from the deck of the destroyer to the captain standing on the bridge above.

VANCOUVER NORMAL SCHOOL

There were no tears in my eyes when I left North Van High for the second and last time. And I did not have to wonder much about where the members of the class of '38 were headed. We had become a rather tight-knit group and knew quite a bit about the hopes and aspirations of each of us.

The group bound for normal school had shrunk a bit and was made up mostly of a North Van contingent. All of us congregated on the same ferry that September day of first attendance. Overall, the class of '39 assembled in the auditorium that morning was over five dozen strong, women outnumbering men by nearly three to one. Yes, we were now men and women, preparing to be of value. Most were, of course, from Vancouver, but they came also from small towns and rural areas scattered across the province. Two women who had just graduated from the University of British Columbia thought they wanted to teach children rather than adolescents, and so they had come to the provincial normal school to gain certification. There were other older people among us, but these two stood out for their sophistication and clothes that few had money enough to buy.

Mr. Lord, the principal, welcomed us and then turned the gathering over to others of the teaching staff for further welcoming and the delivering of relevant information. More men than women, they were pleasant, well groomed, and articulate. The men were in the middle to upper range of middle age, the women somewhat younger. The married couple responsible for women's and men's health and physical education instruction, respectively, were as handsome, trim, and coordinated as an ice-skating team. The opening assembly was fun.

We then went through a strange exercise. We all took the Seashore Test for Musicality! This was new. I do not know what procedure had been used previously to divide us into two classes, but I feel sure it was more commonly routine. Mr. Lord, it became apparent later, was quite attuned to the ideas of Beverly Sharp, the music teacher. Apparently, she thought that the anticipated range of musicality among us would be so great that a measure of homogeneous grouping was required. Why it had to prevail for all things all year was anybody's guess.

A few days later, we realized that the taking of the test had not been a passing whim. The two groups into which we had been assembled were rearranged into the top group and the bottom group of test performers. Much to my surprise, I was in the top. But not for long. A student in the bottom group had withdrawn; I was assigned to her vacated place. Through no volition of my own, I had gone overnight from the bottom of the top track to the top of the bottom. I had moved only one small notch in the musical hierarchy but a long way down in the perceived social pecking order. Schools function by a strange set of norms. A school is a school is a school, whether or not a normal school.

At that time, I had read nothing about the history of normal schools. Indeed, this history was at the time largely lodged in the letters and diaries of those who had been closely involved with them. Now their passage to teachers colleges, state colleges, and state universities is well documented. Teacher education is not the only purpose they had served. They had provided for many the rudiments of the subject learning commonly associated with general education at the secondary and even elementary school level. I was surprised that this was much of what the one I attended did, only by way of review. There was little of pedagogy—that is, of the art and science of connecting the mind to the systems of knowledge and knowing that embellish the human conversation. John Dewey campaigned at the University of Chicago for pedagogy as a discipline in its own right. That was at the beginning of the twentieth century. It would have been a novel idea at my normal school four decades later and largely remains so in the halls of academe today.

What we did get were assorted overviews of elementary school curricula; smidgens of activities we might replicate in our classrooms; self-improvement exercises in handwriting, music, health, and physical education; lessons learned from the experiences of our teachers; detailed instructions for scheduling and managing the many subjects and graded lessons of an eight-grade, one-room school; and a modicum of instruction in teaching technique. We varied widely in our eagerness to store away acorns to nourish the learning of our pupils on long winter days yet to come.

ON TEACHERS AND TEACHING

During the twelve years of school that had preceded, I paid a lot of attention to my teachers but little to their teaching—that is, to what they did to entice me into learning what they were trying to teach me. Now I found myself doing just that. I have never believed that teachers are born, not made, and my observation strengthened this belief. There were no "naturals" among them. Careful observation revealed that those who were good at it, worked at it. Those who were not, did not.

Studies of secondary school students reveal that interest in and liking for physical education, vocational education, and the arts top those of all other subjects. But one must be careful in crediting their teachers. These are fields in which efficacy is directly experienced and the steps to it quite easily observed. I have enjoyed the hands-on satisfaction involved while ignoring poor teaching. But it was obvious that the couple teaching physical education liked what they did and worked at it. She was a little more carefully planned than he and demanded more of her students, some of whom thought she expected too much. Both did what they expected us to do and gave reasons for it. I wondered how their teaching styles would have to be changed with their aging.

Mr. Hall taught with finesse. His field was English literature. Although he lectured most of the time, interspersed with some readings, he provided openings for questions and discussion. I think it was listening to him that introduced me to having extended muted conversations with lectures and books. I prefer to converse silently with a good lecture any day rather than carry on a verbal conversation with an overly opinionated boor. For me, Mr. Hall's pedagogy was obviously but not annoyingly deliberate. He positioned himself comfortably for a time and then, during an appropriate pause, moved several yards and repositioned himself. He was careful never to be off balance; such is very distracting to an audience. He did not put a foot on the rung or his knee on the seat of a chair. Nor did he engage in that annoying habit of pacing sideways to his audience, to the left and then the right, looking to the floor and then to the ceiling, as though for an oracle through whom a deity would guide his thoughts. Mr. Hall appeared to be a very normal human being.

As the year progressed, it became increasingly apparent that our teachers were not people who had prepared diligently by dint of study and experience for the role of teacher educators in which they now found themselves. Most of the men and one of the women had been former school inspectors, and some were still so engaged part time. The normal school assignment was a kind of reward for years of traversing the province, observing in classrooms, and passing judgment on teachers, particularly beginners. No doubt the "old boys club" played its part in the selection process.

Together, the faculty represented, somewhat unevenly, the subjects of the school curriculum. Several had written textbooks and other materials adopted for the province's schools, Mr. MacLean's manuals on penmanship, the nibs, pen holders, and other paraphernalia being the most obviously lucrative. Some made cameo appearances. I am not quite clear on why Mr. Winslow showed up from time to time, and I am not sure he knew. I guess his occasional sessions had to do with art appreciation. He was one of Canada's famed Group of Seven. His stunning paintings of stormy shores and beached driftwood gleaming on a snowy beach were priced at thousands of dollars. Only a couple of our teachers left the impression of having struggled as ordinary teachers during the depression, now beginning to recover from its lowest ebb.

The essence of being a teacher and teaching was missing. There are today, of course, many books on schools, teachers, and teaching. I do not know what were available then, but I do know that there were relevant diaries and novels. Teachers College, Columbia University, was drawing thousands of teachers to the classes of William Heard Kilpatrick, George Counts, Harold Rugg, John Childs, and others who were generating a stream of books and articles on school curricula, pedagogical theories, human development and learning, and alternatives in educational philosophy. And, of course, the sharply differing views of Edward L. Thorndike and John Dewey, housed on opposite sides of 120th Street in New York City, were stirring a debate that is still alive today.[3] It passed us by.

A Hint of Progressive Education

I think we came dangerously close to being caught up in the perennial controversy over what are conventionally referred to as traditional and progressive education. It came from an unexpected source late in our academic year. I do not think I had seen this relatively young instructor before. I think she represented that sometimes-maligned field that came to be known as the social studies—what some scholars have referred to as a corruption of the social sciences. Miss Porter lacked the credential of experience as a school inspector. The impression lingers that she had returned from studies at a university in the United States.

I do not remember much about the class, but there were references to John Dewey. I drew one of his books from the library but did not stay with it. With student teaching now behind us, I was getting somewhat bored and a little careless. I did not want to mess up my chances of successfully graduating, but I wanted classes over with so that I could get into my own. Suddenly, we were into something interesting that turned my attention to the potential realities of next year.

Miss Porter observed that jobs were scarce. The best hope for most of us was in the faraway Peace River District coming to economic attention for its production of award-winning hard wheat. Then there were scattered rural areas where male teachers were likely to be chosen before women. Some of these would have significant proportions of Native North Americans in the classroom mix. They had rich cultural backgrounds and tribal customs that we should get to know something about, said Miss Porter. Then she said that we would dig into some of this and think up creative ways to bring it into the understanding and appreciation of all children. The standard history of westward exploration and economic development of the region just would not do. This was pretty gutsy stuff for the time.

We had gotten into some discussions of hands-on approaches to traditional classroom fare and learned a little about Kilpatrick's project method. We stayed pretty much on the surface of pedagogy, not digging into the highly controversial distinction regarding the learner as a reasoning being with skills already honed in the processing of experience. We did not enter into any of the great debates. The project method was another acorn to add to the educational menu on rainy days.

Nonetheless, we entered vigorously, noisily, and sometimes creatively into our projects. Miss Porter employed that old pedagogical bromide: we were to imagine ourselves being nine- or ten-year-olds. I decided to make a dugout canoe and brought a chunk of clear-grained red cedar for this purpose. Some others were into the cultural significance of cedar and salmon, and so, with my modeling of a canoe, we had the subject matter of communion.

Our classroom was, I think, what had once been a high school lab, and so we had tables and benches to accommodate our activities. It was on a day that Miss Porter apologized for having to be gone for a time that I decided to be authentic. I had read about the hardening effect of the burning out process in the making of a dugout canoe. In a mood of careless frivolity rather than devotion to tradition, I set out to kindle the necessary fire. By now I had a supply of shavings and the floor of our room was concrete. I sidestepped authenticity and lit a small bundle of paper to get things going. I had not counted on the volume of smoke produced while, in panic, we stamped out the small blaze.

The blue haze still circled the room and some of us were still coughing when Miss Porter returned. Surely my normal school days were about to come to an abrupt end. No, I was praised for my keen attention to factual detail! But my custodianship of progressive education and the project method suffered a blow. That old normal school building is probably long gone. If not, there undoubtedly remains a concrete floor marked with a dark memorial to educational innovation gone awry.

STUDENT TEACHING

We had been a couple of months into the fall schedule before being sharply confronted with the realization that schoolteaching involves classrooms and students. Over a period of several weeks, we were scattered about for two or three visits to classrooms, each of several days. There was consistency in our being assigned to only one teacher and one classroom. I say "visits" because mine were not much more than that. On the first, I only observed and the time went slowly. I was in the second grade of a school next door to the normal school building. Accommodating aspiring student teachers over the years had become routine, as had the habit of introducing us to the class as such—an introduction that automatically reduces one's authenticity. I felt peripheral.

My second and third short visits involved teaching—first a reading and then an arithmetic lesson. I did not know what to look for in my observations, and the lesson plans for both sessions were handed to me by the teacher the day before. I was not comfortable. The report of my efforts that was shared with me was rather innocuous except for the observation that I might experience some difficulty with discipline.

That was the welcome end of teaching experience until March and then April-into-May of the next calendar year when student teaching was scheduled. I was elated that both placements—each a month in length—were in North Vancouver where I still lived: the first where I had once been a pupil, Ridgeway School, and the other at the small Lynn Valley School, near the end of the streetcar line of the same name.

Ridgeway Elementary School

I encountered none of the teachers with whom I had associated at Ridgeway. Nonetheless, I was welcomed as an alumnus. There had not been in my time a class like the one to which I was assigned. The energetic, middle-aged Mrs. Baker was enthusiastic about it. The lowest-achieving third- and fourth-grade pupils (and, I think, a few from the fifth grade) were grouped together in what she referred to as an Opportunity Class. I had not known then about such an arrangement, but I was chilled by the idea. Opportunity for what? Decreasing self-respect?

I lacked honed skills of pedagogical diagnosis, but I did not need them. The sorry circumstances jumped out at me. There were fewer children than were then common in a class, but because of the near-constant milling about, there appeared to be more. Mrs. Baker remained enthusiastic and smiling most of the time, but never before had I been in a classroom of such frequent shushing, her voice at high decibel levels to get over the babble. And never before or since have I heard so much praise for mediocre work. The children had given up seeking her attention at their desks and came in twos and threes for her approval. The children who might have served as role models in many things were elsewhere.

We had been strangely tracked at the normal school. But this was my first introduction to tracking in an elementary school. There were no marked changes from the usual in curricular content, teaching methods, or materials. There was simply more of what had not worked before, especially of coloring in workbooks. The class bespoke failure and of more to come. The other teachers must have been pleased to have had these children bypass their classrooms.

Mrs. Baker took seriously her tutelage of me. I asked many questions that I thought might give her some discomfort, but they did not. She took them for genuine innocence and sought to put me on an understanding track of what was intended and going on. I hunkered down to help and asked questions less and less. The most promising thing I sought to do was individual tutoring, which she very much appreciated. Mrs. Baker was as generous with her praise of my efforts as she was of those of the children. I think most of my teaching of the still-graded groups was to little avail, but I remained high in her esteem. Perhaps her evaluation helped me get my first teaching job.

Actually, the busy, bustling atmosphere of the classroom helped to balance the depression of my out-of-school thoughts. The children and I got along well, perhaps because, as with my Mr. Terry, I was their first male teacher. I began to flow, flotsamlike, with the classroom currents. But I was glad when the four weeks ended.

Since then, I have given muted thanks many times for that experience. I learned a lot, mostly about what I hoped never to let happen. I felt bad for the children, but what had gone on there would have gone on without me. What I badly needed was a chance to talk things through with someone of experience and insight who shared some of my concerns. I was visited only once—by a person from the normal school whom I had not met before. It would have been inappropriate to engage her in the kind of conversation I wanted. My next assignment straightened out a lot of things for me anyway. But a question that arose in my mind then has been with me ever since: How much of a child's self-respect are we willing to sacrifice for what amount of a school's progress in academic achievement?

Lynn Valley Elementary School

Lynn Valley Elementary School was a joy. I had been well aware of the profound cultural differences among classrooms, and now I began to realize how profoundly different the cultures of schools can be. My month at Ridgeway had created nervous anticipation, but this was washed away during my first day at Lynn Valley. Edwin Cowan, to whom I was assigned, and Stanley Morrison, the principal, saw to that. Almost raucous in their bantering of one another, they set a tone of caring and civility that permeated the whole school, affecting adults and children alike. Parents came and went as I had not seen before, knowing that they were welcome and would be listened to.

Ed was a decade older than Stan. He had not risen to offers of a principalship. He obviously loved teaching and seemed particularly to enjoy his relationship with boys and girls aged eleven and twelve. Following convention, Stan taught the older children in the seventh and eighth grades. He was replaced regularly by the same, obviously competent, female teacher during quite frequent absences. Ed picked up his principalship duties. Stan was a primary, part-time executive with the embryonic British Columbia Teachers' Federation, soon to become a powerful force in the unionization of the province's teachers.

I was gone on Thursdays. Several months earlier, a charismatic enthusiast for radio as an educational medium had approached Mr. Lord to request the assignment of a student to his pioneering effort. Thanks to his entrepreneurship, the Ministry of Education had allocated funds for the startup of the British Columbia School of the Air. Programs would be broadcast across the province from a studio in downtown Vancouver.

Characteristically, this venture would begin with science—a half-hour lesson for the upper elementary school grades every Thursday morning. Needed was a School Radio Postman who would seek to answer, during the program's concluding minutes, questions sent in by student listeners. Mr. Lord sought the advice of Beverly Sharp, who, to my complete surprise, invited me to take on this role of modest notoriety and no money. Apparently she held nothing against me for failing to show

up for thrice-scheduled demonstrations (required) of singing and playing on the piano "Hickory, Dickory, Dock," the simplest ditty I could
conjure up.

For someone with so little competence in both science and music, I
do not know how I managed over the years to get so tangled up in both.
I had been involved in creating the noon-hour music programs and
had managed them during my senior year at North Van High: I had
given up on both my mother's violin and organ, in spite of her patient
tutoring, long before encountering Miss Sharp's requirement of a
command performance from all of us. Some of my classmates gave
wonderful performances, but I had botched what I had elected as minimally acceptable. Miss Sharp assured me that it was a voice and little science that was required of the Radio Postman. And so, each week
throughout the second half of my year at normal school, I selected and, on
Thursday mornings, answered those questions for which I thought I
had acceptable responses. The experience added a little spice to my year.

Ed Cowan made no mention to the class of my being a student
teacher. The circumstances of his sometime responsibilities as principal
left me with more responsibility than is usual for a student teacher and,
given his propensity to share and explain, some sense of the school's
total functioning. I was included in meetings with parents and of the
small faculty. Since the school functioned smoothly, a single teacher
took on a week of noon supervision of the entire entity, while the rest of
us usually engaged in wide-ranging conversations while eating our
brown-bag lunches.

My classroom—it was mine in my mind much of the time—was quite
large and cluttered with creations of instructional usefulness. And with
flora and fauna requiring tender loving care. Those plants and animals
that needed daily care over the weekends were taken home by children. It was obvious that Ed Cowan was hooked on science. Consequently, I was surprised when, near the outset of our relationship, he
turned over to me the whole of its curriculum and teaching for the
entire month. Perhaps he felt best prepared to judge me in his most
comfortable domain. It was obvious, too, that he wanted to stretch me,
and so I felt on my own much of the time while he was gone or worked

at his desk. But at the end of nearly every class day, he startled me with his awareness of and insights into what I had been doing. While I appreciated this keen, caring mentoring, I did not know then how rare it is and how lucky I was.

The month went quickly. Ed and Stan both expressed regrets that a vacancy they thought was pending in which I might be interested now appeared not to be forthcoming. Had it occurred, I am confident that there would have been others with priority on the waiting list. North Vancouver was commonly regarded as a choice district. Ed wrote a long and glowing report for which I was very grateful. Several years later, I had the pleasure of joining and bantering with him and Stan and others in a crowded carpool commute each day of a summer to our classes at the University of British Columbia.

There was, even during those dark years of deep economic depression, a continuing hard core of respect for "learning for its own sake." It was not new, and it was not confined to an elite class that could afford "the higher learning." Nor was it confined to the halls of academe, although it was believed to flourish there. The aforementioned Mr. Gray was granted respect for assumed wisdom gained in earning a master's degree at the exalted University of Edinburgh. Years ago, members of the working class read Locke, Marx, Rousseau, Milton, and Shakespeare. It is reported that three hundred unemployed Welsh coal miners drew five hundred books from the library each week. Liberals read conservative tracts, and conservatives read the social, political, and economic treatises of liberals. And heated discussions of them in pubs, kitchens, and the workplace were common.[4]

It is difficult to retain an ethos of learning for its own sake when schooling is purposefully vocational and economic. During my eleven years of attendance at elementary and secondary schools, there was little need or justification for making them instrumental to jobs. There were none waiting for us. The goal of graduation was a modest incentive because we were aware that the certificate might someday be a passkey into a desired career. The unfortunate reality was that this expectation was still the tradition for only a fortunate few, as I previously stated. There were no creative stirrings of and imaginative additions to the curricular pot geared to the realization that these years would be for most of us our last opportunity to be introduced to the richness of the human conversation for its own sake—the social and communicative, the economic and political, the aesthetic and creative, the scientific and technological, the spiritual and philosophical, and more.[5] Instead, we got what most pupils get still—the leftovers from others' intellectual feasts from which the spirit of romance had largely evaporated.

We were still ripe for the joy of learning for its own sake in Senior Matriculation, but the context had sharply changed. We were preparing to be useful, for which our learning was to be instrumental to vocational and economic purpose. Since then, these circumstances have expanded to squeeze out almost all else. Much of the higher learning for its own sake has been replaced by the prevocational and preprofessional, after which there is scarcely any. The lower schools have become farm clubs, with their test scores determining where in the hierarchy of academic institutions they will play ball.

The test scores correlate hardly at all with the noble and virtuous traits embedded in the rhetoric of school purpose we consistently espouse. The time has long been with us for setting aside a period of several years solely for cultivating the sensitivities and sensibilities, the sense of self-respect and worthiness, and the civil and civic dispositions required of citizens in a free and just society. I would set aside the years from four to sixteen, now of little economic value beyond consumership, for the necessary educating and make them off limits to all else. Given our worship of the higher learning, now given over largely to vocationalism and credentialing, this may look like the long way around to ensuring the social and political democracy that is our most vital work in progress. I am confident, however, that beginning with the young is not just the shortest but the only way to this end. I would then leave to the graduates of this educational apprenticeship the wise honing of the later years.

It is necessary to adjust our educational thinking to a new reality: A combination of transition into adulthood in the late teens and societal pressure for this age group to become vocationally and economically useful is undermining the traditional concept of reserving the liberal studies for higher education. The last chance for general education not to be corrupted by the presence of economic utility may now be in the secondary school years, with these years terminating at an earlier age than now prevails. The secondary school that hardened into place in the 1930s is not the best place for today's seventeen- and eighteen-years-olds to be. They need to be in a deliberately educative adult environment unlike that of today, which is so little geared to learning for its own sake. My fellow students and I at the normal school, finding ourselves in a cultural ethos of soon-to-be economic utility, had little interest in or expectation for further immersion in liberal studies. Similarly, many college students heading for admission to the professional schools are impatient with general education requirements and commonly choose course alternatives that will enhance their chances for meeting the academic requirements.

I look back with some embarrassment at how critical my fellow students and I were of our normal school teachers. I think we expected them to prepare us for all the exigencies of any classroom and school in which we might find ourselves. Such is the commonly misguided image of vocational and professional education. I still look back in puzzlement over being introduced not at all to that rich philosophical debate over the ends and means of educating that was taking place in centers of inquiry around the world. The neglect was not, I think, solely because of our geographic location on a slice of the northwest coast of North America. I think it was more the result of a policy view of the practical, vocational purpose of preparing teachers. With a couple of exceptions, our teachers at normal school were not scholars. They were neither prepared nor interested in the theory that generates the concepts and principles that, in turn, provide sound, practical answers to matters otherwise invoking trial and error. The conventional policy view, still prevailing, was that normal school teachers with years of teaching and supervising were those best able to pass along "what works." I used hardly any of it in my student teaching, but I began to become aware of what good teaching requires and was awed by this awareness.

The Remains of the Year

The year sort of died out like the embers of a campfire. Veterans of our first short bout with teaching, we came back together again with much to talk about. The going had been rough for some who doubted they would ever teach again. It was good to face this decision now rather than later. We all had experienced both ups and downs; most of us were at least mildly enthusiastic about what lay ahead. The chances of getting a job dominated our conversation. What most of us shared was current boredom. We wanted to get on with our teaching.

Although not yet teachers, we were no longer pupils. Those of us who had come as teens were now adults, whatever our age. Adulthood is a state of mind that conveys into daily behavior a sense of who one is. The mindset of being a teacher began to flow into my concept of self.

A committee of faculty and students made quite a thing of our parting ceremony, balancing somewhat my earlier missing of a high school graduation ceremony. We were both tearful and surprisingly boisterous. We sensed that we were leaving a lot behind—life in school as students for starters. We promised to come together again, and many of us did in a reunion decades later that I was unable to attend. We went out in a gala parade, with one of us, Myrtle Dewar, in the lead, Scottish kilt and all, playing the bagpipes magnificently, as she might never have played before or since.

Part Two

As a Teacher

Woodward's Hill School
(Courtesy of the City of Surrey Archives, British Columbia, Canada)

Chapter 5

Chalk Dust

Outside the cottage, I had nothing but my school; but having my school I had everything.

SIR ERNEST BARKER[1]

ANTICIPATING

A few hundred yards from the little gray building, I was able to discern through the drizzle the composition of the dark mass on the stairs and porch leading to the entry door. At least fifteen bodies of varying sizes were huddled there. The mass parted into two rows as I drew near.

There was little auspicious in my beginnings at Woodward's Hill School. Summer warmth had faded for the third and last time over the Labour Day weekend. I poorly planned and poorly executed on Sunday evening the first of the many trips I would make from North Vancouver to my lodgings near the school. Earlier that day, Great Britain and France had declared war on Germany. This momentous occurrence was very much on my mind as I spent Labour Day preparing my class for that first day to follow. Yes, Labor Day—as it is spelled in the United States—is a holiday the two countries share. As with many districts in the United States, the Tuesday following this holiday was opening day for the schools of Surrey municipality and the rest of British Columbia.

I had been lucky to get a position that was close enough to permit my coming home on weekends. This was the good news.

Early in the summer, I had heard of a couple of vacancies in Surrey and applied. Surrey stretched for miles to the south and southeast of the mighty Fraser River, to the border between the United States and Canada, and to the rich farmlands and grazing land to the east. The smaller farms of Surrey produced most of the fruit and vegetables for the markets in New Westminster and Vancouver to the west and north-west. Except for the new King George Highway that put concrete over farmland from the border crossing just north of Blaine in Washington State to the bridge crossing the Fraser at New Westminster, roads were narrow, winding their way around farm configurations. Family budgets favored agricultural equipment over automobiles, the latter far out-numbered by tractors and horse-drawn wagons. The lifeline to New Westminster and Vancouver was the interurban electric train system that served a chunk of the lower Fraser valley and delta.

Early in August, I had taken that train to Cloverdale, the municipal seat, to be interviewed by the school board. My letter of application—the only one I ever wrote—had gotten me this far. The waiting room was full: at least two dozen women and three men—the lanky basketball player, John Lancaster, who had been a fellow student the preceding academic year at the normal school in Vancouver; me; and a small, nervous-looking man a few years older. The interviews were short. The choice job was that of teaching an eighth-grade class in the district's largest elementary school in Cloverdale, the nearest thing to an urban center, at a salary of $800 (per year, not per month!). The other was that of teacher-principal at Woodward's Hill School, wherever that might be, at $780 per year.

The board dispatched its business quickly once interviews were over, hours after beginning. To the hushed crowd, the secretary-treasurer announced that the jobs had gone to the two Johns—the first to John Lancaster, the other to me. It took a while for the light to dawn. Two men, both with athletic experience on their vitas (Lancaster's in basketball, mine in soccer) got the jobs. The values of the social and civic surround are powerful determinants of winners and losers. The crowd fell apart, some of its members in tears. Were there not in it better prospects for teaching in elementary schools than John Lancaster and me?

A friend borrowed a car and drove me to Woodward's Hill later in the month. Here I confirmed the boarding arrangements I was lucky to get, just a short walk from the school. Mr. and Mrs. Hornsby lived on a small farm but were not commercial farmers. The precise Mr. Hornsby, narrowly but properly read, had a military pension. He had been disabled in the war. He presided despotically but benevolently over wife and son who together took care of house, garden, chickens, cow, and the drawing of water from the well. My room was available because of the departure of the Hornsby daughter to pursue a nursing career. Room and board would be a dollar for each day of the month, whether or not I went home for the weekends.

The school was gray, not red, an adequate playground sloping toward it, two outhouses to the rear. The janitor, Mr. McKay, took time from his garden to give us a quick look inside. He told me that some supplies would arrive during the first week of school when the precise attendance would be known, and that he would get the mouse nest out of the cupboard before the babies were mobile. My companion and I didn't talk much during the drive back to North Vancouver.

I realized that there wasn't much I could do to prepare for the first day of school on the Tuesday after Labour Day. I decided to board the train early Sunday evening in order to have Monday as a day of orientation. Midway, there was what the airlines now refer to as a mechanical or technical difficulty. We were delayed for nearly an hour. Each of the few stops was at a covered platform, often bearing the name of the nearest long-term farming family. My stop, "Sullivan," boasted no lights or other amenities. The night now fallen was pitch-black and moonless.

During the visit a few weeks before, I had not noticed the distance between the Sullivan stop and my new place of residence. Nor was I now aware of how quickly the hours of daylight had shortened. I could scarcely see my feet and barely distinguish the road. My two large suitcases got heavier. Why I had not brought a flashlight I will never know. But I would have needed a third hand to use it anyway. There were no lights along the way. There was one light in the living room of my destination. Mr. Hornsby was scarcely civil in telling me that everyone was long in bed. There was a chill in the air. I thought at first that the large pan of cold water set at my bedroom door the next morning was intended to be punishment for this tardiness, but it proved to be routine for the prebreakfast wash.

I spent most of Monday at the school. Everything—floors, chalkboards, desks, outhouses—was scrubbed very clean. Mice and nest were gone. Mr. McKay performed his duties very well.

Dinner was special, more fitting for a Sunday than a Monday meal. I sensed that the Hornsby family anticipated my presence for the evening, and so for one of the very few times during my stay, I did not return to work in the classroom. They had, I think, looked forward to an older man, certainly someone who had traveled the world further than from North Vancouver to Surrey. Their questions brought out nothing to enhance their status for being host to the teacher. Back in the "old country," my mother's little-schooled parents went up a notch or two intellectually on Burra Isle in the Shetlands through boarding two successive, highly regarded female teachers. Had I been female, I would have been under the protection of the Hornsbys. Had I been older and had the education to be a high school teacher, especially of English or mathematics, I might have been a fitting companion and perhaps even tutor for their son, David, several years of age beyond my just-turned nineteen.

Clearly, the evening's conversation did not come up to their expectations. I had not read much of the nineteenth-century literature well represented among the several hundred prized volumes on the Hornsby bookshelves. My reading had been more of the eighteenth and twentieth. Mr. Hornsby graciously invited me to read from them at my pleasure, and as a matter of fact, I often did so after returning from the school when all were in bed. Much of our talk was of the new and past wars. The Hornsbys were, I think, disappointed in me. With the passage of fall into winter, I was gone. The sudden illness of their daughter brought her home to the room I had to vacate. There was little doubt that they missed my monthly payments in cash more than my presence. Had my credentials been more impressive, Mr. Hornsby might have considered adding a room. I don't remember any good things about the one to which I suddenly (was) moved. The school became my sanctuary.

OPENING DAY

As I drew closer over the rough graveled road, a dozen or so more boys and girls joined those already gathered on the steps and porch.

I had risen early, planning to head off such a gathering by getting to school well over an hour before the nine o'clock opening bell. But one should not underestimate the curiosity of pupils in a one-room country school, anticipating the first day of a new school year with a new teacher.

I was only six or seven paces from the steps when the flock parted like the biblical Red Sea. The thought that cricket bats and sticks might suddenly appear to hasten my walking the gauntlet to the door momentarily passed through my mind. I reached and unlocked it without incident or sound.

Inside, profound stillness and a dampish chill, a little less severe than the one I had endured the previous day. This last weekend of summer freedom had been unseasonably cool and wet. Mr. McKay had planned the small fire, laid in the bulbous black stove promptly at six, to burn out several hours later—enough to warm the room a little. Then, bodies would take over; no point in depleting the year's allocation of coal. But much more fire and heat would have been required to temper the melancholy of a bleak schoolroom absent of any other than rodent occupation for ten weeks.

In my inspection several weeks before, I had been dismayed to find only a few very old "spellers" and "readers," some chalk and erasers, and some paper of different colors. The major part of my inventory consisted of thirty-five desks, fastened in threes or fours to wooden runners, and, of course, that monumental boiler-stove (destined to become an antique collector's cherished possession), sitting on magnificent cast-iron legs directly in front of the center aisle of desks.

I had been informed officially by now that necessities would be delivered in a few days and that parents were well informed about the purchases they must make. As things turned out, into the second week of school and utter desperation, a new car-owning colleague, Marshall, principal of a four-room school in the same district, drove us to the board offices where we were fitted out with the basics by the secretary-treasurer—yesterday's surrogate for today's superintendent. One essential I had plenty of was blackboard ("chalkboard" in later vernacular) space: nearly twenty feet across the front of the room, thirty or so along the windowless wall, and another twenty across the back. On Labour Day, I had filled the whole with exercises and directives designed to keep each grade group reasonably busy for the foreshortened first day of school that lay ahead—several hours worth of my manuscript and cursive writing that filled all but a one-by-three-foot patch, front and center, reserved for special announcements and, later, my teaching of spelling.

Either the solemn gloom of the immediate surroundings or the continuing drizzle or both prompted my decision to bring in the flock a little early. (Very soon after, I assigned the handbell clanging to eager pupils and eliminated the longstanding regularity of keeping everyone out until nine o'clock.) They dripped in and soon were huddled about the stove. It is said that one does not get wet in the Scotch mist of the Northwest coast—so named more because of legendary Scottish thrift than climatic similarity with Scotland's dells and lochs—but one gets very wet when messing or standing about in it for a time. Pity today's teachers, deprived of that thoroughly unforgettable, unique smell of wool sweaters and jackets soggily drying in the warmth of a friendly stove, the privilege of so many of us once upon a time. I place it in olfactory power and penetration well above the odors produced in Mr. Shaw's chemistry lab.

The desk arrangement, no doubt repeated year after year, inspired my detailed seating map: little desks for little bears along the window side of the room, big desks for big bears along the inner wall, and middle-size desks for middle-sized bears in the rows between. I had prearranged each child's seating from the roster sent to me: the five first-graders in the row by the windows, then the two second-graders and the four third-graders, after that—moving closer to the nonwindowed wall—the three fourth-graders, the five fifth-graders, the five sixth-graders, and the two seventh-graders (identical twins). The eight eighth-graders occupied all of one row along the wall and part of another. I quickly learned that my predecessor (perhaps predecessors) favored the same plan. The ministry of education's expectation was, of course, that pupils were to be taught the content specified for their particular grade and then ranked with their grademates on "the normal curve"—5 percent getting A, 15 percent B, 60 percent C, 15 percent D, and 5 percent F, as I recall. An interesting challenge! "One size fits all" strikes again.

My chart was largely a waste of time. Quite quickly and with unerring accuracy, each of the thirty-four settled into a seat. Subsequently, I made a few changes, such as moving the twins to the two front instead of the two back seats of the row they had chosen. But nearly all remained with their first choices.

In retrospect, I realize that I should not have been as startled as I was. I was the inexperienced newcomer, a tourist in territory well known to almost everyone else. My acquisition of practical knowledge was beginning. When it comes down to the nitty-gritty of school life, students are the best informed and their knowledge and insights the most ignored. When it comes to the conduct of schools, well-established systemics and regularities take over. Breaking out of them means going against the grain. John Dewey had something to say about the extent to which most teachers are doomed to repeat the ways of their first year of teaching for the rest of their lives. It was just my first day and I was being relentlessly molded.

Ernie

On that first day of school in September, Ernie once again performed the feat of easing into the seat along the window row where he had sat and squirmed for the seven preceding years. Small for his age—more like an average-size boy of ten—Ernie nonetheless found it necessary to project both knees into the narrow aisles. There simply was not room for these bony protrusions under the shelf of a desk intended for the first grade.

These knees were especially prominent because Ernie wore "stove-pipes," the standard uniform for all boys until emancipated for obscure reasons at some magical age between eight and ten. The time of transition depended primarily, it seems, on the strength and stubbornness of a boy's drive for freedom. Stove-pipes were short trousers, usually reaching to or just below the knees but sometimes sagging to midshin. They climbed higher, usually to several inches above the knee, as the boy grew. The more impoverished the family, the shorter the stove-pipes appeared to be; most were above the knee. Boys of my generation, overlapping in age with that of the boys now in my daily care (the oldest approaching eighteen, just fifteen months younger than I was), had considered stove-pipes to be an emancipation from the knickers earlier worn by older siblings.

Ernie's pale, very freckled face was topped by a tousled crop of carrot-colored hair. Most of the time he smiled somewhat vacantly; his eyes were rarely steady. Quite frequently, his facial expression changed to a scowl, he lowered his head, and slumped in his seat. Sometimes on these occasions, he moaned softly, the volume sometimes rising to a kind of forlorn howl.

Little wonder. Ernie had begun school with most of the eighth-graders now in big bear desks on the other side of the room. All had long outgrown stove-pipes and wore "long pants"—"denims." Since several of these had been nonpromoted and were now beyond the normal age of eighth-grade enrollment, Ernie was not the only one to have spent more than a year in the same desk. Frank, my near-peer in age, had experienced this several times. (I had just missed one such first-grade experience at North Star School, thanks to my parents.) These older pupils knew Ernie well, of course, took care of him when necessary, and tolerated him without criticism or comment, although Ernie remained in the status of a kind of peripheral burden to be borne.

Why Ernie's parents continued to send him to school in stove-pipes can only be conjectured. Perhaps the transition to long pants went only with transition to a higher grade. Why my teacher-principal predecessors did not arrange for a larger desk as Ernie grew in size is beyond my comprehension. (Yes, I was classified as principal for certain managerial reasons, but my annual salary of $780 a year was not augmented for the additional duties.) The principals before me were decent, intelligent people. Those ubiquitous regularities of schooling loom large again in one's mind. They are part of that deep structure of schooling.

I lost Ernie by late fall. Over the early weeks of the school term, all of us had grown closer together, like a large family, somewhat in the vision of Jane Roland Martin's schoolhome. The big stove and the morning conversations around it helped. It was a wet late summer and early fall, marked almost daily by the sour smell of wool clothing drying. The possibilities of family-type grouping, the absence of higher authority and other classes, freedom to take recesses when the urge grows strong are among the advantages of a one-room school. Ernie was simply part of the ecosystem, to be accommodated and adjusted to. His struggle was deeper and greater than that of the rest of us.

There had been crises involving Ernie over the years, and apparently, he had been removed from the school for periods of time. The question of his continuing had been raised; and at this period in the educational history of I.Q., Ernie's had been estimated at 65. The question of his eligibility for school had been raised on occasion, and some parent protests regarding his attendance had surfaced.

I'll never know what Ernie thought of me, but at least he tolerated me and even seemed to respect my authority. I don't think he made much more progress with me in learning to read than he had with my predecessors. I had no game plan for him; nothing in my teacher education program at normal school had prepared me for him. I was content when he seemed to be at peace.

Signs of playground incidents increased as we moved into October: a child quietly crying after recess, a bloodied nose, a bruised shin. There was some silent classroom conspiracy to keep the source from me, but evidence of Ernie's involvement grew. Twice I sent notes to Ernie's parents, whom I never met, and twice afterward Ernie failed to show up for several days. Then, late in November, more than a few days went by and Ernie did not show. I never saw him again.

On becoming convinced that Ernie would not be back, I asked some of his classmates. Ernie had been taken away; they knew not where. I was unable to reach his parents. They had never responded to my notes.

I've thought about Ernie often over a period of more than fifty years. I see that pale, freckled face with the near-transparent skin and the hair that matched the freckles as though it was Saturday and I had just spent another week with Ernie and the rest of my large family. That row along the window was never quite the same after Mr. McKay removed the larger desk on its own slats that he had somewhat begrudgingly agreed to provide for Ernie.

Helen and Esther

The unusually prolonged drizzle eased in late September, to return after a couple of weeks of crisp, sunny weather. A soccer ball took care of pent-up energies during the midmorning recess. We had had two soccer balls. A bicycle pump served to keep one or the other somewhat flabbily inflated for an hour or so. Then, into the third week, a smiling Mr. McKay delivered a magnificent new one, thoughtfully sent by a father who wished to remain anonymous.

After a few nights of frost in early October, the ground still soaked from September's rain, the sun turned it into deep mud by recess time. The soccer ball took on a new color and a larger sphere, looking very much like its two predecessors. There is nothing quite like a soccer ball to keep a playground of children running back and forth like ants after booty. Rules are of no interest. They remove the anticipation of returning a lofty kick to whence it came with one still better. In the mud, the whole activity moved in slow motion; the kicked return just slithered. Generous chunks of mud then joined us in the classroom where it caked under Mr. McKay's desks.

For reasons I'll never know, it was more fun to boot the ball in the growing warmth of the morning than in the lazy haze of the afternoon. But we all needed a break. I already had learned what not to do. Early on, I had developed an unjustified faith in the proclivity of children and youths to be decorous even in the absence of adult supervision. Perhaps because I was only a little more than a year older than the oldest, I saw myself as more their leader than their teacher, and so I could set rules that would prevail for the gang. I simply didn't realize that Frank neither knew I was nineteen nor saw me as such. Nor did any of the others. My authority over their behavior and, indeed, as an educator stemmed from the very fact of my being "the teacher." Too many teachers forget this in seeking "to get close" to their students. There is little respect in our society, particularly among the young, for adult reversions to child-hood and youth.

My mistake—and it seared into me too deeply to be repeated—simply was in assuming that my instructions would prevail over the creative deviations of adolescents on their own for a time. A couple of weeks into the school year, and desperate for time to concentrate on the learning of some children without the distractions of all the rest, I sent the ten seventh- and eighth-graders into the surrounding woods to sketch what might catch the eye. They returned at the scheduled time but sans the masterpieces I had hoped for. Several presented blank pages. It was a silly assignment; they knew it. Worse, I had not developed with them a frame of reference for school-connected activity deprived of the presence of my authority as their teacher. My anger with them was really anger with myself. (What might be the consequences today of any comparable foolishness?) I don't think I ever came even close to such a caper again.

An important learning for me by the end of September, much of it from the misadventure in the arts, was that breaks without the soccer ball or the equivalent must be carefully planned *inside the classroom* before fresh air flushes the creative juices. I think Miss Hamilton had understood this. For a few minutes each afternoon, then, weather per-mitting, we rehearsed an activity to be performed outside for fifteen minutes or so, building up a repertoire from which later choices might be made. (How are children to make intelligent choices among alter-natives never experienced?) On a nice Tuesday in October, we planned for the anticipated nice Wednesday afternoon to follow. We went through all the rules and steps of a total class potato race, lining up volunteers who would bring the necessary tablespoons and egg-sized potatoes. (There was no dearth of potatoes in this area at that time of year.)

Wednesday afternoon was come. Squinting into the sun, I gave a few last-minute reminders. The children, clustered in predetermined teams, were lined up on the shady side of the building where the crisp autumn leaves had blown deepest. The first runners were poised, spoon and potato in hand, ready to begin the relay race. Tense and silent, they awaited my signal. One could hear a pin drop, but that is not what dropped. There was no mistaking the dribble of water on the dry leaves. Heads turned. Little Esther had wet her pants.

Fractions of seconds hung in the air. There was a titter from somewhere. Lungs were taking in air; perhaps they were only mine. What do I do?

Before lungs could push out their noises or I could blunder, Helen had Esther's hand in hers and they were off toward the girls' outhouse, Helen not hurrying Esther along but just chatting to her as though they were going to the store for ice cream. I gave the signal and the potato race began.

Helen was fourteen going on twenty. She was not just physically mature; she had an adult bearing and wisdom that went with it. Although not a quick study in schoolwork, she was a conscientious student, doggedly sticking with it and usually reaching a point of mastery that made her a resource for others, just as she was a resource in most matters. Frank tried from time to time to upset her calm demeanor, no doubt vying for her natural leadership role. He invariably came away the loser, but never Helen's critic. Helen would become the kind of adult about whom relatives, friends, and neighbors would say, "Let's ask Helen; she'll know what to do."

In appearance, Esther could have been Ernie's little sister: slight of frame, transparent-looking freckled skin, fine hair, more toward pink than Ernie's carrot-colored top. But there the resemblance ended. Esther was very bright and alert, her eyes and ears following everything that went on in the classroom, as she tossed off her own assignments with ease. I could never find enough for her to do. She finished my assignments in about the time it took me to write them on the blackboard. Esther was what was referred to in those days as "high strung." Beginning school had been a long-anticipated and much acted-out forthcoming adventure. She writhed in embarrassment the several times she threw up during the first few weeks. It usually was one of the twins or Helen who cleaned up and took care of her.

I do not recall thinking specifically about Esther, Helen, Frank, Ernie, or the twins and their differing individualities when I came up with the curricular innovation that improved their daily lot in the cramped quarters of our classroom. I was thinking about me. Nor did I know much about the work and ideas of those who had found similar answers before me. That knowledge was to come later. Necessity—no, desperation—is the mother of invention.

CURRICULUM

We were well into the second week of the school year when desperation and Marshall's small car took us to the warehouse where the secretary-treasurer of the school board doled out some of the essential materials, mostly textbooks. "Meager" is an overly generous description. Further, the interface with grade enrollments was casual. The district supplied the very basics: graded readers and arithmetic texts, blue spellers, MacLean Method writing manuals, crafts paper, rubber bands, paper clips, and, of course, chalk. One was never sure of the inventory and learned to ask for more than the first handout. What one got on asking varied from asker to asker but usually exceeded what one got from not asking. Parents were required to purchase a few special books—usually those not graded or not much discounted—and pencils, pens (a standard, miserably ornery nib was part of the handout), "scribblers," atlases, and dictionaries (the last two items usually entering the list in the upper elementary school years and expected to last for as long as one continued in school).

By the time most of this potpourri was assembled, I was well into the habit of projecting the daily curriculum on the blackboards (and well into the allergy to chalk dust—and to almost all else but the basic components of air—that was to plague me for years to come). I usually began by 3:30 p.m. after most of my crew had gone (some hung around until I eased them out), took a break for the never-varying early suppertime, and then continued until 9:00 or 10:00 in the evening—across the front, down the side, across the back, except for that space on the front, now shrunk by encroachments, for teaching spelling. At first, not knowing my habits, passersby were critical of Mr. McKay and me for being careless about turning off the lights.

Instead of making this work unnecessary, the availability of a few instructional materials provided more flexibility. Instead of writing questions and directives on the blackboard to be answered in students' scribblers (notebooks), I could now assign pages of books to read or refer to questions at the end of textbook passages. I could now more easily address daily, period-by-period, grade-by-grade, subject-by-subject curricular coverage. Making a weekly schedule for all grades and all subjects of an anticipated one-room school in some remote part of the province proved to be one of the very practical things I had learned to do in normal school.

My peak effort for a day was 56 blackboard assignments; 224 for the peak week. It must be remembered that my family spread across eight grades, each getting daily doses of most of the following subjects: spelling, arithmetic ("mathematics" is more modern terminology), reading or some derivative thereof (such as what Robert Maynard Hutchins referred to as "that abomination, the language arts"), handwriting, composition, science, history, and geography. My three courses of study handed down from the ministry of education—one yellow, one green, one blue—also specified so many minutes a week for art and music and for health and physical education. For a brief period, I enjoyed the luxury of my eight eighth-graders heading off for some place or other one afternoon a week for home economics (girls) and manual arts (boys). Logistics and budget restrictions ended this by mid-fall.

This never-ending backdrop of blackboard assignments left me with the luxury of carrying on conversations with successions of grade groups about topics specified in the relevant course of studies. Then, a couple of times a week, I read to the entire class. I had tested this out early in the year with the lower grades and the works of A. A. Milne. But "Winnie the Pooh" attracted all ages, and I found even the eighth-graders to be abandoning their assignments to listen in. I never quite grew accustomed to the attentiveness of Frank, a diffident scholar, whose eyes were level with mine when he stood and would be looking down at me by year's end. Toward the end of the fall term, there was daily demand from all for at least a few pages of *A Christmas Carol*. I was an easy touch; these sessions were a relief for me as well as for them. I had learned much from Miss Hamilton.

But my readings were not the only occasions of cross-grade interest. The blue, upper-grade course of study for grades seven, eight, and nine (there were now a few junior high schools in the province, especially in Vancouver, the major city) alternated history and geography, the former with a geographic perspective and the latter with a historical perspective woven in—social studies was about to come on the scene. The eighth-graders and I were deeply into England, Scotland, and Wales: climate, cities, industries, exports, imports, with some attention to the why and how of the emergence of the British Empire—all of which ultimately would lead us to Canada and our own British Columbia.

Our daily conversations usually were quite spirited (even Frank entered in occasionally, usually after a bit of prodding from me). So spirited sometimes that I failed to note the full compass of inclusion. The twins in the seventh grade were the first to enter in; both were very bright and probably would have led the eighth grade academically had they "skipped" a grade somewhere along the way. And then fourth-, fifth-, and sixth-graders joined the conversation (and no doubt the lower three grades followed along without speaking up). I suddenly found myself responding to the interlopers, countering their contributions with comments and questions. More often than not, when I tried to tease out some more subtle point or unique explanation, the most interesting responses came from some of the younger pupils. Perhaps the years spent by most of the eighth-graders in moving along from windows to wall, row by row, seat by seat, had dulled their creativity and spontaneity. These cross-fertilizations occurred with increasing frequency and combinations of participants as September merged into October.

I continued with my fifty-plus blackboard assignments each day. But my spirit for it was waning. Increasing fatigue played a part, but a kind of unease became my daily companion.

I went home on weekends, even though the round trip by train, ferry, and streetcar (San Francisco's cable cars share a kinship) took several hours. And the modest costs bit sorely into the few dollars left over each month after paying my dollar a day for room and board and a little into retirement and tax. The break from sponging off each morning from the basin of cold water (it toughened one, I was told); a diet heavily oriented toward potatoes, beets, and cabbage; the same phonograph records played over and over; the somewhat strained supper conversation; and avoiding the cow dung in the darkness of my after-supper school-to-farmhouse walk each evening was worth the time and cost.

My plans for this particular Saturday night back home in mid-October had fallen through. As usual, I had played a game in one of Vancouver's soccer leagues that afternoon—another round trip on ferry and street-car. I was tired and bored. The cream-colored door between kitchen and hallway in my mother's house no doubt has been painted many times but the indentation from my kick probably remains. It was a kick of freedom leading to emancipation from fifty to fifty-six class periods a day. I had had enough of them.

On Monday morning, I went across to the school before breakfast, catching Mr. McKay just as he finished stoking our stove and laying out our allotment of wood and coal for the day. "I want a table along the wall as long and wide as can be fitted in, with sides at least eight inches high all round." Mr. McKay's automatic first response always was negative. This time, it was mere incredulity. After all, our total space for thirty-four desks and students and the small table we used for a library was only about 780 square feet. We had come to respect one another; he knew I was serious. He was challenged.

The table was waiting for us the following Monday morning: four feet by eighteen, with sand halfway up the sides. Mr. McKay had lined it with heavy tarpaper to retain the water I said would be used at times. All the aisles were narrower now. For the first time, Mr. McKay didn't complain about the desks being on skids instead of screwed to the floor "the way they're supposed to be."

One of the peculiarities about all of the intended school curricula I know is that they repeat certain topics several times in the stretch from grades one to twelve. One of the things the British Columbia ministry of education intended to plant in our minds was the shape and general contents of the province. In my own progression through the grades, I had learned to draw a map quite accurately from memory: the forty-ninth parallel and the dip down around the Gulf Islands, to the south of Victoria, the capital; the curve of the coastline with Vancouver Island nestled into the bight; the Fraser River flowing westward from the Rockies and then the bends to the south and west for the long sweep to the delta, Surrey, New Westminster, and then Vancouver. We memorized a host of facts that later would not be facts about towns that scarcely existed but were meticulously placed on our maps. We didn't learn much about life there, why there was a town, or where it was in relation to anything else; the "facts" were sufficient. I was pretty good at what we were supposed to learn. The woman I later married was better at it. She always got an "A" in geography, but when called upon to give directions, some friends tell her to point straight up for fear of gesturing in precisely the wrong direction.

Since the eighth grade and I had now gotten from the British Isles to British Columbia and the fifth grade was about to get into the wonderful story in their green geography book (that I still enjoyed) about the life of a chinook salmon from egg to spawning, it appeared to me that some kind of joining should be attempted. And there would be some interesting catch-hold points for others in my planned creation of a sandbox replica of the mighty Fraser and the towering mountain ranges. There would be need for careful hands. We would be reading about the different ways the great red and yellow cedars, Douglas firs, Sitka spruce, and hemlock are brought to the mills and become lumber or pulp for paper. Hemlock, although not the kind of literary fame, would lead us to that legendary drink and dastardly human deeds of power and money. There would be myths uncovered, songs to be sung, flowers and leaves to draw and paint. And all of these we would write about. What hath subjects and grades to do with such adventures?

Esther was soon in her element. She had learned to read before coming to school and was bored with first-grade fare—and, I think, with most of what I had foraged for her. She had been somewhat more nervous and introverted since the potato race incident; now she worked joyously beside Helen whenever the opportunity presented itself. She got very much into flora and fauna, nerving herself to read to us all her report on fungi. Ernie idolized Frank, but in school, it had been at a distance; on the playground, it was Frank who kept him in check (most of the time). I think it was Ernie's intense interest in getting into the sand and drawing his strange pictures of what he saw taking shape there that changed Frank's attitude toward it all from "kid's stuff" to genuine involvement. We were well into the sand table and British Columbia when Ernie was taken away from us. I still feel pain over the loss and a sense of failure.

That brief bout with progressive education at normal school had made some impact on me. (The model canoe-burning incident was still fresh in my mind.)[2] The sand-table saga proved to be just part of a departure from the regularities of schooling to which I had grown accustomed. One of the major things I had going for me in the enthusiasm of my students was the absence of attractive distractions in their lives outside of school. I can only guess at the pressures they put on their parents to supply so much of what we needed that simply did not exist in the district's inventory of instructional materials. A couple of them even brought in radios—for a purpose that astonished me.

As earlier described, during the second half of my year at normal school, several months before, I had been called upon to be "the radio postman." A bright and shining media star in Vancouver believed that educational radio for schools was the wave of the future, destined to solve the problem of getting needed information into the classroom. Not surprisingly, science was chosen for the opening salvo. How incredibly repetitive the saga of school reform! The first round would provide a half-hour science lesson every Thursday throughout the school year for every tuned-in classroom in the province of British Columbia. School boards were requested to supply the necessary technology, but not provided with additional financial resources. Cities, the most information-rich centers, did so; the relatively information-poor, resource-poor rural areas did not. Vancouver did; Surrey did not.

On beginning to teach, I had forgotten about the B. C. School of the Air (or whatever its title). We had no radio in the classroom; radios were commonplace in homes at that time—major sources of information and entertainment. Into many of these homes each Thursday morning came the School of the Air. Some parents were surprised that their children's classroom was not tuned in. With radios now available, thanks to them, we listened on a few Thursdays—all of us, not just those in the grade for which programs were intended. The scheduling proved to be awkward, requiring us to cut off whatever we were doing. The younger children fidgeted; the older students talked and frequently attended to other things. As I recall, the decision to drop the program from our schedule was unanimous. Neither radio nor, later, television caught on as an instructional medium in schools. Given the rapidity with which communication technologies become commonplace in the home, it is strange that so many of us view schools as behind the times if they don't quickly follow suit.

At first, the sand table was a kind of magnet, but more and more, it became generative. Although learning about the history and geography of British Columbia had inspired its installation, its use penetrated most of the curriculum. When we got into mining, lumbering, farming, and fishing, students of all ages brought books, pamphlets, photos, and more. They read and they wrote; the two were intertwined. The measuring, adding and subtracting, and other manipulations of numbers were not, in my judgment, sufficient learning in arithmetic, and I retained my daily teaching of twenty-five words to spell per grade, per week. I was now able to spend some concentrated time with my non-readers, all but Ernie quickly becoming readers, far more because of what the sand table spawned than from what their "readers" inspired. The children read and wrote, wrote and read, to one another as well as to me. They slipped into reading very much as, earlier, they had slipped into oral language, just as most children do in all literate societies.

What captivates me most in retrospect was the profound shift in the ethos of the classroom. Before the novelty of the sand table wore off, there was constant babble, some natural to the ongoing activity, some boisterously unrelated. I was still the authority figure from whom control was expected. With the more individual and small-group work generated by, rather than focused on, the table, the students established an acceptable level of noise and nature of discourse. They hushed one another. There emerged a high but normal decibel level maintained by the class, which intense concentration blocked out, except when I was occasionally called upon to intervene.

I had found in my desk at the outset a short, rather thick, leather strap bearing signs of use and wear. It remained there. High on the problem list of beginning teachers is "discipline." The problem lies primarily in the educational ethos of the classroom rather than in difficulties inherent in "controlling" children. Unfortunately, many of the regularities of schooling exacerbate the latter, making it difficult for teachers to create the caring, participatory culture that sets and maintains the necessary controls.

Mr. Calvert

On a Monday morning in late November, a boy on a bike showed up at our schoolhouse door and pulled a note from his pocket. Telephones were not part of the issue to schools. Getting to serve as message-runner from school to school was a much-sought, cherished reward for dependable boys who owned bicycles. Unknowingly, these favored few were the critical communication links among several like-minded, small-school principals, including me, who planned a monthly bash for the first Saturday night after payday.

But this was not the message in the sealed note. Mr. Calvert's black coupe had been spotted, parked at the school nearest to that of my new friend, Marshall. A little fortuitous checking had revealed that the trail led toward my door. Mr. Calvert, the gray ghost, was a provincial school inspector. His report—a copy to the ministry, a copy to the secretary of the local school board, and a copy to the victim—sealed one's future. A negative report meant the end of one's appointment and, possibly, teaching career. But the research of a resourceful sleuth had revealed a rosy side: Vancouver and a few of the larger cities sometimes underestimated their need for teachers. Being jobless and footloose at the end of the year was an asset in getting an eleventh-hour appointment with a higher salary and city amenities. Indeed, getting fired often shook one

out of the slow route to advancement locally and into first-time ownership of an automobile.

But, being a sensitive sort when contemplating this kind of disapproval
and faced with spending my meager savings (yes, even on $780 a year) on
two successive summer sessions required for permanent certification, I
anticipated Mr. Calvert's visit with trepidation. His car pulled in at
9:15 on Wednesday morning.

Mr. Calvert was thin and stooped; his hair was gray and he wore a
gray suit. His face was interesting and friendly, his handshake firm. He
roamed the room quietly, trying to be inconspicuous, but he might just
as well have been swathed in neon lights. I remembered Mr. Calvert.
He had visited my class in North Star School in North Vancouver; I was
in the third grade, I think. And so I knew that he would get around to
addressing the class and directing questions at specific students. They
would think that *they* were on the line. I knew differently.

Mr. Calvert spent a lot of time at our sand table. Of course, I had
temporarily abandoned it and was back into my 56 lessons, but the
artifacts remained. I think he read quite a lot of what I had written on the
blackboards; I think he was impressed. But he had a fixation on that
table. How badly had I blown it?

After a short session with the children, he asked me to dismiss the
class for recess. We talked, or at least he did and I gave short responses.
Recess was so long that curious children opened the door and peered
in from time to time.

Mr. Calvert wanted to know why I had the sand table. Nervously, I
scaled down my emphasis and the time spent with it. He asked if I knew
about John Dewey and William Heard Kilpatrick. I said that I had heard
of Dewey in a class at normal school. Yes, I had scanned one of his books
but found it to be quite impenetrable. Yes, we had done a "project" at
normal school, and I had smoked out the room through imitating too
literally how cedar logs were burned out in the making of dug-out
canoes. He smiled that slow, enigmatic smile that one could interpret
many different ways. "Mr. Goodlad," he said, "I very much like what you
are doing. Just always make sure that your pupils do well in arithmetic."

Nothing in my entire career has contributed more to my views on the conduct of schooling than my brief apprenticeship in a one-room school. I have been more than a little amused during subsequent years by the resistance—sometimes angry and bitter—of many of the teachers who have found themselves assigned to a class of just two grade levels. Deliberate creation of multi-grade organizational structures, sometimes chosen by teachers in innovative schools, often is threatening to teachers of single grade levels. Teachers often refer to themselves as fourth- or fifth-grade teachers, but an elementary school would need to be many times larger than any I have seen to make possible the deliberate grouping of entire classes of equal-performing pupils. Of course, one could reduce the prevalent diversity in achievement somewhat by locking many children in closets and keeping them there until others, one by one, caught up. There simply is no such thing as a fourth-grade class other than for numerical classification.

With the introduction of Mr. McKay's sand table into the classroom and its dominance in daily learning, it was impossible even for me to know where individual students fit into the prescribed curriculum. Students of all ages and grades worked side-by-side, often reading the same books and listening to one another read what younger as well as older classmates had written. They made and carried out plans together, unmindful of their differing grade classifications. I've often wondered what they shared with parents, how much of what was going on was known to parents, and what they thought about what they thought they knew. I did, as already stated, continue to teach graded spelling and arithmetic. But what students learned of both spelling and arithmetic in the context of the sand-table curriculum probably transferred more directly into their lives outside of school. I never knew or thought about such matters in those days—certainly not enough to think I needed to explain to parents something that might have appeared to them to be novel or innovative. It didn't change the nature of what they saw each month on their children's report cards.

What strikes me as extraordinary is that only one parent visited me in Woodward's Hill School throughout my stay—a father who asked me to ask the district office (one more time) to install "SCHOOL—GO SLOW" signs on the nearby public road. Motored traffic was steadily increasing. We still had no signs when I left. Nearly all parents attended our primitive, hastily put together Christmas concert that I had forgotten about until the eleventh hour. Beyond that evening, parents were faceless. What I learned about them—and that was very little—and what they learned about me—probably a good deal—came from the students. Mr. McKay was my weather vane with respect to parents' school-directed climate and probably parents' weather vane regarding me as well. Through him, I knew that they were watching.

On further reflection I have come to realize that this ethos of virtually no teacher-parent communication (other than through monthly report cards and handwritten notes), accompanied by sometimes-eerie parental watching, characterized my several years of apprenticeship in public schools. The parent-to-teacher limited relationship continued, but as I describe later, it was primarily parent concern that pushed a negligent principal out of one of the three public schools in which I taught.

My experience with such an ethos was not, I think, unique. Perhaps it was an accompaniment of a prevailing school-community compact regarding the dual but near-autonomous role of school and home in their respective domains of rearing the young. The decisions of the board of education to hire or replace a teacher were respected, however, and the teacher who experienced board disapproval was soon gone. And, of course, distance, the rarity of automobiles, and the absence of telephones in elementary schools of the time contributed significantly to teachers' isolation from parental concerns.

There is a considerable recorded history of schooling and education in the United States and Canada. Largely missing in the history, however, are treatises (other than diaries) on the community ecology of which schools were and are an important part. Largely missing, too, are artifacts and analyses of such that would help today's teachers place themselves in the contextual continua of their occupation, still struggling to become a major profession. When I stroll through historical museums, I am saddened by the general absence of such artifacts and accompanying narratives seeking to describe their context. There usually is, however, no dearth of such with respect to military events, their leaders, and their artifacts.

Next to the weather, school is the topic of everyone's conversation—a subject of nostalgia. But, unlike the weather, the present condition of each of our schools is not part of each morning's electronic news. Such is too much to expect for a cottage industry, just as it is too much to expect this cottage industry to drive a nation's economy.

Chapter 6

Promotions

*Lack of attention to the rhythm and character of mental growth is
a main source of wooden futility in education.*

ALFRED NORTH WHITEHEAD[1]

GOODBYE, YOUNG FRIENDS

My river teeth of memory include a well-preserved whorl for Woodward's
Hill School: for Ernie, Esther, Helen, Frank, the twins, and others
more chimeric. Helen planned to become a teacher. Did she? She
would have been a good one. What difference did I make in and to their
lives? Ernie made an enormous impact on mine.

The crossing in our lives turned out to be brief. I was "promoted." Mr.
Calvert's caveat was to embrace much more than arithmetic.

Three routes were considered ones of promotion in the Surrey
school district and most other districts of the kind then common. It
simply was assumed that a teacher completing a bachelor's degree (in
summer sessions and through correspondence) while teaching in an
elementary school would be offered and would accept a position in his
or her field in one of the two (soon to be three) secondary schools.
This promotion brought with it a significant increase in salary. The second route was from teacher-principal of a one-room school to princi-
pal-teacher of a larger elementary school and then, perhaps, one still
larger, each move accompanied by a modest increase in salary. The
third was geographic. It simply was expected that all but the few who
had come home to teach where they had grown up would jump at a par-

allel position that took them from the very rural to the less so—to a small village or hamlet.

My promotion was of the third ilk. Actually, it came about for interests beyond my own but was presented as if earned. I don't know if the board's secretary-treasurer knew then that the $20-a-year raise in salary that would come with the move was about to become standard for all teachers with a year or more of experience. There had been wrangling over an increase with the local teachers' association soon to be embraced by the fledgling British Columbia Teachers' Federation. I was seen as fitting a need in the White Rock Elementary School, commonly regarded as rather choice. I came to suspect later that the move also accommodated my being replaced by a teacher from another district lobbying to return home.

My guess is that I would have accepted, in spite of my sadness in leaving Woodward's Hill, even if the roof over my housing arrangement, problematic from the outset, had not collapsed. The coming home of the Hornsby daughter changed my daily routines. She needed my room, and quickly. Without specific notice, my belongings were moved between the time I left for school one morning and the time I returned for dinner that evening.

Mr. Hornsby had been kind enough to seek out and arrange the only possible housing alternative. Lacking wheels, I had no choice. A nearby farmhouse, set back from the graveled road I walked to the schoolhouse each day, had an extra room, with its own outside entrance. I would sleep there and continue to take my meals with the Hornsby family.

My daily walk now became triangular rather than linear: From a quick sponge-off from the cold-water basin (yes, again) unfailingly left at my inner door each morning, to the Hornsby house for breakfast, to the schoolhouse carrying the worker's lunchbox Mrs. Hornsby unfailingly and quite tastefully stocked for me, back to the Hornsby family for dinner, back to the schoolhouse and the blackboards, and then, in pitch blackness, to my sleeping quarters (more often than not, after wiping the cow dung from my shoes in the grass before entering). Most of us see cows only at a distance and are not adequately aware of their size and prodigious processes of digestion. Reality sets in when a huge shape rises from the footpath with a grunt just a few feet ahead, dark and towering against the night sky. Once more I wonder: Why did I so unfailingly not avail myself of a flashlight or the much more common kerosene lantern?

But much more than my itinerary changed. My room at the Hornsby house had been furnished only with a bed, a small mirrored dressing table, and a narrow wooden chair. There was neither shaded light nor place for reading. Yet, the family was quite literary in its reading habits and tastes. The shelves in the living room, to which they retired after dinner, did contain some fine pieces, I eventually discovered. Their routine rarely varied: the news by radio (television had not yet come on the scene), a half-hour favorite program, when available, or a record or two on the phonograph, some reading, and to bed. All were retired or about to retire by the time I returned from my evening chores at the schoolhouse. The living room was then mine for a couple of hours of reading. But now, at my new sleeping quarters, I came directly into a stark room, with its bed, small chair, and dim lamp. I stayed later and later in the schoolhouse, stumbled through darkness past the cows, and to bed.

There is something strange and unnerving about living for seven or eight hours out of each twenty-four with a wall separating one from family life sometimes heard but never seen. I saw the elderly couple only once, when I was first shown the room. I never really saw the house; it was in darkness when I came to it each night, and my back was to it when I left in early morning (in darkness again during the winter). I have no other memories of them or it.

My romance with Woodward's Hill School and my weekend trips home were insufficient to overcome the sheer melancholy of my non-school hours. But I soon began to wish that I had taken the entire class with me when I left. I always have viewed Woodward's Hill as my school and its children as my family.

HELLO, ATLANTIS

The change in my out-of-school life was stunning. White Rock was at that time largely a family summer resort, with a touch of honky-tonk. I don't know how much of the rumored goings-on at such establishments as the Blue Moon café, bar, and sometime hotel and dance hall were myth. At any rate, unlike Plato's Atlantis, the gods never found it necessary to sink the small town into the sea. My fortuitous year-round boarding status at the circumspect White Rock Lodge brought me one of the two choice front rooms. From its deck, I looked across the road, the boardwalk, and the railroad tracks to Semiahmoo Bay.

Blanche and Jack were wonderful hostess and host. Blanche cleaned, cooked, baked, and frequently substitute taught in various schools. She had brought with her an exemplary reputation as a teacher in a town close enough for the news to carry. No subject or grade level fazed her. Blanche's cooking and baking were on a par with her teaching reputation. Her cuisine predated today's preoccupation with diet and nutrition. Had I stayed more than the few school years I did, I probably would have met the fate of Adele Davis's husband—before she became a world-renowned nutritionist—and died along the banana cream pie route. Jack, ever good-natured and retired from "the feed business" (cattle), as he put it, puttered and reminisced.

Andy Richardson, the new bus driver, joined us early on. There were only four of us most of that first school year, and so the single guest bathroom proved to be only a minor inconvenience. (The romance with bathrooms in our society was yet to come.) I still paid a dollar a day for room, huge breakfast, Blanche's very special brown bag lunches, and those magnificent dinners. But I paid only for days there, agreeing to let my room be used for carefully chosen patrons as needed on weekends. My monthly bill dropped from a regular $30 or $31 a month to $22 or $23—more than two months of savings for the nine-month year. And what a difference in ambience and lifestyle!

My monthly paycheck of about $65 was a source of fascination, near-sardonic humor, and occasional outrage for Andy. He and that other Andy, my brother, were good friends. Both had hated school, dropped out early, and had begun driving for the fledgling Pacific Stage Lines at an early age. My new friend, now high in seniority, could command almost any run he chose (except for the one on which a passenger's counting out of a full fare in pennies had provoked Andy's tossing them all out the window and, consequently, his removal from the route). The White Rock–Vancouver run was a dream: into Vancouver in the morning (not early), a few hours layover there, and out in the evening (not late) for ten days, then four off and the cycle repeated—not more than fifty hours of driving every two weeks.

At the end of each two-week cycle, Andy showed up in the lodge with cash, cleared a space on my work table, and counted out in small bills about $80, some $15 more than I made in a month. He had been making about this much for years and was appalled at my salary and my estimates of prospects for the future. I found myself arguing, somewhat lamely, the nature of the work and its importance to society. This was the kind of rebuttal he hoped for, and I usually fell into it. Now street-smart and worldly wise, he was able to pick up my argument and develop it much more convincingly. As a youth, he had stepped over the line into self-confessed delinquency. A talented, self-taught drummer, he had found no support for his musical abilities. He considered our society to be upside-down, giving only lip service to what should be most valued and reinforcing all the wrong things. Blanche endeavored to be an objective referee but clearly was biased toward Andy's views.

REGULARITIES REVISITED

For reasons I understand now better than I did then, there was little synergy between my new class and me, let alone the new school and me, during that first year. There was good chemistry with some individuals and even clusters of pupils, but it never reached the same level with the entire class group.

There were really two White Rocks: the "town" fringing the bay with small rental units scattered up the hillsides, bringing high rents in the summer but cheaply available the rest of the year; and the more rapidly developing "suburb" above, on the plateau where my new elementary school was located. The boardwalk and the small shops gathered together at town-center drew a steady stream of walkers throughout the summer. What was below the plateau was far more interesting to the young people than was the staid residential community above. The town ambience stimulated the juices of budding adolescence in particular. And budding adolescence was what was taking over in some of my sixth- and seventh-graders—the stage about which Bruno Bettelheim said that teaching anything to a mixed group of boys and girls is impossible.

My "promotion" was itself an interesting reflection on Andy's upside-down society. I had left a little school not more than a thirty-minute drive away, so isolated that Mr. McKay and the Hornsbys were the only adults I talked with each day, for one so different that it seemed to me to be hundreds of miles away in a different school district. Located in a growing population center, this eight-grade elementary school was treated almost as favorably as a high school. No going off to the school board's warehouse for supplies; they were delivered on regular drop-offs. Supplies were not bountiful, but they were sufficient by comparison with what I had at Woodward's Hill School. And there were enough graded textbooks in every subject for every pupil. Some people with clout lived in White Rock.

The school was fully graded in expectations, organization, subject-matter coverage, and promotion practices. I got the impression early on that there was to be no time in my class for deviations from courses of study and textbooks such as the ones in which we had indulged in my rural schoolhouse over the horizon. Miss Storm (whose pupils clapped and cheered when her occasional absences for illness were announced) made it clear that she expected pupils to be prepared for her fourth grade. There were to be no prior intrusions by the third-grade teacher into fourth-grade texts, and her pupils were to be ready for the fifth grade or retained in her class for another year—this last threat intended to goad even reluctant scholars into frantic effort. Fortunately, Miss Scott was between Miss Storm and me. Miss Scott taught part of the sixth grade (sharing it with me) and all of the fifth. My class included all of the seventh. The increasing population of the area was now warranting a full grade per class at the lower levels. Miss Scott and I shared certain commonalities of educational belief and opinion that included a dim view of our principal. It was apparent that, in her six or seven years of teaching, Miss Scott had become superb.

Principal Bannock and that school that year presented a paradox that has puzzled and intrigued me ever since: the incredible importance and the monumental neglect of a school's culture in its daily conduct. I rarely saw Mr. Bannock, a mild and gentle man. He smiled a hello when we passed in the hallway. He admonished me once for being overly harsh, in his view, with my treatment of a couple of boys who, in my judgment, had gone beyond the pale in their inclusion of a popular female classmate in a licentious poem they had written and circulated (up to the point of my intercepting it). Mr. Bannock was kind almost to a fault with all students, male and female—a source of frustration for all my colleagues and particularly Miss Storm. All but Miss Scott and I sent him a steady stream of classroom offenders who received a pat on the shoulder and the admonition, "I know you'll not do it again." But, with increasing frequency, he arrived late in the morning when the long wait for his disciplinary services had diminished the need. His small eighth-grade class was surprisingly patient in its wait, in part because Miss Scott, growing increasingly impatient with Mr. Bannock, looked in on it from time to time. Mr. Bannock had learned to rely on this capable young teacher and not my predecessor, even though he had taught in the adjoining classroom, now my daily abode.

So far as I can remember, Mr. Bannock never called a staff meeting or any other meeting. This was not because he was taking good care of the school as its chief worrier. We received occasional written notices from him. On the surface, one might have thought this absence of our participation in school affairs to be ideal and that we were free to teach. But the systemics and regularities of schooling ran the school like a faltering, halting, battery-operated child's train. So far as I know, there emerged no public clamor regarding his tardiness, usually a couple of days each week, and sometimes for a couple of hours into the morning; occasionally a substitute for the day was summoned. Yet, his delinquency was common knowledge, and parental concern was palpable. He was removed at the end of the year, not without some parental

protest, I was told. There was only a small, innocuous newspaper notice
of his end-of-the-year departure.

SANCTUARY REGAINED

The upside-down nature of our value system with respect to schools
and schooling mercifully removed me from systemics and regularities
early in my second year at White Rock Elementary School. Junior high
schools were just coming into vogue. The rhetoric of justification was
replete with all the right concepts regarding the frequently bewildering
passage from childhood to adolescence. But the real motivating factor
for junior highs usually was enrollment growth. Such was the motivation
for the junior high being built on adjacent land.

Like most such projects, it was not ready on schedule. Organizational arrangements already were in place for the school's opening in
September: the new junior high would absorb our seventh and eighth
grades, add a ninth, and enroll some students in these three grades to be
bused in from crowded schools some distance away. Now, with the new
school building not ready, portables were brought in so that the anticipated junior high could begin. There was a net shortfall of one classroom.
In the resulting scramble, someone in authority hit on the idea of moving
one of the elementary school classes to a local church; the then-vacated
classroom would substitute for the one more portable needed for junior
high students but not available. Overall, an interesting conceptual
transformation was occurring: placement in a junior high rather than an
elementary school would hasten the young toward adulthood. The seventh and eighth grades would now be more secondary than elementary.

Our school's enrollment had grown to pick up the slack of losing two
grades; we teachers simply moved down a couple of notches on the
graded hierarchy. I drew a fourth- and fifth-grade combination of girls
and boys at that wonderful age of nine and ten. And as the only male
other than our delightful new principal, I drew the church for my classroom. I benefited enormously from this common practice of favoring
the secondary school. After just a few days in the classroom we were

vacating, my brood and I picked up our belongings and trudged to the church on the flats just east of the town center.

Paradise regained. I do believe that the little church had once been a one-room school; it even had a cloakroom, just like North Star School. The classroom was no larger than that of Woodward's Hill, but I had a half-dozen fewer pupils. I would have settled for Thoreau's lakeside hut. Other than this one room, there was no space for the congregation, which, apparently, had found another location.

This group and I had hit it off from the beginning. Pubescent juices had not yet clogged the academic thought channels. I was a unique phenomenon: their first male teacher. We were now completely on our own. Not Mr. Martin, the new principal, and not anyone else from the school on the plateau or the school district visited throughout all the wonderful months that stretched from the anticipated three to almost the end of the school year. The prospect of going back was something we didn't talk about.

Nearly all the children and I lived west and northwest of our new home. Small clusters found their way down the hill by various footpaths to the boardwalk and then, at its end, on to the side of the main road that then passed the school. It didn't take them long to figure out my timing. There was only one route; I simply crossed the road in front of the lodge and took off along the boardwalk. After the first few days, a cluster awaited me; we were joined by others as we moved eastward. Most of the class was trailing along by the time we reached our destination.

Since it was no longer necessary to spend more than an hour at the blackboard preparing for the next day, and since my living quarters provided such a pleasant place to work and read, I headed back sufficiently early for some of the children to find it worthwhile to hang around to wait for me until I locked up the building. The grounds surrounding the church, with the old basketball backboard and hoop and the public softball diamond adjacent, provided good play space. I sometimes joined those still at play. The numbers remaining after school steadily grew. Soon, I was repeating my Pied Piper routine of the early morning late in the afternoon.

The word got around. There were other comparisons, such as to a mallard adult leading a brood of ducklings, stopping traffic when they crossed the street. Parents were delighted; they had few fears about their children's safety going to and coming from school.

Unlike at Woodward's Hill, we soon had a few parents visiting from time to time. Some of them had automobiles, and the little church was just a hundred feet off the road leading to most of their destinations. But it started with the children. Billy, whose parents owned the Blue Moon, asked if he could bring his mother to observe. A precedent set, others followed. Children and I agreed on some rules for visitation. I was in Woodward's Hill all over again, without the isolation and that nightly loneliness.

The major crisis of the year grew out of a combination of my inexperience and the too-little-examined norms of schooling. Ellen thirsted for recognition, especially from her male teacher. She was a plodder in her schoolwork; numbers were her nemesis. She could add, subtract, multiply, and divide—not easily—but, like a good many children of this age, she was thrown by problems requiring her to figure out which of these manipulations was required. I don't yet know why we so discretely separate the teaching of each of these operations, but that's another issue. Ellen's repeated tribulations with my old friend, arithmetic, frustrated and embarrassed her.

Suddenly, she got it. She came to school triumphantly with homework neatly and correctly done. This happened several times in succession. I was concentrating elsewhere at the time, with others' learning problems, depending on assigned exercises to keep Ellen and some others busy. And then I turned once more to a situation that required some mathematical reasoning by Ellen. She couldn't; she burst into tears and the whole sad story poured forth.

She and several classmates were getting together in the evening to do their homework. They all shared in the near-perfect results. Ellen was now in the devastating situation of confessing to cheating and implicating her classmates. "It was just to please you," she sobbed.

My mind was racing. Academic efficacy ranked high in my priorities. It now ranked high in those of my effervescent family. We worked hard and played hard. We were good at what we were doing and each success brought praise, not just from me but from the group's ethos, and more effort. Ellen and some others were slowly drowning. They were desperately reaching out for something to hang on to.

I said something like, "Let's talk." All work stopped and we held a powwow. More details regarding the evening get-togethers came out. They were quite widespread. They sounded very much like what many college students do together in preparing for their finals. Nobody calls that cheating. Why is it cheating when children do their homework together?

We developed a kind of compact. Helping one another is not cheating; indeed, it is desirable. But turning in work with solutions claimed to be mine, but that are not, is not honest. Nor is it a sensible thing to do. I needed to know the difficulties being encountered so that I could help. And there would be work from time to time to be accomplished entirely alone so that I could make individual assessments and intervene accordingly. But the basic ambience was to be one of cooperation, collaboration, and mutual assistance. The goal was not to please me but to gain insight and efficacy.[2]

School is conducted as a highly individualized, competitive affair with goals that bespeak democracy and teamwork. There is a disjuncture between ends and means, with the means converted to ends. No wonder that success in school predicts success in school and little else. To say that schools do not and should not teach values is nonsense. They are teaching values all the time—but not necessarily those a democracy espouses.

In my school in the church, I had seen no need for something akin to the sand table at Woodward's Hill. Perhaps this was because the latter had been so obviously segmented into its eight grades; we needed an organizing center to bring us all together for the creation of a guiding classroom ethos. I had not fully anticipated the amount of curricular and instructional fallout that resulted. I had only two grades in my new sanctuary that merged into one for most activities. Everyone could now read well enough for a good deal of independent work. I had less need for older mentors such as Helen and the twins. However, I believe that the inclusion of such from time to time, perhaps as aides seeking to determine if they wished to become teachers, would have been both an instructional bonus and a way of mitigating the need for my approval.

We now have plenty of evidence to support the creation of buddy systems that connect children with adolescent counselors who have had a little training for their role. Both age groups benefit.

I resorted more and more to selecting curricular topics, such as the relationships between the location of towns and environmental circumstances, that occupied the attention of us all over a period of several weeks—the approach that had emerged from the sand table. There commonly was one of these per month, since about a week between each was required for an ending and a new beginning: some kind of culminating activity that emerged rather naturally out of the ongoing work followed by a tooling up that brought artifacts from home to make up for the absence of materials other than those tied specifically to the graded curriculum. Each new unit emerged from a topic specified in the yellow guidebook, almost always in social studies or science, and extended into arts and crafts, occasionally our own dramatic creations, and the basics in language arts: reading, writing, and spelling. But those basics were also what the rest of each day accommodated in traditional fashion. An insightful school inspector—none visited that year—would have viewed the ongoing program, I believe, as a combination of traditional and progressive education.

What I most carried away from that wonderful period of almost a school year was the remarkable energy and focus of nearly all the children. They appeared to want to learn—anything and everything. I have never understood why the trajectory of school-based learning is calibrated to a graded curriculum and graded tests. We were not allowed to use the public softball diamond for soccer but were permitted to use it for softball in the spring, but not after school hours on those days when an evening adult game was scheduled. This left us primarily with the basketball hoop for organized sports. Basketball had never been my game, but I knew enough to teach the fundamentals. I was amazed at the skill and dexterity these young people developed, and the encouragement they gave one another. The ethos in class was very much the same.

I still have much to learn about why it was that they enjoyed each dawning recognition of personal efficacy. In his book *The Aims of Education*, philosopher Alfred North Whitehead tied his educational cycle of romance, precision, and generalization to successive stages of human development, whereas I have tended to view them as the desired cycle of each learning experience. My year with these nine- and ten-year-olds suggests that there is much to commend in what he wrote and, also, that my interpretation of his view is not off base.

I had only a little association with my colleagues during the year, nearly all of it social rather than professional. As with Mr. Bannock, Bernie Martin made no effort to address our school as a culture, to consider its mission and how we might work together toward it. Apparently, he was connecting well with the other teachers from whom I was now separated, but he and his wife, Mary, brought us all together socially on a couple of occasions during the year. I was invited from time to time to make up a foursome for an evening of bridge. My early passion for whist had not carried over into bridge or poker, the two card games that took up so many winter evenings in White Rock homes. Backroom poker had long and frequent runs at the Blue Moon, I was told. Fortunately, the Martins' bridge games were primarily a foil for conversation. Bernie is the only human being I have met who, I think, would have at least kept up with the now-deceased educators, Paul Woodring and Frank Keppel, in the rapid-fire coining of puns.

Bernie thought he was conveying good news when, in April, he told me that I should prepare to end my exile early in May. The disappointment among the members of my classroom family was palpable on getting the news. There were some tears. I wondered if people noticed how we shrugged off expressions of sympathy for the hardships we had endured. I have no recollection of experiencing these concluding weeks in the normal environment of school.

TREADING WATER

I don't remember much about that next year, either. I had half of my former class back with me again. I was out for the month of January, recuperating from a near-fatal ruptured appendix. Blanche took over. After being with her, I'm not sure the class was enthusiastic about my return.

I had learned during the previous year that Bernie and his wife, Mary, had "come out" after a long stint in the Yukon. He suffered severe migraine headaches and longed to go back. "It's the people there," he said. I don't think he ever called a faculty meeting, but he was always present and accessible. Bernie reminisced a lot about the Yukon, in school and during the evenings of conversation and bridge. I learned that I could quadruple my income by teaching in a one-room school there, earning room and board by serving as my own janitor, and keeping the post office open for a couple of hours each day after school. He figured that, by staying in for three years, I could come out with a fortune of more than $10,000. I thought about it.

Things change. The new junior high and our elementary school had been somewhat alien from the beginning and remained so. None of us held a college degree; most of the teachers in the junior high did. All were paid more. We sensed that our status in the community had dropped a little. Bernie was bright and capable; he probably was managing the school better than most principals did, but it was obvious that he had no plans for its future. The Yukon was on his mind.

My energy was surprisingly slow in coming back; the walk up the hill that I previously had enjoyed was, for at least another month, a burden. And I was seriously behind in a relatively new undertaking. I had not, after my first year in White Rock, gone back to summer school in Victoria for the second year of credits required for a permanent teaching certificate. Instead, I enrolled for the longer summer session at the University of British Columbia in studies that could lead to a bachelor's degree. After the summer, I was into the maximum of year-long correspondence courses allowed and again to summer school—a regimen that would continue throughout my school-teaching years to the master's degree, and then to an abrupt departure to the University of Chicago for studies leading to the Ph.D.

Sometimes I wonder about what was missed by my never "going to college." Gained, of course, in the seemingly endless reading and writing was deep appreciation for the written word. Lost for a time was reading by choice and happenstance, but how could I completely resist some books of my time such as Hemingway's *The Old Man and the Sea*, Stapledon's *Last and First Men*, Steinbeck's *The Grapes of Wrath*? And there usually was plenty to interest me in the reading lists of the courses I took.

My professional preoccupations were not all that were changing. Andy Richardson chose to leave to pick up another bus route. News of the amenities (other than bathrooms) of staying in the White Rock Lodge had gotten around. A male and a female teacher at the junior high, both with college degrees, picked up his room and the one adjacent. That propinquity and their mutual charm stirred a courtship that was consummated in marriage within a year. After-dinner conversation with them, Blanche, Jack, and other patrons of the lodge delayed my getting to books and papers, shortened my sleep, and probably reduced my effectiveness as a teacher during the year back with my colleagues—my last at White Rock Elementary School and the equally memorable White Rock Lodge. But the memories have enriched my life.

The promotion that came at the end of that year was of the conventional kind in the education business—a good deal more responsibility and a little more money. I was offered the principalship of a four-room elementary school, Wellington Road, close to the municipality's northwest boundary in an area that would, within a few years, become a suburb of New Westminster. I took it. The courtship there never quite matured into a romance, but I learned a lot about keeping school.

THE EGG CRATE

There is no better way to disassociate from a school's culture than to commute. With wheels I would have had choices, but an automobile cost more than my new $1,000 a year salary, and I had to save for summer school. There were no motels or boarding houses anywhere in this newly developing area. I learned that Mr. McCormick, an English teacher in the just-opened Queen Elizabeth High School down the road a piece, drove to and from Vancouver each day, passing not far from my school and my mother's home. (She had moved from North Vancouver, and the ferry trip no longer was an added inconvenience for me.)

Mac informed me that he had tried a passenger before, and it didn't work. Mac was precise in all of his habits, and the passenger had been careless with time. But, my contribution to the gas bill would help;

however, if he had to wait for me just once, the deal was off. I got wet often, standing early beside the road in the rain so as never to be late. The enjoyable, twice daily conversations with Mac are the only memories of that year at Wellington Road School having some continuity in my mind. He was not merely much-schooled; he was well-educated. Other memories are jumbled and disconnected.

One memory is the show-off bluster of Teddy before the opening of school on the first day, telling classmates how he would take care of the new principal, not knowing what I looked like and that I was in earshot. I guess I looked too young to be a school principal. I was now experienced enough not to rise to my natural instincts in challenge. Instead, I enlisted his help right off in some organizational matters, and he was my proud, right-hand man for the rest of the year. I was the full-time teacher of the fifth- and sixth-grade classes. Why the principal always was expected to teach the oldest children I'll never know.

A second memory is the mud. The rain and fog that stretched unprecedented that fall from September through December were broken by a severe frost in late October. The playground soil, soaked deeply, rose six inches each night and subsided into deep mud in the morning sun, chewed up at recess by sloshing boots chasing that ubiquitous soccer ball. The soccer ball was the opiate for frazzled teachers in small rural schools.

The third recollection is resuscitation of the message service that had connected my car-owning buddy and me that first year. We expanded it. Beyond the usual planning for Saturday night in Vancouver, we exchanged books. We had discovered this mutual interest during my stint in White Rock where Marshall lived. He was now the teaching principal of a six-room older school down the King George Highway several miles. Neither of our schools warranted a telephone. Since we were reasonably close, we planned some interschool soccer games during the fall and softball games during the spring. His enthusiasm for these waned, probably because of his consistently losing. I don't think he knew that soccer and fast-pitch softball had been addictions of mine since boyhood; I was arrogantly confident that I could train my boys (the girls were enthusiastic fans) to beat any school of twice our size in both games. And that I could train his boys to beat mine.

I shall linger on the fourth recollection since it has to do, once again, with the puzzling neglect of school culture, as well as with sex stereotypes in the social context. As more and more schoolwide irritations piled up, I decided that it was time for my colleagues and me to address them. I called my first and last staff meeting. The three teachers—all female—arrived with their purses in hand. They didn't put them down, an ominous sign. Jean Schwartz spoke. She let me know in no uncertain terms that she had quite enough to do with her class and needed to be planning for the next day right at that moment. The issues I had summarized in my planning note (that also asked for other suggestions) had nothing to do with her classroom; furthermore, they were my responsibility as principal. The others nodded and my first foray into schoolwide planning and renewal was over. I don't think I would have gotten very far under the best of circumstances with my perceived effort to share schoolwide responsibilities, even though topics such as how to handle tardiness consistently did affect us all as teachers. Relationships between Jean and me had been strained from the beginning. This was particularly puzzling and upsetting since she appeared friendly and outgoing with colleagues. She was a good teacher and the children liked her. I found out later that she had had her heart set on this principalship and had been passed over. There were a few elementary schools in the district headed by very senior women, but able, experienced young women were regularly passed over in favor of young, relatively inexperienced men, especially those with athletic interests and abilities. The customary explanation was that men would be firmer disciplinarians. It is of interest to note that men dominated the school boards of the era.

My fifth memory is of report cards. Perhaps it was population growth in the attractive southwest section of British Columbia that was contributing to the growth of bureaucratic practices in the school district. Standardized testing was on the rise and, with it, the concept of the bell or normal curve. As noted earlier, I had encountered at Woodward's Hill School the expectation that I would assign 5 percent As, 5 percent Fs, with an ascending and then descending percentage of Bs and Ds above and below a large percentage of Cs. How does one deal with this piece of nonsense when one has three or four or even eight pupils in a grade?

At White Rock, there had been a brief flurry of pupil report cards with qualitative judgments regarding "improvement," "needs improvement," "dangerously low performance," and the like in several categories that included academic and social behavior. I didn't pay attention to the bell curve and relied heavily on short notes to parents to recognize outstanding or troublesome performance. Each year at both schools, I monitored the taking of one standardized achievement test, bundled the lot for pickup, and heard nothing more about them. I can think of better ways to handle standardized tests, but faced with a choice, I'll take yesterday's over today's practices.

The monthly demands of report cards, attendance reports, tardiness, and truancy were virtually the only school matters two of my three colleagues chose individually to talk about with me. Clearly, my road to approval was to provide answers to all four. Yet, I had the strange feeling that, were I able to eliminate such annoyances from our lives, the result would be comparable to taking away the weather from the conversation of the populace. The sharp distinctions between the grade levels enrolled in each class, the daily roll call, the taking home and taking back of report cards, the isolation of miscreants to a corner of the classroom as punishment, the keeping "after school" of the tardy to make up time lost, the dependability of the timing of the bell to signify the beginning and the ending of recess and noon hour—these and more were not just the regularities of school but the regularities of my two most experienced colleagues to which the third, in her second year of teaching, was rapidly growing accustomed. I began to see and, I think, even to understand the threat in the agenda of possible change that I had sent to them for our first and last faculty meeting. The certainty of even annoying regularities plays a stabilizing role in our daily lives.

Did I give in too readily (perhaps willingly) to my colleagues' rejection of my plan to address schoolwide matters together? Our lack of connections with parents was on my list. There was, as yet, no organized parent group in this new school. Or were we all—children, teachers, and parents—better off with the retreat of the four of us into our classrooms, each a cell in the egg crate? Except for a few of the regularities that go with school as a place, each of us was very much on her or his own, as I had been at Woodward's Hill and my class in the church. Regarding my performance as a principal, I think that any competent school superintendent or professor of educational administration of today would give me, at best, a D.

With the coming of the year's end, I sensed that I would not be back. During the first few weeks of summer school, Wellington Road School was uncomfortably on my mind. It did not beckon. Once again, I had enjoyed the children in the classroom and on the playground, but they and I seemed to disconnect from it, probably because of the anonymity of simply disappearing each day. The "community" had as yet no roots. Gertrude Stein would have viewed it as having no there there. My communal base was elsewhere. Halfway through the summer, on the eve of the deadline for such action, I dropped my letter of resignation into the mailbox.

INTERLUDE

There was something strangely different and relaxing in being out of a job for a while. The feeling of freedom was exhilarating—perhaps similar to having work after a spell of being without it. Thoughts of how to avoid ever working again passed into my mind and then shimmered away in the sunlight. Years later, I was reminded of these thoughts in conversations with the superb surgeon in Los Angeles who took care of my hernia. He asked me if I had ever thought of being a drifter—a bum, as he put it. His view was that he had to be either that or excellent in his calling; nothing in between would satisfy.

I had found something else to do at the University of British Columbia, in addition to taking classes. I was a member of the summer students' council. Teachers from all over the province dominated in the student body, the next largest group being students who had flunked a course or two during the regular academic year and needed credits to be back on schedule. Unlike these, we had no class year to march with. We were a polyglot group lacking academic identity. Perhaps we were trying to make up for what we thought we had missed in not going on to college as regular undergraduates, and so the all-teacher student council sponsored a lecture and musical entertainment series and maintained the tradition of a summer dance. With no obligation to do so, the alumni office gave us welcome support.

With my financial resources rapidly running out, I don't know why I wasn't worrying about getting a job and spending my spare time seeking one. My feelings of carefree abandon dissolved on the second to the last day of summer session, just as I was beginning to sense that my contacts were about to scatter. Lunch in a place of one's choice with other adults was and still is a rare privilege for most elementary school teachers. There was a tug on my arm as I passed a table in the campus cafeteria.

It was Stan Morrison, former principal of Lynn Valley Elementary School, who had just assumed a full-time role with the British Columbia Teachers' Federation, the organization he had worked so diligently to help develop. He had heard about my unemployment and wanted to know if I still needed a job. His office had received a call the previous day from George Ross, head of the Provincial Industrial School for (delinquent) Boys—a.k.a. "reform" school. The director of education, the only schoolteacher, had unexpectedly requested an indefinite period of sick leave. Was I interested? And, by the way, I was told, it pays $1,500 a year plus free room and board. I met with Mr. Ross the following day; I took the job.

The way certain patterns take hold in one's life is more than passing strange. On reflection, I realize that this is the serendipitous way jobs have come into and facilitated my work. And the way most partners in marriage come together. After employment at Woodward's Hill, I never thought to cruise the want ads. I was near a first retirement before I discovered the incredible array of worldwide opportunities offered in the *Chronicle of Higher Education*. Did I miss joy or torment in failing to follow up on a few? The selling of one's self that goes on today is not attractive. But the tradeoff is that so many people overlooked in the past for very wrong reasons now get a hearing. But, in taking most of the serendipity out of the old ways, the new have yet some distance to go in taking the inequities out of both the old and the new.

My mother had been shocked by my decision to resign from the principalship of Wellington Road School, which I shared with her only after I returned from the mailbox. She had never had the security of a steady household income. But now she had a new worry: I was to be with the "bad boys."

Chapter 7

Loss of Innocence

If the child experiences failure in school during these five years (from age five to ten), by the age of ten his confidence will be shattered, his motivation will be destroyed, and he will have begun to identify with failure.

WILLIAM GLASSER[1]

BISCOQ

The British Columbia Industrial School for (delinquent) Boys was located about an hour's drive from Vancouver, up the Fraser River on the edge of the town of Port Coquitlam. The need for brevity in referring to it had produced BISCOQ—pronounced *bisco*. Several other state institutions were located between New Westminster and Port Coquitlam: a fortresslike prison, a companion correctional facility to Biscoq for girls, a hospital-like residential entity for severely mentally retarded children never seen in public schools, and more.

A belt of woods separated Biscoq from the main highway. School property took up a considerable chunk of acreage: a small farm, large playing field, and well-worn buildings—the main hall (for eating, sleeping, administration, and twenty-four-hour-a-day confinement as required); motor mechanics, tailoring, and upholstering shops; various storage sheds; and a rather large building containing two small classrooms, gymnasium, swimming pool, and tiny library. Entry through the library (for which I was responsible) provided considerable privacy for my very limited bedroom-bathroom living quarters.

Biscoq did not have the physical restraints of even a minimum-security facility. There were no surrounding walls or retaining fences. During breaks in the daily schedule, a couple of boys sometimes hastened down to the highway in the hope of hitching a ride and, if unsuccessful, getting back before being missed. More often than not, the driver picking them up lived in the area, recognized what was going on, and simply returned them to the school via the next turnoff. On several occasions, these unwelcome services were provided by Mrs. Ross on her way to town.

Institutions of this kind often turn out to be essentially pre-prisons. The recidivism rate for them was, and probably still is, high. During the four years I was there, the youngest boy was eleven; those boys not released by the age of eighteen were transferred to a more prisonlike adult institution. Some boys were returned to Biscoq up to three times after their first incarceration, resulting in their spending more than half of their years between twelve and eighteen in Biscoq. Some were far more comfortable being there than in the environments from which they came and regarded the time spent out as a kind of vacation from their daily circumstances. There were those who broke down in my presence (not that of fellow inmates) in tears of despair in seeing no future other than that of alternating between a "home" environment that didn't want them and a "school" environment that offered only a temporary alternative. For every new arrival brought to us, there usually was the return of one who had spent a year or more with us before.

Such institutions are incredibly costly. I don't recall our population exceeding about five dozen boys. Their care, supervision, and education required a considerable staff over three shifts day and night: a superintendent spending a good deal of his time with external affairs; an associate superintendent occupied primarily with program and other internal matters; a manager of the day shift when most activities were carried out; a nurse-nutritionist; a secretary and an assistant (there was a considerable amount of paperwork to take care of); an instructor in tailoring and upholstery, another in motor mechanics and carpentry, one more in gardening and grounds maintenance (the actual work of maintaining buildings and grounds, apart from major repair, was part of the boys' work schedule); at least three men who came on in midafternoon for recreational activities and getting the boys settled into bed and another for maintaining order after lights out; a cook and an assistant; and then—with more and more boys over the compulsory age of sixteen deciding during my second year to go to school—an additional teacher for the following year. Perhaps I left out a couple. Clearly, the ratio of staff to inmates was close to one to three.

Compare this to the public schools of the time, usually lacking super-intendents and with teaching principals, a secretary or part-time secretary in high schools but rarely in elementary schools, no lunchrooms in the latter, no nurses, and only rarely special educators. Then add to this cost the loss of property to which much of the delinquent behavior was addressed, that of apprehension and court procedures for incarceration, custodial transportation to Biscoq, and then of prison terms for a very large percentage of its "graduates." The misplacement and folly of our attention to the young screams out at us. The cost of our ways in human lives is incalculable.

PEDAGOGY OF THE DAMNED

Inside the Biscoq classroom, my Woodward's Hill experience served me well. But this time I had twelve not eight grades: the larger group—all elementary—from 8:30 to 12:00 in the morning; the smaller—grades seven through twelve—from 1:00 to 4:00 in the afternoon. Actually, I wasn't sure of the grade classification of any of my pupils. The records that sometimes arrived with them rarely were adequate; most reached me months later. Accurate or not, records and pupil claims of grade level rarely aligned with attainment. By the age of fifteen, most boys had repeated at least two grades, but even after such retention, all but a few were still below what I concluded to be the "correct" grade desig-nation—as best I could determine through the not-very-reliable stan-dardized achievement tests I administered.

The criteria these boys used in sizing up an adult, especially a teacher or some other in authority, were different from those I had experienced, or at least differently weighted. Few excelled academically, but they had plenty of "street smarts," with "street" expanded to include their entire surround. Many seemed to have a well-honed practical awareness of their immediate space and circumstance, accompanied by an incredible ability to beguile one into trusting them. Most, on concluding that you had passed the test—often quite subtle—rewarded you with the giving of trust. But, oh my, one could be let down. What some of the most dispirited had learned was that they had used up their cupful of letting people down, and there was no more water in the spigot. At this point, there was nothing to be gained by telling the truth, and so deceit became habitual.

Promptly at 8:30 on my first day, one of the morning staff delivered my class of twenty or so ranging from eleven to perhaps fifteen in age. One of the things I was yet to learn was the degree to which Biscoq, perhaps necessarily, ran by the clock. Once again, I had used up the generous amount of chalkboard space available in preparation, but this time I had textbooks and other materials for everyone. The group made heavier and louder use of their bodies than I had experienced before, but the morning passed without memorable incident until almost noon. My predecessor, over his dozen or more years at Biscoq, had developed a few interesting strategies for daily survival. One was a block of wood drilled to hold the pencils given out and returned each day so as to facilitate a quick tally. I was one short in the end-of-the-morning check.

I said that we would not go to lunch until it was recovered and in its slot. Someone told me that Mr. Evans, manager of the day shift, would not be happy with me for holding up lunch. Mr. Evans had no authority over my teaching responsibilities, but he was responsible directly to Mr. Ross with respect to his authority over the daily work and schedule. I ignored the warning. Time passed—probably not more than a minute or two. Then Ray suggested that all be released from their seats to look for the truant pencil. I told him that this would be confusing and suggested that *he* look for it. He did. All eyes were on him. Ray was clever. He leaned down behind a desk as though to look under a radiator and, presumably, somehow disengaged the pencil from his person and came up with it, triumphant. I thanked him; we went to lunch (and, yes, Mr. Evans reminded me of the necessity of getting my class to lunch on time so as not to hold up the kitchen staff).

I don't know how much that incident spared me difficult times in class. After all, I had behind me the considerable authority of the institution. Nonetheless, Ray had been outwitted in his little caper and not further embarrassed by any claim to victory on my part. Most groups develop codes and respect their observation. Luckily, I had passed; presumably, several years of teaching had honed some "school smarts." Still, I was let down several times, quite hard.

Two years later, a couple of boys I counted on most messed up the near-antique little Ford coupe I had just purchased in their aborted attempt to use it for a getaway. And, when I relaxed a little the second year, rewarding all the pupils with an "off-campus" picnic, two boys strayed out of sight long enough to break into a nearby residence and put an end forever to such excursions.

Instructional resources were not abundant, but they were more than what I had available in my three previous schools. And my freedom to teach was restrained only by a kind of built-in sense of loyalty to those three courses of study that emanated from the Provincial Ministry of Education. For my first two years, when enrollment did not warrant a second class, the grades in my care spread across all three. My main problems in seeking to respond to the intended curriculum came with the afternoon class composed of the oldest students.

I had not previously taught above the eighth grade. Early on in that first year, I didn't need to worry much about higher grades because only a couple of boys over the age of sixteen—the end of compulsory attendance—chose to attend school, and so the eighth grade was near the upper end of my curricular responsibilities. But I quickly became aware of a major fact of individual differences: the range of academic achievement within one student often approaches the range of a "graded" class. Just as the range in tested reading achievement in a sixth grade class is at least six grades, the spread between reading and mathematical scores for some individual pupils in that class sometimes is as much as six grades.[2] And so, although the average achievement of my afternoon class corresponded to that of upper elementary and junior high school grades, most were able to function several grades higher in at least one subject. Even in this first of my afternoon classes, with fewer than twenty pupils, the spread in most subjects was from elementary school grades to at least the middle of the tenth grade.

Another circumstance added to the complications of pedagogically addressing this problem of academic diversity—one that exists to a similar degree in most schools but is disguised by the prevailing grade stratification and the reinforcing influence of graded texts, graded tests, graded promotion and nonpromotion for pupils, and indeed, graded teachers. My predecessor openly admitted to me that he was burned out. He had been contemplating sick leave for quite some time; he just didn't feel well and admitted to discouraging the attendance of boys over the age of sixteen—an attitude favored by most of the day shift staff. The recently appointed associate superintendent, Hugh Christie, placed education high in his theory of rehabilitation. He encouraged me in my desire to encourage school attendance for all.

Older boys began to trickle in as the year progressed, increasing afternoon class size and otherwise complicating my daily life. Experienced as I was personally with the correspondence arm of the University of British Columbia, I turned to the parallel school arm of the Ministry in Victoria, the provincial capital. The service was splendid. Although students not enrolled in a school were required to mail in completed lessons for marking and approval before getting the next lessons, my intervention assured a steady stream with little in-between delays in the supply of lessons. Just as I was connected with a responsible professor for each of my own correspondence courses, boys with part of their daily schedule geared to such had access to my tutoring.

From my perspective then, the correspondence lessons that augmented our learning repertoire were about as pedagogically sound as the two-dimensional page permits: amply illustrated, replete with practical examples, satisfactorily sequential, and with appropriate tests. They provided me with models that inspired my development of parallel materials at both elementary and secondary levels. There always was someone ready to take over my hand-printed "software," place it on the "computer"—a pad covered with a purplish genre of jelly—bring down the press, and produce a few copies. A messy business, at best. Over time, I built up a substantial paper curriculum for most subjects and most grades (all eventually typed and mimeographed by the office staff), sequenced in several boxes that, I learned later, were used for years by my successors as instructional kits. These and the province's extension services saw me through. Today's much-touted distance learning is not exactly an innovation.

The burden of increasing class size in the afternoons proved eventually to be self-serving. Also, for reasons not clear to me, enrollment in the morning class grew during my second year. The case for a second teacher was easily mounted and then approved. Nell Thomas, an experienced elementary school teacher, joined me at the beginning of my third year, taking over two classes a day of the youngest boys. The older half, divided again into half, constituted my morning and afternoon classes. I was, once more, a teaching principal, a role that left me with more discretionary time than had those excruciatingly demanding first two years.

My shortcomings in the content of some subjects, particularly of the high school curriculum, were not high on my list of worries. By now, becoming a partner with my pupils in the adventure of learning had become habitual. My constant need—indeed, ever-pressing demand—was for some flash of pedagogical creativity that would bring to flame whatever spark of interest or curiosity flickered for a promising moment in any one of my pupils. Few such flashes served more than once; never before had I been so sharply aware of individuality.

I was with Tony day after day for months without seeing a spark. Had there once been burning embers, they had grown cold and dark. With Blake, the sparks popped like burning cedar kindling, but rarely carried flame to larger logs. I sat with him again and again in the evening, responding with increasing reluctance to his plea: "Just listen one more time," he enticed. His face became ecstatic as we listened together, one more time, to Artie Shaw's "Stardust." I've long been a fan of Artie Shaw and his orchestra, but enough already. I envisioned the bridge over the garden wall in the song to lead to a lush garden of learning beyond, but we never got there. It was the same with his barrage of questions to me about the toughest trucks in the world. We never managed to get them on a road to other learnings—about transportation, for example. Blake's knowledge was a bundle of disconnected information, not at all encyclopedic in that it was heavy on detail in one small segment, but missing in all others. Blake would have had fun today on the Internet.

Tony's mind was hard to plumb. Was he in deep meditation or just mentally blank? Clearly, he was dangerous. Strong and quick, he lashed out when provoked, his provocation rarely predictable. More than any other boy, he brought on the necessity for physical restraint and days of confinement. The older boy whose attention he most cultivated and by whom he was most consistently rejected was Charlie, whose long-term commitment to Biscoq was for attempted bank robbery and for his role as accomplice in the murder that accompanied it. His slightly older accomplice was in prison. The last thing Charlie sought was any altercation with peers or staff. Charlie was by far my best student, with clear signs of genius in mathematics. When he reached eighteen, the courts would make a decision about his future: imprisonment or restricted freedom. It was scary to think about why Tony was so intrigued with Charlie and fascinating to sense with Charlie the danger lurking in association.

There was affinity with my Ernie of Woodward's Hill in the challenge presented by Tony. But whereas Ernie stirred compassion, Tony promoted antagonism; he lived in deep, dark pools of the most damned, resentful and threatening. Nobody in his now-disintegrated home environment— never stable—loved him, nor he anyone. There were some remaining connections with a sister. Tony just missed being handsome, in a menacing way. His shifts in temperament were meteoric. He was smilingly delighted when, on his return from sick bay, I said that I had missed him. The next moment, he was snarling at the boy in the desk behind him. Tony had chosen the front desk in the center row from the beginning and protected it like a fortress.

Tony was fourteen, claimed to be in the fifth grade, but could read only his name. He seemed to take pride in the claim that no teacher had been able to teach him to read, and I couldn't either. To a lesser degree, this trait was common with quite a few boys: their nonlearning was the fault of teachers and a triumph of their ability to keep teachers from the satisfaction of teaching them something. This trait was a kind of badge of damnation.

I have written much about the humane ends of education not warranting the inhumane means we commonly use to attain them. Consequently, I reflect frequently on some of the ends I have used, with Tony often coming to mind. Months into my first year with Tony, I fanned what I believe was one of those sparks I continuously looked for. Although written announcements for both boys and staff members appeared from time to time on the bulletin board in the main building, those to the boys almost always were posted following an oral statement during one or more of the routine roll calls taken several times each day. Tony had been in confinement during the oral presentation and posting of one—still on the bulletin board—that, because of his disregard, turned out to affect him negatively. He was very angry. "Doesn't anyone know that I can't read?" he complained.

I bided my time. Institution-bound much of the time, most of us did favors for one another. Some people, boys and staff, added up a tally of favors, sometimes reminding one that he owed. I printed out a list of "favors" I had done for Tony, all of which I considered in my normal line of duty but for which he now "owed"—not in return favors, but in dollars. I had learned of the high value Tony placed on money. I don't know what reason I gave Tony to get his signature on a promise to pay, with interest. He was outraged. He envisioned the small account to which the school contributed from time to time and maintained for each boy to be virtually consumed by his debt to me.

I told him that neither his earlier unpleasantness nor this one would have occurred had he been able to read and that, in all probability, there would be more such occurrences in the future. Learning to read was in his self-interest. "I trusted you," he screamed. Shame crept over me. I had cheated him, however well intentioned my aim.

Tony said not a word to me for days. Then, he asked if there were some books—not "little kid" stuff—in the library that, with my help, he might be able to read. I forget what I picked, but I recall that the first was along the lines of the early "bad guys, good guys" silent movies—

short, simple sentences under pictures devoid of ambiguity. I owed him, I knew, and I was willing to struggle with him for as long as he maintained interest and effort. Both faded after several weeks but not completely. He began to pick books on his own, addressing with expletives the many with few illustrations. He did learn to read a little, but if required to pass a test in reading for promotion to the third grade, he probably would have remained in the second forever.

No, the degree in the social sciences I earned with honors a few years later—which many people would think should entitle me to teach—would not have helped me much in my teaching at Biscoq. Mastery of subject matter is desirable but insufficient preparation to teach. What I needed desperately were the insights and the myriad necessary ways to restore confidence shattered and motivation drowned in the despair that accompanies those human beings who perceive themselves early on to be culturally damned. Whether I helped or hurt Tony I'll never know. I, too, was desperate—in my desire to teach him to read.

INSTITUTIONAL CULTURE

Institutions create their own norms, exacerbating some and virtually ignoring others characterizing the larger culture of which they are a part. Schools, for example, reflect the dominant extant beliefs of their surround, while developing and observing regularities that have little currency elsewhere. Institutions with largely residential inmates tend to be most extreme and, indeed, bizarre in some of the norms they create and massage. Biscoq was no exception: to the casual, short-term observer, surprisingly normal and rational; to the long-term analyst, a nest of contradictions and disproportionate weightings of priorities.

Needless to say, both juveniles and adults brought to the establishment and maintenance of institutional culture various bits and pieces of the cultural surround to which they variously belonged. Several members of the staff shared the external conventional wisdom regarding juvenile delinquents: they were born bad and likely to remain so. I finally gave up trying to advance an alternative view when my Saturday night friends raised the question one more time: "How are the bad boys out on the farm?"

Juvenile delinquency was becoming a field of study, but the insights being gained were confined primarily to sociological and psychological literature. The ethos of Biscoq had, since its founding, been custodial. Most of the staff at the time of my coming shared the conventional wisdom of the larger culture: rehabilitation was unlikely. And, with longitudinal data that encompassed repeated sentences—including being sent to prison after the age of eighteen—revealing a recidivism rate up to 70 percent, refuting the view of inherent incorrigible badness was not easy. The counterargument that a *custodial only* environment was an unlikely route to rehabilitation usually brought forth only anger. The strong believers in the "bad from birth" theory were quick to put down contrary views. If some among the older staff members had once believed in the corrective purpose of Biscoq, they now kept silent, awaiting retirement.

Nonetheless, fresh breezes were stirring and beginning to reach policy circles. The work of Emile Durkheim of France, Cyril Burt of England, and Ernest Burgess of the United States pointing to cultural cause-and-effect—such as poverty, homelessness, and parental neglect—was entering criminal theory and practice. The no-security Borstal system in England for late teen and young adult offenders was being considered in British Columbia as a way station between the industrial school (earlier termed "reform school") and the penitentiary. The new winds signaled the possibility of a shift in ideology at Biscoq.

Hugh Christie had preceded my coming by only a couple of years. His predecessor in the deputy post was a charismatic individual known to the public for his basketball skills but with no experience or professional credentials for the position—a rather typical choice for a quite high-level civil service post of its kind. He had been popular with the boys who were sorry to see him go. Christie was of a different genre. In his studies at the University of British Columbia, he was into the frontiers of thought in social work and criminology. And he was a lightning rod for inevitable controversy at Biscoq.

Before Christie, there had been no strong spokesperson for the educational side of the custodial-corrective purpose that marked the beginning of schools in the Western world. The issues involved were now heating up with the increase in juvenile delinquency in urban centers. The growth in the number of boys sent by the courts from the province's largest city, Vancouver, was beginning to exceed Biscoq's capacity. Further, they were changing institutional culture in various ways, some subtle, some not. The challenges to Christie were quite different from those of his predecessors, in part by his own choosing and persona.

With educational-corrective ideology weak, Biscoq had fallen into orderly custodial routines. Boys had been coming from scattered locations across the province, more from Vancouver and New Westminster than from anywhere else, but not disproportionately. They commonly were strangers to one another. There was no strong "boy culture" apart from institutional culture. Successful runaways had been few. Most had only one neighborhood, reservation, or town to go to, in which they were quickly picked up and returned. Twenty-four-hour days of confinement were immediate; the privilege of short "vacation" trips home for good behavior suspended. Christie's predecessor apparently had many outside interests and expectations to address. Much of the daily operation was left to Syd Evans, third in command: the competent, firm, but regarded as quite fair, Mr. Evans, a confirmed believer in the intractability of the bad-from-birth syndrome. He took great pride in running a tight ship, was admired by his fellow believers on the staff, and respected in a careful way in his authority by most boys.

But Biscoq was changing—in its juvenile population, in its staff, and in its ethos. Juvenile gangs were not yet viewed as a public menace, but they existed and were growing. Those boys who came to Biscoq from gangs brought some of their gang culture with them. They were mostly boys for whom belonging to a gang was their strongest bond of belonging—more than to home, school, and church of a past that was to become increasingly nostalgic rather than embracive for many adults, in both Canada and the United States.

Boys who identified strongly with the gangs from which they were temporarily separated managed to maintain at least a thin line of communication. How they did it would in itself be an interesting study. All incoming and outgoing telephone calls and letters were carefully monitored. There existed none of today's almost instant means of communication. And yet, a kind of metaphysical message ran through the institution from time to time regarding the pending arrival of a gang leader known to someone. Fascinatingly, much of the prestige and power enjoyed by a gang leader on "the outside" came with him into the ethos on the inside. One could sense the growing on the inside of an increasingly cohesive boys' culture that in no way replaced the imposed custodial culture, but was to a considerable degree separated from it. Leaders of what might have been rival gangs on the outside were leaders of a common culture on the inside. There is much in the literature of criminology and adult prison life on similar phenomena.

But now—about halfway through my four years at Biscoq—I was beginning to see emerging a fascinating struggle of ideologies and the personalities attached to them for, shall we say, the soul of the institution. My fascination has increased over the years because I have seen the struggle in so many different kinds of institutions, including, of course, schools and universities, both public and private. Clearly, this struggle is most severe in settings with individuals whose lives center almost exclusively on or in them and not much beyond, as is so often the case with those that are largely or entirely residential. Interestingly, these many struggles, each of small physical scope, are essentially the struggles of democracy writ large, given the degree to which, as Loren Eiseley once wrote, institutions are the bones of our civilization.

IDEOLOGICAL DISSONANCE

I strolled unwittingly into the then-embryonic struggle on my second teaching day at Biscoq. There is, I think, an acceleration of bantering behavior among people at work when there is common reluctance to engage in talk that might open wounds. My parents had warned me to be cautious in instigating conversation on politics and religion with people I didn't know well. I had visited and talked with staff members a couple of times before my duties began. There had been a good deal of bantering, part of which picked up on the probability that, as an educator,

I would side with a few colleagues whose heads were askew. I was already being pigeonholed.

The pencil incident caused me to be quite late for lunch on my first day of teaching; most of my new colleagues had left the lunchroom. On the second day, however, I arrived precisely on time and joined the only two others in the room, seated at a table for four. A few minutes into idle chatter, I was nicely told that I was sitting in Mr. Henderson's usual chair, but he wouldn't mind. I moved to the fourth chair. Mr. Spence's disposition was, however, of a different order. I knew just as soon as he looked at me after coming in the door that he minded a great deal my usurping "his" chair. Seemingly small matters can become a big part of institutional culture. I moved to one of the still-empty other tables in the room; Spence hesitated for a moment and then went silently to his accustomed place, completing the table of four.

When the next person entered, I welcomed him to my table. The nurse, Amy Frandsen, and Wally Bowen of the afternoon shift joined us soon after. There were some comments regarding some change in usual seating that apparently had occurred and some expression of appreciation for my role in it. I left the matter alone and didn't ask questions. I still don't understand why a couple of people not even there at the time congratulated me for exposing and shaking up a situation that had grown silly. But I was now more precisely pigeonholed—not just as a soft-and-tender educator but as a Christie recruit. Shaking up the routines is what he did (and enjoyed) quite regularly.

That I shared Christie's educational orientation was, of course, a given in my mind, but I had never before—and not now—perceived myself to be on one's ideological team. Nor was I aware of the underlying staff tension and how, in turn, it was affected by the ecosystem that accommodated the boys, an ecosystem that would intersect more and more with the ecosystem that accommodated the staff as internal connections to external gangs increased and Christie's influence spread.

Hugh Christie exuded leadership: physically magnificent, bright, basically cheerful and optimistic, and, with a wry sense of humor, determined. He walked like a panther and talked in whatever use of language the circumstances appeared to call for. He gave little ground when it came to principle. Even boys who ran up against his tough side respected him. His well-honed "progressive" views on rehabilitation through capacity-building sharpened the formerly near-dormant ideological division in the staff.

There emerged two divided sectors in the adult ecology: the initially small group of Christie believers that steadily grew in size with the addition of the "academic types" Christie was able to bring in, and the hard core of "custodial types" who, in their own eyes, kept the work schedule, the very spine of the school, afloat. These were the staff members who complained about the increase in school attendance taking away their workers.

This initially larger group reported directly to Syd Evans. Even though Hugh Christie was second in command and, technically, represented authority above that of Evans, he rarely exercised it and never in public, another mark of his wisdom. Christie seemed to sense the rather delicate balance that George Ross had to maintain in his essentially public office. Ross had no professional training in juvenile delinquency, but his experience with boys' clubs put him on the educational side Christie represented. The general public and those in political office to whom Ross was responsible were nervous about such things as runaway young criminals from Biscoq being at large. They favored strict control; Syd Evans represented such. There is a parallel here with schooling, of course. Retiring military personnel are still viewed as promising candidates for teaching in public schools and, especially, administrative posts. Hugh Christie recognized the undesirability of forcing a showdown in Ross's office over his own and Syd Evans's authority. I am convinced, however, that Evans was waiting for the kind of incident—perhaps a massive runaway—that would strengthen the case for his own ideology over that of Christie's. Later years have revealed to me that the situation is not novel, even if somewhat more intense than is commonly encountered in institutional life.

The economic times were tough. Staff members valued their jobs. Few of those who enjoyed the fresh breeze of change represented by Christie possessed evidence of special expertise, other than experience, for their work. They saw Christie as having the right mission but undoubtedly were a little uneasy over the young professionals he brought in whenever the opportunity to do so came along. It was best to remain silently supportive, but their loyalty increasingly became assumed. The bantering began to have a sharper edge, something Evans seemed to enjoy.

The two sectors of the adult ecosystem moved carefully around each other, continuing to sustain cheerful bantering. I sensed Christie's frustration, but he managed to contain it, except for moments of candor with those of us he trusted most—and, even then, he avoided placing blame. Indeed, I think he even admired the degree to which Evans stuck to his guns and managed his responsibilities. Christie's enormous presence enabled him to appear to be almost ubiquitous in Biscoq even when absent in his studies at the university and engaged with others on the cutting edge of theory and practice pertaining to juvenile affairs.

Although in a hurry, Christie appeared acutely aware of the cultural realities and the ties to them of personalities that make institutional change so difficult. He harbored no villain theories. His was the burden of all change agents who believe their views to be authorized by serious inquiry while butting up against the institutional circumstances that provide security even for those colleagues who empathize with the mission of renewal. It takes courage to risk one's job for loyalty to principles, especially in times of economic depression.

Homeostasis amid Dissonance

Hugh Christie, with support and help from some of the rest of us, was steadily pulling on the membrane between the two sectors of the adult ecosystem to give that of the boys more dignity and decision-making space. I am more aware now than I was then of what delicate business this was, especially given the degree to which newcomers among the boys remained connected to a volatile sector of the juvenile population outside. Should there be staff-inmate altercations on the inside, Superintendent Ross would have been forced into a clampdown mode. Christie and his theories would be discredited, and we would be back to ground zero in the change process. He probably would then consider it to be to his own and the institution's best interests if he were to leave, even if not asked to do so.

We probably were saved from a major crisis by the very characteristic of institutions that makes change so difficult—the fear of change itself and the need for sufficient homeostasis to ensure that everyone maintains largely familiar routines. Most of us seem to adjust more readily to the mind-boggling changes that advances in science have produced than to changes in our daily habits. As I stated earlier, the boys had plenty of street smarts. They were smart enough to know the direction toward which Christie was pulling and welcomed it. Some probably were even smart enough to know the degree to which this direction threatened the status quo they had figured out how to cope with and triggered retaliation from the other sector of the staff ecosystem—most of which would fall out into increased restrictions on their daily existence. Fear of the unknown often makes the known more tolerable.

In effect, nobody stood to gain from Biscoq in turmoil, so far as I know. What appeared to me at first to be an effort on the part of both sectors of the adult ecosystem to gain the support of the boys seemed to slacken, the banter to increase and to take on an even sharper edge of one-upmanship. This, I now realize, was healthy. The late historian, Lawrence Cremin, asked and then answered his own question: "What do we do in our society to resolve tough issues?" His answer: "We talk." We endeavor to communicate in order to keep dissonance from getting out of hand. Banter appearing to be light on the outside can carry deep messages on the inside.

Another powerful factor helped to keep the lid on. I realize in retrospect that most, perhaps all, of us had a deep affection for Biscoq. In spite of the profoundly conflicting ideologies that so separated the two adult sectors in regard to both ends and means, we all wanted the boys to "make it." We cheerfully greeted those boys returning for a second or third time, but their recidivism tugged at our spirits. Those staff members just waiting for retirement enjoyed recounting earlier romances with Biscoq. And even those who claimed allegiance to the "born bad" ideology defended "our boys" on encountering this view in their off-campus lives. We were a family, and blood is thicker than water.

Although Hugh Christie and I both lived very demanding and quite parallel lives, I think our activities on the outside helped us with our perspective on the inside. Several years older than I, he was further along with his university studies, completing his bachelor's degree and then earning his master's before I left Biscoq at the end of four years. Ownership of a motorcycle enabled him to pursue erratic but residential studies and manage a great deal of commuting (through rain, sleet, and snow in the winters) between Biscoq and the university on the far west side of Vancouver. My college campus was Biscoq, where my correspondence studies went late into every weeknight.

I recall with awe and appreciation the personal way in which both the government's selective service office in Vancouver and officials of the University of British Columbia conducted their wartime responsibilities. Hugh Christie and I were involved with both. Several years into World War II, Canada's selective service agency governed both the military and the civilian lives of young men in line with Britain's expectations of its Commonwealth countries. Not yet overwhelmed by military humanpower needs, the expectation was that the infrastructure for resource productivity would be maintained.

Christie and I regularly received notices to report to Mr. Bromley, director of the selective service office, who made sure that we were still doing what we had been told to do. And we were told to keep doing it until ordered otherwise. The university's military responsibilities, including leadership of its ROTC, were handled by a professor of physics, a veteran of World War I with the rank of colonel. Military training was part of academic life. Christie and I did not cross paths in reporting to different lieutenants and for drill. As a more-or-less regular student, Christie was part of a regular ROTC unit. As a maverick, I was part of a polyglot of university employees and part-time students that clearly was a challenge to the lieutenant in charge. We drilled and trudged on Saturdays, often in rain and mud that further bedraggled the coarse khakis that, I believe, were leftovers from World War I.

Communication between the university and the downtown selective service office was amazing, especially given (or perhaps because of) the relatively primitive state of technology at the time. Christie and I never appeared together in the line of men always waiting to report to Mr. Bromley. He seemed to know a good deal about us—our work and our studies—but I always had to tell him that I was not "the crazy fellow" who regularly traversed by motorcycle the distance between Biscoq and the university. The Great Depression had stagnated movement in the population. We were now all in the same mess together and needed to take care of one another. Mr. Bromley and the ROTC lieutenant cared.

In my second year at Biscoq, my life on the outside grew much more interesting, necessitating my lengthening the hours of work and study each weekday in preparation for the weekends. I found that I could manage for days at a time on about five hours of sleep. How we take being young for granted! My friend Hal, a high school teacher in Vancouver, and I double-dated toward the end of my first year at Biscoq. His date had been cool to the idea and, as the evening progressed, warmed not at all to me. Months later, she confessed that people she disliked at first often turned out to become her best friends. I became her one and only husband.

By early fall, we were engaged, setting the wedding date almost two years hence when, if all went well, I would have completed requirements for the bachelor's degree. Christened Evalene, she was Len to family and friends and later, in the United States, the abbreviation became Lynn. Her role as manager of the Alma Mater Society of the university had brought us together during the preceding summer and quickly smoothed out what had been a bad start months earlier. I should note that Hal and my date on that fateful evening were married months before Len and I took the step. Yes, many of the most momentous happenings in life are serendipitous.

Up to this second year at Biscoq, I had returned from weekends at my mother's home early on Sunday evenings. Now I took the last bus, arriving there after midnight. Happily, Andy Richardson was the driver. He enjoyed this run because he liked driving more than he liked passengers, and he had only a few to deal with late at night. On the return ride from Chilliwack the next day, he would be at his taciturn best with a full load. The hour-long drive to Biscoq provided me with a very welcome nap, but knowing that Andy had a bad memory and might forget to wake me at my stop, I dozed lightly.

Purchase of the nice little 1934 Ford V-8 coupe, with a "rumble seat," gave me more flexibility in my third-year schedule. Automobiles were hard to come by, even if one had the money for purchase. I should have known that the newspaper advertisement that sealed my owner-ship was intended to attract the mechanically naive for the fair price of $400. But the little car's not-noticed cracked engine block did survive until Len and I met the challenge of crossing the Cascades two years later en route to the University of Chicago.

For three years at Biscoq then, until marriage just before the fourth made me a daily commuter from Vancouver, I lived very much within the press of its systemics and regularities and accompanying tensions. I lived within an infrastructure I had no need to challenge in order to carry out my responsibilities. My interface with the regulatory aspects of the culture required only that of meeting the schedule of boys delivered to class and boys returned each weekday. Nobody interfered with what I did in my box.

It is somewhat ironic that I was the one who came close to seriously disturbing the degree of homeostasis necessary to keeping ideological dissonance under control. In my own defense, I think that the near crisis I unwittingly engendered served to release some of the pressure and relieve the tension.

The rubbing together of the membranes separating the several insti-tutional ecosystems reached its greatest intensity in my third year. I think that the parallels in our lives outside of Biscoq had brought Hugh Christie and me more together in our perspectives on the inside. I sensed in our candid discussions his awareness of not being opposed by villains and of the mutual respect between him and Evans, in spite of their differences. Christie had been somewhat amused by my uninten-tional exacerbation of these differences late in my second year, but not at all amused in the third.

I was closer to my pupils at Biscoq than I had been with any before—even those in the school in a church. This was largely because I was there day and night from Sunday evening to late Friday afternoon and occasionally on weekends, except during that fourth year of daily commuting when I was virtually certain that my romance with Biscoq was coming to an end. I often took part in their late afternoon and early evening recreational activities and, of course, connected with several through my library duties. Each week, a different boy cleaned, more or less, the little library and my living quarters. We had many interesting conversations that included offers of lessons in practical matters I wish I had accepted, such as in how to pick various kinds of locks. Few of the boys—"incorrigible from birth"—were hard to like.

Toward the end of that second year, I thought it would be nice to break the institution's afternoon and evening routine with a picnic off the premises for all who attended school classes. I checked with the kitchen staff and learned that packing a picnic supper would be no problem; they were rather intrigued. I reported only to George Ross and Hugh Christie, and so I asked and got the latter's permission. Technically, Evans was supervisor of the recreational staff during the two hours—two to four—when its members took over the daily work program from the morning shift. We were into that ambiguous territory where Christie had chosen not to insert his authority into Evans's.

All went well, to everyone's relief. We played softball, ran some relay races, enjoyed our supper, and were back on campus by 8:00 p.m. without incident. Evans was livid but held his temper, while letting it be known on the following day that our caper represented the height of stupidity. He directed his remarks around Christie in referring almost solely to my softheaded, academic impracticality. Christie had not brought my request to Superintendent Ross, who probably would have overruled the approval. The next year, things went quite differently.

Almost from the beginning of my third year, a clear message circulated. We must keep a low profile and the lid on. News of runaways, for example, invariably appeared in the papers of the so-called lower mainland. The roll calls sharpened; there was an immediate check on any boy missing. Whereas before the staff had waited somewhat casually for boys to line up—even for those who had managed to get to the highway and back to hitch a ride, hoping for their absence not to be noted—now a staff member was sent on a quick search. More than before, Christie led a team of staff members and trusted senior boys to search the surrounding woods for the missing—like a pack of dogs to ferret out the foxes. I always was amazed at how much the boys enjoyed the chase and being part of a capture. Sometimes the capturer was next time the captured. Part of my enjoyment of Biscoq and Hugh Christie were the idiosyncracies and internal contradictions. He seemed to enjoy the hunt as much as did the boys, but the institution's image was uppermost in his mind.

Late in my third year, Christie once more approved my request, hesitantly and with words of cautionary advice. We were a much larger group this time, but I was joined in supervision by my new teaching colleague, Nell Thomas. And Christie added Kyle, a relative newcomer to the recreational staff, for added insurance. We returned on time and without incident, or so we thought. I realize, in retrospect, that our supervision was at times a little casual. The previous year, on my own with a smaller group, I had been very much involved. This time, we were more spectators, taking advantage of the opportunity to chat, as colleagues tend to do on such occasions. During refreshment time, we were distracted sufficiently, I think, for a couple of boys to notice and slip away. In minutes, they were inside a house we didn't even know was nearby. They took only a little money but left clear evidence of forced entry. I'm sure that both boys took considerable pleasure from the opportunity to practice the art that had caused their presence at Biscoq in the first place.

Within hours, the trail led to our door and the telephone calls to the Ross home up the road a piece. I had three separate encounters on the following day. George Ross was not outwardly very upset with me; he was a kindly man and we had a good rapport. He was relieved that newspaper reporting was kept to the routine. Given the fact that neighbors were uneasy about the school's presence anyway, there could have been an outcry. I was not even to ask to do it again next year.

Hugh Christie was sympathetic. He had liked the idea from the beginning; the warnings had been only in the call of duty. He was a little saddened, I think, over the fact that the degrees of freedom for pulling on that membrane between the ecosystems of staff and inmates toward his mission had been lessened. We had lost a little ground; some custodial norms had been strengthened a bit.

Syd Evans chose a public occasion for his rebuke. He had no line authority over me and my program. But he did have authority over observance of the regularities. I'm sure that he was pleased not to have had the authority to deny or grant permission for what I had done. He certainly was smart enough to see his possible personal benefit in Christie's having granted the permission. My screwing up would add another example to his views on the favors you should not grant to boys you could not trust. And I had screwed up. Of course, I would have done something along the lines of that outing the following year, had that option not been closed off. Evans's loud accounting of the whole at lunch the following day was directed only to the people at his table but was intended for all, especially Hugh and me, to hear. It was jocular in nature; victors can afford to be generous.

Readers familiar with or connected to schools and some other institutions will have little difficulty recognizing the roles portrayed and perhaps even identifying with the actors. Educational literature is awash with descriptions and explanatory theories regarding the difficulties in seeking to bring about significant institutional change. But what this literature sorely lacks is some way of accounting for the disparate personalities of key players and how they choose to play their parts.

GOODBYE, BISCOQ

I was deeply touched and saddened by the response of the boys to news of my pending marriage scheduled to take place in late August, two months after the close of the schoolrooms that third year. Something about their individual responses brought home to me the depth of the ethos that I had had to cope with and get above each day. For want of better words, I shall call it an ethos of defeat.

The swaggering, blustering behavior in which so many of these boys engaged—and so many others I've seen marked with failure—suggested disdain for and rejection of conventional norms. But buried below was that melancholy ethos of defeat. They were, I deduced, strongly envious of my pending marriage, a deduction that strengthened in my mind when we came together again in September. I thanked them for the little wooden tray (which we still have) that they had purchased, wrapped, and sent with a card as our wedding gift. This elicited surprising queries about details of the wedding itself—getting to the church, the number of guests at the reception, whether there had been dancing, and more. They wanted what most people see as normal participation in the human conversation, but the coming together represented by love and marriage was not seen by most as likely to be in their cards. What brought me up short years later was learning of generations of unemployed black men in urban settings missing such in their life cycles.

Few things disconnect one from a school's culture more than a daily commute. Commuting throughout this final year eased somewhat my departure from what I did not know then would be my last year of earning a living by teaching the young. At the end of a day in June, I drove off from Biscoq for the last time. For me, the day had been very much like that last day with my covey of young pilgrims in the church converted into my school. Teachers, too, get the blues.

Part 3

As a Hybrid Educator

Miller Hall at the University of Washington
(Sketch by Mark Elster; reproduced with permission
from the University of Washington College of Education)

Chapter 8

The Higher Learning

Once I got over there in the actual presence of the classroom buildings and the library, it seemed to me that I hungered and thirsted to hear somebody talk about books who knew more about them than I did. I didn't mean I wanted to be a schoolteacher. I just made that my pretense to be there, for I had never heard that anybody ever went to a university just to read books. There had to be a real reason—namely, something you wanted to do later.

WENDELL BERRY[1]

A strange, disconcerting thing happens in the twilight years of a continuing lifetime career. One finds it necessary to give up more and more of things enjoyed, and yet time management remains a problem. Each day gets a little shorter, and the realization that one cannot quite do today what one did yesterday creeps into one's being, softly as misty rain creeps over the headlands into the fjords of the Northwest coast.[2]

In these twilight years, one often looks back in awe of the miracle of once being young and in wonderment over balancing and accomplishing so many things then. We accomplished a great deal during that first year of marriage—Len's last year at the university's Alma Mater Society and my last at Biscoq. Housing being tight in the aftermath of the war, we moved three times, each an improvement over the last. Len's commute by trolley and bus and my hour-long drive each way gave us long days that, in winter, began and ended in darkness.

Most nights, I wrote and Len typed my master's thesis—a study of incarcerated delinquent boys based on a sample of those at Biscoq.

Letters inquiring into doctoral programs went off to a half-dozen U.S. universities and one Canadian. Anticipating our return and probably a high school teaching job in Vancouver, we visited a few of the fledgling new housing developments and talked about what we might be able to afford and where we might want to live. Our goal was to finish the master's degree requirements at summer's end of that year and be on our way back home in a couple of years with the doctoral dissertation still to be finished.

My mother's concern for the boys I worked with at Biscoq had been from the beginning marked by the spiritual: She prayed for them. Mine was of the rational idiom: I would lead them to other roads on which to experience life's journey. My mother prayed for us, too, when we set out for the University of Chicago nearly three months after that last day at Biscoq. For her, Chicago was sin city.

From time to time in later years, Len has said to friends, "Had I known then that we would not return, I would not have gone." Many times I have thought about my not knowing that there would never be another class of children to add to my whorls of memory. Was the deep melancholy I experienced on driving away from Biscoq that last day a premonition? I was to have quite different romances with schools, learning, and teaching.

CHICAGO BOUND

We left for Chicago in mid-September, exhausted from working late into preceding nights. Thanks to the suggestion of my adviser, Professor Fred Tyler, we had dropped off the thesis at his home late in the evening two days before, anticipating several more days of revision. To our astonishment, he said that he knew enough about the manuscript already. "Get going," he said, "I'll see to its binding and placement in the library." If there is anything teachers should learn from their teachers, it is to carry the baton to tomorrow's teachers. The tributes to their mentors that graduate students write in the first pages of their theses attest to the sturdiness of the tradition.

The slow distancing of a land journey from its beginning to its end tends to lessen the trauma of leaving—unlike the trauma of departure and quick separation of a sea voyage. There was an awareness among immigrants crossing the Atlantic or the Pacific Ocean by ship that there would be no going back, that they might never again see parents, relatives, and friends or even hear their voices. The jet plane and easy telecommunications were yet to come. The known was being left behind; the unknown lay ahead.

Those of us who lived most of our lives in the twentieth century in North America and were first generation Americans in Canada, Mexico, or the United States had no depth of understanding or appreciation of what our parents suffered in this parting, often undertaken for their children's future. Some sense of it came to me as a child when the occasional departure of one of those large Australian steamships from Vancouver harbor got me thinking of that long voyage to Sydney and its accompanying human rites of passage. But, as a child of eight or nine, when I came home from school to find my mother weeping at the kitchen table with a letter in her hand, I had little comprehension of the depths of her grief. The mother she had visited only once since leaving the Shetland Islands and coming to Canada—and that visit taken many years ago—had died.

One of the thoughts from which my parents took great comfort was that they and their three sons would never have to experience such a separation. But, with that other war to end all wars now over, Len and I were not the only ones packing to go elsewhere. The children of those immigrants were on the move. With a land journey, there is no sudden picking up of lives led in a familiar place and setting them suddenly down in an unfamiliar one. Much of what one is leaving merges with where one is going. Even if the stay in the new is to be a long one, there is little sensation of giving up chunks of one's past. Rather, the experience is more transcendental—of both keeping and getting. This first move of several major ones yet to come, however, proved to be such a watershed in our lives that I'll slow down to tell of it before picking up the tempo to move more quickly through some of what followed.

Our journey was more slowly transitional than anticipated. Fred Tyler's thoughtful gesture turned out to be serendipitous. We were able to leave a few days earlier than planned, and we needed all of them. Although it was planned to take five or six days, the trip consumed ten. Nonetheless, we managed to reach Chicago a few days before the beginning of the fall quarter.

Trouble began early. We were just climbing the western slopes of the Cascades on the first day when we suddenly realized that the friendly passengers in passing cars were not waving at us but pointing to the trail of steam behind our cute little coupe. By dint of frequent long stops for cooling and the careful use of the water we carried, we made it through Snoqualmie Pass. We managed to find more water, but no mechanic, on the mostly downhill drive into Ritzville at dusk.

We had not spoken much. Twilight added to our gloom. The distance still ahead was many times greater than the little left behind. There was no beauty in the dry, treeless terrain. And Ritzville was no oasis.

The scene was surreal—surely the movie set for a western shoot-'em-up in the making. Peering through twilight laden with yellow dust, we concluded Ritzville to be a boomtown in the making: tractors, trucks, bulldozers, picks, and shovels at work. The decibels were high. Men and women shouted at one another; children played noisily in the dirt. Were we encountering the early stages of post-war mobility and migration to promising new settings? And why Ritzville? What did it promise these newcomers who were so hastily building platforms and erecting temporary shelters? Today's population, according to available records, is about 1,750 children and adults.

There was no horse-drawn stagecoach at the steps of the little hotel to strengthen a movie-set hypothesis. The clerk at the desk apologized for the size and condition of the one remaining room. But we had no choice. His news of a good automobile repair shop just east of town cheered us a little. Even though we had parked the car in a lighted place, we carted up everything except what was out of sight in the packed rumble seat. We neither talked nor slept much during the night.

Morning brought no joy. We left the car with a mechanic and walked to where he said we might get some breakfast. On our return, we learned that we would have to wait awhile for some goop to dry that he had poured into the engine's cracked block. Why had we set out to cross the Cascades and the Rockies with a car in this condition? I was embarrassed to confess my ignorance. A more mechanically experienced eye than mine would have noted at the outset the relatively new paint on the engine and the slight ridge under it. The mechanic said that his job was better than the original repair, but advised us not to drive over forty miles an hour and to carry some water with us. "Good luck. You'll have flat country once you get beyond the Rockies."

We were learning that there is very little relationship between the geography in school texts and the real thing. Len had been a straight-A student in geography, and I had taught it to children and youths of all grade levels. We made it over the mountains to where the flat country stretched endlessly ahead of us. We should have known enough to take a more southerly interstate route at that time of the year. We were lucky to encounter no snow, but the wind blew endlessly, mile after mile. Back home, the leaves would have just begun to change color. Crossing Illinois, we were startled at every gas stop by signs advising the purchase of antifreeze—and it wasn't yet October. We were to learn how cold it can get in Chicago in wintertime and how hot and humid in the summer. Our innocence in many things was monumental.

THE UNIVERSITY

Our long-distance efforts to secure housing near the University of Chicago had been in vain. Friends of relatives had kindly offered a temporary room in their suburban home, some thirty-five miles from the university. We learned soon after arrival there that the boxes of our belongings shipped some weeks before were languishing on a railroad siding somewhere in the country, but nobody was able to tell us where.

My first visits to the university brought greater disappointments. My plan was to study with the eminent sociologist Ernest Burgess (whose work on juvenile delinquency I had read avidly), with scholars in the department of education, and with a few in other departments whose names I knew. The divisional structure of the university appeared conducive to interdepartmental exploration. I was to have an assistantship in the famed Orthogenic School (for autistic and variously disturbed children), headed by Bruno Bettelheim.

Professor Bettelheim was out of town, and so I sought the office of Professor Burgess. I found him on his knees packing books. He had just retired! After listening to my suddenly aborted intentions, he suggested that I go over to Judd Hall, the home of the department of education, and visit with his good friend William S. Gray. It was many months later that I figured out that Gray's simple tales of Dick and Jane were a major part of the now decades-old conflict over phonics and the whole-word approach to the teaching of reading that had its genesis at about the time I began school. What kind of workshop on reading had Miss Laing attended in midyear, and did it have something to do with plunging me into the darkness of nonreading?

I was not interested in becoming a specialist in the teaching of reading, but the conversation with Professor Gray was very helpful, nonetheless. He had been dean of the college of education when it once existed and was very knowledgeable about requirements for the Ph.D. I knew what was involved by the time I met with Professor Bettelheim and knew soon thereafter that our priorities were incompatible. I had been given only a two-year student visa; he had children with very special needs to be taken care of. In addition to probing into students' reading and writing abilities, the doctoral qualifying examinations tested some nine domains of educational understanding. There were no specific course requirements, and so one need not take courses that clearly reflected these domains. But one would be a fool to ignore them, especially if the fool were a foreign one. It was abundantly clear that the work schedule Professor Bettelheim outlined would permit me, with luck, to attend no more than one of the nine courses each quarter. The fit that had appeared symbiotic, given my experience with emotionally disturbed delinquent boys, dissolved as he and I talked. What to do?

I made my first of many appointments with the second Tyler in my life—Ralph W. (no relation to Fred): dean of the division of the social sciences, professor and chair of the department of education, university examiner, and head of the then-completed Eight-Year Study (the fountainhead from which has flowed the very concept of evaluation in education and schooling). I presented my problem and began an education that was to be confirmed over and over in later years: In ten minutes of listening and occasionally questioning, Ralph Tyler could clear one's head without proffering advice or telling one what to do. After a few departing pleasantries at his office door, I knew from his two concluding sentences that only one rational decision was open to me: "Mr. Bettelheim is a reasonable man. He will understand."

I walked around the campus for quite some time, trying to figure out how best to break the news to Mr. Bettelheim. I had quickly concluded from my brief conversation with Mr. Tyler that, at the University of Chicago, faculty members were not addressed "Doctor" and only rarely "Professor." Several years later, I joined Bruno Bettelheim as a faculty colleague, and we became longtime friends. Fortunately, as I learned much later, he never connected me with the eleventh-hour staffing crisis I had, as a student, thrust upon him.

With the bottom fallen out of our financial plans, we were faced with a dilemma. Clearly, I could now step up the pace of graduate studies, but the not adequately anticipated inflating cost of living would soon siphon off our modest savings. I rejected Len's suggestion that she go back to work in Canada while I sought a low-cost room in International House on the university campus. Then came the good news. Immediately after the setback regarding the Orthogenic School, I had applied for a tuition scholarship. It was granted. Now we just needed money for the basics. Len sought employment, as permitted by the permanent resident status that inexplicably had been granted to her but not to me.

The job market was rapidly improving, and Canadians, especially those with experience and education in business, were very highly regarded. She soon found work with a small washing machine company. Her employer found us an unfurnished apartment, still quite far from but much closer to the university, with Len's workplace more or less along my daily route. The little car had indeed survived the journey across the plains. We settled in.

The time restraints of a two-year student visa necessitated my getting at least approval of a dissertation proposal before returning to Canada and forced me to gamble. I decided to take the grueling four-day qualifying exams scheduled for the coming February, although by then I would have completed only three of the critical courses and be only a little along in another three. I was short on specifics regarding education and schooling in the United States. Fortunately, writing and reading paid off, and such had characterized my largely nonresident, correspondent program of studies at the University of British Columbia. I passed.

Our resolve to get all but my dissertation behind us before leaving had been sorely tested the previous December, just after the fall quarter ended. We received a letter from Maxwell Cameron, chairman of the department of education at UBC, saying that he and Mrs. Cameron had decided to send it in lieu of a Christmas card. It was an invitation to join the faculty there by the next academic year as an assistant professor. I had not dreamt of such a possibility, even with the doctorate completed.

Our first reaction was a surge of utter joy. There appeared to be nothing in the way of penning a jubilant letter of acceptance. But then doubt began to enter the conversation that dominated our holiday lives into January. There is a story of Sigmund Freud being approached, following an address, by an admirer who said, "Dr. Freud, it must be wonderful to have your insights. They must make your decisions so much easier." Freud pondered the implied question and replied, "There are two kinds of decisions in life. For the frequent daily ones, I simply list the pros and cons and follow the guidance of whichever is the longer list. But then, there are those difficult, life-changing decisions. These I make first and then list the pros and cons."

We decided not to accept and then agonized over all the obvious benefits of going that so appealed to us over the one reason for staying. Ironically, as things turned out, we left Chicago for a destination still further from home at almost precisely the same time we would have been settling down in Vancouver and the University of British Columbia, had our decision gone the other way.

A CULTURE OF INQUIRY

For most of my years of teaching school, I had worked late into the night on correspondence courses of the University of British Columbia and then attended summer sessions there. Although this schedule took away most discretionary reading, much of the work was reading and writing and lacked some of the pressures of several courses packed into quarters or semesters of attending classes. Nonetheless, what turned out to be only one year of full-time attendance at the University of Chicago was sheer luxury. I had what Wendell Berry's Jayber Crow had sought—learning for learning's sake. Such has, I think, suffered decline in recent years.

The experience was aided by winter's hostile weather and by being separated from routines once grown familiar. Such is the benefit of travel and study abroad. Free of the security blanket of daily routines, one is opened up to new realities and possibilities, such as subjecting one's hardening "truths" to fresh examination. But there was another powerful contributing factor: The career goal did not go away, but it faded into the background.

It shifted, of course, after encountering the unanticipated retirement of Professor Burgess. I no longer knew *what* I wanted to get the degree for. I opened myself up to unknown possibilities. This is what I have tried to do since then with my own graduate students, nearly all of whom have come with precise career goals in mind. This gets in the way of learning something for little other reason than wanting to. Such learning is mostly what renewal is all about—whether of the self, a program, an institution, or a culture. Unlike reform or projects, renewal is never finished. Projects and reform begin to deteriorate the moment pronounced "done."

My days were now more enveloped by the department of education than I had intended. There was a cornucopia of diverse talent in the faculty. Of the twenty-seven I am able to recall, only one is still alive, so far as I know. But the writings of most are cited in the journals of today, even though referencing contemporaries is more politically correct.

Ironically, I doubt that more than three or four would get high marks for their teaching from evaluating observers. I recall only one whom I would classify as a scintillating lecturer—the often-cited criterion of good teaching.

But this is to miss the critical educational point. The milieu was the great teacher. Asked to define it, I would first resort to Lionel Hampton's reported response to the query, "What is jazz?" His frequently quoted reply: "If I have to tell you, you'll never understand." I fear that many of the students now seeking degrees through today's "distance learning" likewise will never understand the power of learning in a richly educative cultural milieu. Distance learning has its uses but is only part of what should be on one's educational plate.

The whole was much more than the sum of the parts: the morning coffee-time conversations in the commons room, casual conversations anywhere including in the restrooms, hot arguments over lunch, faculty voices in disagreement drifting from a meeting place, one-on-one discussions with advisers—the entire ubiquitous surround. It was everywhere across the campus. The question of a professor in the natural sciences to a student defending a point was a campuswide legend: with a heavy accent he asked, "Vat is de evidence?"

Is such a culture the prerogative solely of higher education? Surely not. Indeed, the openness of the young to learning is a given. It needs no transplant to a new geographic and social setting. And yet, we waste this greatest of learning opportunities by presenting the young with precooked, prepackaged fast food easily confirmed by tests of mental digestion or indigestion. "Reform" in the quest for "world-class schools" mandates more of the same. Reformers, year after year, parachute their packages into schools without any consideration for or knowledge of the cultures there, and then they wonder why nothing happens. Sadly, many school principals are as ignorant and neglectful of their school cultures as I was of mine, largely because our meager preparation and subsequent experience offered little opportunity for inquiry into their nature and the conditions necessary to improvement.

People who look at schools from a distance have scarcely a clue to comprehending how incredibly difficult it is to develop learning cultures in our schools. Much of what the young believe and value is brought with them each day. With "good-looking kids" and "athletes" far ahead and "gang members" ranking about even with "bright kids" in the popularity polls of secondary school students, it is an uphill struggle to move academics to the forefront. But cultural renewal of schools by teachers and principals is off the screen in the lexicon and practice of so-called school reform.

Had I been traipsing into the university to take classes in the late afternoon and evening after a trying day of coping with a classroom filled with turbulent adolescents, I probably would have looked to each session for practical help and criticized it for not providing it. But I had left most of the memory of such far behind me and far away. Some of my student colleagues were not so fortunate. Their complaints were of not seeing an immediate close relationship between the curriculum and their career goals or of not getting answers to the problems presented by their past and, for some, their present daily work. They just didn't get it. These are the complaints commonly voiced by candidates for professional degrees and credentials, whatever the field. If stockpiling answers to problems of current practice is to be the mission of professional schools, we do not need them. Trade schools outside of universities will suffice. Doing well what practitioners always have done will constitute the zenith of the aspirations of both the institutions and their clients.

ROMANCES WITH IDEAS

Given the time pressures imposed by the two-year student visa and the implicitly high standards of the University of Chicago, I don't know why I experienced so much of the luxurious freedom usually reserved for sabbaticals. I read the works of scholars that I had heard about and many who were new to me, sometimes right through the time of classes not attended. And there were no classes during the last two weeks of each quarter! The time was set aside for reading. Jayber Crow would have liked that. Very little of it touched directly on my school experiences, but I found myself thinking about them nonetheless. Much of what had frozen into my store of conventional wisdom began to shake loose.

A teaching experience of a decade ago comes back to me. It happened in the final evaluative session of a graduate seminar on the moral dimensions of schooling and leadership comprising eighteen would-be principals. Most of the sessions had been devoted to what they considered to be moral dilemmas encountered in their internships as assistant principals. Paul suddenly spoke up with passion. "I have been encountering in ten years of teaching the very immoral practices we have been discussing as though they were simply part of the reality of schools, that this is the way schools are. It was immoral to allow me to become a teacher unprepared to recognize that these things should not and need not be. Now I understand that school culture must continuously be under scrutiny and engaged in renewal." Paul was having the "aha" experience I was having time after time during that memorable year at the University of Chicago.

With the coming of the summer quarter, I was startled and pleased to learn that the three classes for which I was registered would bring me up to the minimum required. After that, I need only sign up for independent study and the dissertation. Later, I learned that the minimum course requirement was set according to some formula of the percentage of students' financial support necessary to sustain the faculty. The university was not interested in "seat time" as a *curricular* requirement.

I was beginning to think about potential research problems, and it was this that most connected my thoughts with past teaching experiences. Reading Dewey's *The Sources of a Science of Education*, my attention was drawn to the practical context of educational research:

> Educational *practices* provide the data, the subject-matter, which form the *problems* of inquiry. They are the sole source of the ultimate problems to be investigated. These educational practices are also the final *test of value* . . . of all researches.[3]

Virgil Herrick, my adviser, led me out of the first few problems I brought to him for discussion. He warned against studies that required the tracking of several teachers engaged in markedly different teaching methods or others that depended upon people who might leave during the designated time period, become ill, or change their ways. "Be as confident as possible that the circumstances necessary to the study will still be there at its end," he cautioned. He gave good advice.

I moved closer and closer to what had been cluttering my mind for years: the retention and grade repetition of children progressing slowly. I had experienced the spurting of children who had not been doing well the previous year but had not been retained. I had seen the deep sense of failure in Biscoq boys who had been retained several times in their slow progress through school. Were there better alternatives than this annual exercise of promotion and nonpromotion? I had gone back in time to my own early roots in schooling.

Writers often are advised to write about what they have experienced. Herrick rose to my proposal of comparing a group of nonpromoted and another of promoted slow-learning children on an array of criteria. He was less than optimistic, however, about getting it approved for conduct in Chicago schools. The several universities in the area already were overloading the system with such requests, according to those responsible for giving the necessary approval. And intensive scrutiny of my request was assured because of the likelihood of my conducting some student testing. The problem was resolved in a surprising, unanticipated way.

ATLANTA

At the end of a session with Virgil Herrick, he said that there was a man visiting the campus whom I should meet. Floyd Jordan, from Atlanta, Georgia, was seeking graduate students at the dissertation stage who might be interested in a fellowship with a unique collaborative venture, the Atlanta Area Teacher Education Service (AATES). I saw little reason to meet him, but I agreed to talk with him anyway. And I did, that afternoon.

Jordan smoked cigars but had the decency always to do so outside. We walked around the campus. He already had recruited a fellow from The Ohio State University and hoped to complete the roster of two with someone from the University of Chicago. Half of the time was to be free for research, and there would be a fellowship stipend of $400 tax free for each of nine months. I was astounded. The cost of living was rising, but in those days, that appeared to me to be a lot of money. At the end of our walk, he offered me the opportunity. He was leaving the next morning and would wait until then for my answer.

Herrick was still in his office. He thought going to Atlanta would be a good way to get some experience with schools in the United States and, he surmised, would provide access to some for my study. I called Len. She was flabbergasted. I guess I wasn't very clear regarding the specifics, and she interpreted the prospect to be my going to Atlanta and her going back to Vancouver. Learning that this was not to be the case probably caused her to accept the unknown. Atlanta was some far-off place with a past we had seen depicted in the epic movie, *Gone with the Wind*. A few weeks later, almost a year to the day that we had left for the far-off place we had now come to know a little, we packed the little Ford coupe one more time and went there.

During the weeks before leaving Chicago, I learned a lot about the AATES from materials Jordan sent me. It was, indeed, a unique creation, far ahead of its time. My experience with it, over far more years than initially intended, deeply influenced my thinking about teacher education. Many teachers, largely female, lacking degrees and often other credentials, had been recruited during the war. The dynamic Atlanta area was growing rapidly, attracting returning veterans and their families and straining the capacity of the schools. Long a major producer of teachers, the University of Georgia, more than an hour's drive away, simply could not meet the demand for upgrading experienced teachers now pressured to secure the baccalaureate. Few of the smaller, private institutions in Atlanta were equipped to pick up the slack. And, of course, the educational institutions of the South at all levels were still segregated. Georgia Tech prepared no teachers, Emory University only a few, and Atlanta University helped provide for "the colored."

The AATES was the brainchild, I understand, of Lawrence Haskew, director of the division of teacher education at Emory, soon to be gone to spend a long career at the University of Texas. He was later described to me by the dean of Emory's graduate school as the only person he knew who could (and did) dictate thirty-page, clearly articulated "memos" in an hour or two. The plan for the AATES emerged from one of these.

It was to bring together, for degree-oriented teachers' in-service education, six institutions of higher education and six contiguous school districts: Fulton, DeKalb, and Cobb Counties and the three cities located, respectively, in each—Atlanta, Decatur, and Marietta.[4] Teaching AATES courses was to be credited as part of the regular load of faculty members at all six of the colleges and universities, but it was assumed that most would come from the University of Georgia and Emory. Students enrolled in AATES courses could apply the credit, regardless of who taught the course, to the institutions where they were officially registered. The AATES shared office space with the division of teacher education and the psychology department in an old building on the Emory University campus.

Floyd Jordan had arranged for us to occupy a low-rent efficiency apartment in recently constructed faculty housing on the western edge of the campus. It was intended for short-term personnel or until regular faculty members had time to get settled elsewhere. Housing was still very tight. What a change in our circumstances! We were just a couple of blocks from the most-needed stores, a block from the bus that Len would take for soon-to-be employment in the office of a surgeon, and only the equivalent of two or three city blocks to the east side of the campus where I shared an office with the fellow from Ohio State, Larry Metcalf.

We arrived and moved in on a Saturday in September. Midmorning on Sunday, Floyd Jordan called to say that he and Em would be by after church to take us on a drive. We were learning fast. One of the first things asked of us by Georgia natives was "And what church do you belong to?" A Coca-Cola truck drove through nearby residential streets at least once a week, dropping off cases of Coke on lawns and picking up cases of empties. A truck and driver served Emory University full time, ensuring that bottles would be available in the many dispensers scattered across the campus supplying Coca-Cola and only Coca-Cola. Emory's handsome endowment of today is largely a product of the company's largesse.

The Jordans introduced us to Atlanta's then-popular pastime of a "Sunday drive." Automobiles were coming once more to sales rooms, and gas rationing was of the past. Car owners in their Sunday best, in automobiles washed and polished the day before, politely acknowledged the existence of others as they passed on streets of the most affluent neighborhoods where all residents were white. Clusters of women of a darker color gathered at bus stops in these neighborhoods where they worked on weekdays but were nowhere to be seen on Sundays. They had their churches, too, singing mostly the same hymns in praise of the same God.

When we got to know some people quite well, we commented on the front-and-back segregation of the city's buses. Usually, their answers were much like Lionel Hampton's on jazz, "If I have to tell you, you'll never understand." This was very new and strange for us. In Chicago, we had experienced the near panic of house owners and renters in all-white ghettos when "colored" encroached more and more on the edges. But on the commuter trains and buses there was an unavoidable mixing of ethnic groups and races. Nonetheless, there was much subtle evidence of deep racial prejudice. Larry Metcalf had in the North experienced about all he could take of it, and the busing situation in Atlanta brought him almost to a boiling point. He was guided firmly off a bus more than once.

A code of segregation accompanied by an atmosphere of silent acceptance seemed to characterize public places. At teachers' meetings I sometimes attended in Fulton County, segregation was not from front to back but from side to side, with an aisle in between. White acquaintances spoke of their warm feelings toward "nigras," and there were tales of kindnesses on both sides in abundance. Segregation provided the safety net that kept the peace.

In my later teaching at Emory and in the AATES, I became acutely aware of how effectively segregation had done this over the years. Late in the 1940s into the 1950s, my comments about racial equality and of there being only one people in the world to which we all belong brought forth no remonstrances. I commonly accompanied such remarks with the observation that there were undoubtedly people in the room who disagreed. With the passage of the 1954 Supreme Court decision, the climate changed abruptly, and I realized how protected from open discourse segregation had been. Without the new law, there had really been no need to regard me as other than another northerner who did not understand. But now, suddenly, the protective net was gone; economic and ideological diversity in Emory University's classes was rapidly increasing. The GI Bill was bringing to Emory many students who could not have afforded to attend prior to the war. There was an unspoken tension regarding profound changes in the offing that most students, eager to get on with their lives, preferred to leave undisturbed.

Two experiences in particular have remained in my mind. There was a lovely black lady, mother of several children, who could be depended upon to take care of our two when we were gone. After coming home on an evening soon after that momentous court decision, Len spoke cheerfully to Ola about the opportunities her children would now have. Ola did not respond. On the drive to her home in a low-income, segregated neighborhood, she expressed her concern—indeed, her deep fear. Her children would have to find their way, handicapped by color, in what she feared would be a more dangerously divided world in which their white competitors would have all the advantages.

The other incident began with a telephone call from the executive director of the National Association of Elementary School Principals in Washington, D.C. I had been for some years professor and director of Emory University's division of teacher education, an organizational unit that was more than a department but less than a professional school. He was looking for a university to host a meeting of a quite large group of principals from across the country and thought the circumstances were ripe for convening a nationwide desegregated group in the South for the first time in the association's history. Would Emory take it on?

I thought that this would be a timely coup for the university that probably called for higher-level approval. I visited the academic vice president, a very interesting man whose long history there and open mind had been very helpful to me in the past. He listened carefully to my request, swiveled his chair so as to turn his back to me with his face to the window, and began to whistle. I got the subtle, unspoken message, "You never asked me. Do what you wish, but if word gets out to a member of the board of trustees, I'll have to reprimand you." I understood. As it turned out, the meeting had to be canceled, and so I never learned how things might have worked out.

AS GOOD AS IT GETS

The Jordans took extraordinarily good care of us. We had been in Atlanta only a few days when the primary-grade supervisor of Fulton County schools, Mrs. Cooper, invited me to visit schools for the purpose of discussing plans for my study with the principals. Jordan—rarely addressed by his first name—already had cleared the way. Six schools had retained from nearly 13 percent to more than 40 percent (in one school) of last year's first-grade children—a startling statistic in itself. In five others, the range was from just over 5 percent to just over 11 percent. Yet, all eleven schools were in the same school district.

It was not difficult to find in the second grades of the latter group of schools a large number of children described by their teachers as having progressed slowly the previous year. In all probability, most of these would have been retained had they been enrolled in the former group. In classes at three schools in the former group, nearly a quarter of the children were now repeating the first grade. Clearly, these were profound school-to-school differences in viewpoint regarding the respective advantages and disadvantages of promotion and nonpromotion of slow-learning children.

Early on, I set out to establish two pools of children, one promoted and one retained, from which to match groups on chronological age, mental age, and academic achievement, with Mrs. Cooper and I supervising all testing. I then reduced the numbers by eliminating all those with visual, emotional, and other problems likely to interfere with their learning. After dropouts and transfers had reduced the numbers, I was able to have remaining two groups of fifty-five children—five more than my minimum target—to compare on the criteria I had chosen.

The initial task of securing two closely matched cohorts produced an interesting observation. Although the six schools represented in cohort A differed markedly from the five in cohort B in their stance on promotion and nonpromotion, the teachers in all eleven appeared to be remarkably together in their awareness of children making slow progress. They simply differed in their views of whether to promote or not to promote. They apparently did not need a battery of standardized achievement tests to know which children were progressing well and which poorly. They were pretty good at making these diagnoses. Perhaps there are better ways to spend billions of dollars today on children's learning than seeking test scores—especially when test scores apparently add so little to teachers' diagnoses. What the Fulton County teachers and principals needed—and their colleagues in schools everywhere need—was ready access to information about relevant inquiry into school and classroom practices. This message has gained little entry into school policies. The recurring debate over so-called social promotion is little more enlightened today than it was a century ago.

By the end of that school year, I had a great deal of data on how two closely matched groups of seven-year-olds had fared in their second years of schooling—one group repeating the first grade and the other enrollees in the second grade. Included were their responses to the inkblot cards of the Rorschach test, increasingly attracting attention for the insights it presumably provided into traits of personality. Lee Cronbach, a young professor at the University of Chicago headed for scholarly distinction, had used the test the previous year in seeking to determine its potential usefulness for predicting whether we students were more likely to fit into research or administrative careers (a line of inquiry he subsequently abandoned). His interest motivated me to attend seminars on the technique at the University of Georgia and Tulane University. I learned enough to use it with each of the children in my two cohorts.

With all of my data in hand, we were packing one more time—again for Chicago where, as it turned out, I spent the summer and fall quarters back at the university. We took a visit to Vancouver, British Columbia, for a couple of weeks between the two. Although the Cronbachs would be on their way to the University of Illinois in September, Lee continued to be generous with his time. In his backyard on a hot afternoon, we poured forth thought and sweat as, with the help of cold beer, we went over my now "scored" Rorschach protocols of each child that I had obtained near the end of the school year. There were striking examples of "color shock"—commonly assumed to be indicative of possible emotional or psychological stress or disturbance—almost exclusively within the nonpromoted group. The finding was interesting because I had already endeavored to eliminate from both groups children experiencing or living in circumstances likely to produce emotional stress. Was the year of grade repetition a significant contributing factor? Unfortunately, the instructors in the two seminars had not worked with children. I had found only one study (in French) of the use of the Rorschach with children, and it shed no light on the color shock issue. Could its significance in dealing with children be deduced from its assumed significance with adults? Lee recommended that I put the data aside. And so, I left in a file at Emory University what was at the time, apparently, the largest body of potentially useful data on children's responses to the inkblots then available.

I have heard many of Lee Cronbach's students testify to his relentless quest for perfection in research. The field of psychometrics was taking off at the time, and Lee was at the heart of it. I had a rather tricky problem of comparing the performance of individuals comprising the two groups and the statistical significance of the differences. Lee recommended the regression technique, commonly understood and used today but not then. On a visit to the University of Wisconsin, where Virgil Herrick was now a Vilas Professor, I met another acclaimed statistician, Chester Harris, who agreed with Cronbach's suggestion and referred me to a source for the technical help I needed.

But, on each trip to a conference of some sort, Lee came back with an alternative. I have learned since that stalemates engendered in the student-adviser relationship at the stage of the doctoral dissertation sometimes go on for years. There comes a time when one must quit reading and seeking advice and get on with it. And termination of my student visa loomed. I told Lee that I was going with the regression analysis and that I assumed his later students would profit from advances in the field of statistics. I thought it wise to mention the matter to Ralph Tyler, who had assumed the chairmanship of my committee following Virgil Herrick's departure. He smiled and said, "Mr. Cronbach is a reasonable man." Indeed, he was—and one of the smartest I have ever met.

HOME AGAIN, HOME AGAIN, FINNEGAN

We had come to Chicago this time in the Chevy sedan acquired in a trade for the little Ford. It already had been troublesome, but unlike the coupe, there was little about it to love. I should have known better than to buy a vehicle previously used for the daily rounds of a mail carrier. "Fool me once, shame on you. Fool me twice, shame on me." However, it got us to Vancouver without boiling over and with only one stop for repairs that were not its fault.

There was both good and bad news waiting for us in Vancouver. The good news was that the regulations regarding entry from Canada into the United States had eased. I was granted a permanent residence visa. The bad news was in a telegram from Floyd Jordan. We knew that he had been trying to get me appointed to the faculty of the University of Georgia (where he was a professor), with my responsibilities to be at the AATES. This had not been confirmed because of the existing requirement of citizenship. But not to worry yet. He had switched his efforts to Emory.

We had been eagerly looking forward to our first visit home in two years. The experience of going home again ranks not far behind the weather and schools in the conversations of those many adults who, during the era of mobility following World War II, left the places where they had grown up to live and raise their families elsewhere. Today, the ease of travel and communication has softened geographic distances, separations, and to some degree, generational differences.

With our respective families, the dissonance was minor, and more to be chuckled over than discomforted by. We balked a bit at my mother's need to have us seated promptly at the dinner table by five o'clock. She was receptive to the suggestion of delaying it a bit. She did— by fifteen minutes. A big problem with cousins, aunts, uncles, and old friends was that we hadn't time to visit them all. Feelings were hurt. We found ourselves strangely out of sync with several of our closest old friends. Although we still viewed the two cultures overall as very similar, certainly contrasting no more than what we had experienced with the North and South, they saw us as becoming "Americanized." Probing the "why" didn't help much. Our experience had been, whether in

Canada or the North or South of the United States, that the conversation was much the same, varying only in details. The debates over the Liberal and Conservative political parties in Canada were surprisingly similar to those over the Democratic and Republican in the United States. But the absence of propinquity had drawn us apart.

Beyond family, it was an anecdote recounted by Len's father, Harry, that most connected me with what we had left two years before. He and Len's mother lived just a few miles from the White Rock Lodge and even closer to the little church that had been for a time my school. Harry had met Ray, one of the two redheaded boys who had been such a big part of the joy in teaching I had experienced there. Both, now young adults, were working and living in White Rock. Harry, always cheerful and friendly, happened to tell Ray that his daughter and son-in-law would soon be visiting. This somehow led to the identification of me as Ray's former teacher and his recollection of those unusual months of schooling as one of the most enjoyable periods of his young life. School *can* be a place of both learning and joy.

Driving back, Len and I talked very little into at least the second day. Then we both commented on a common internal phenomenon: the tight feeling in our chests was beginning to dissipate. We hadn't mentioned it before. The drive to Chicago took less than half the time it had taken two years before. Foolishly, we drove all day and all night on the last leg of the home stretch.

Years ago, we laughed over a timely "Peanuts" cartoon. Charlie Brown, just returned from a family car trip, is talking with a friend on the front porch: "Some families enjoy things like going to the opera or taking vacation trips in great places. But with our family, it's always 'home again, home again, Finnegan.'" There is that familiar saying, "Home is where the heart is." Since that first of many subsequent trips back to Vancouver, we have learned, not without pain, that our hearts always have been where we lived.

There wasn't much in a material way to come home to. We had managed to hang on to the apartment, miles from the university, where we lived prior to going to Atlanta. Len has always been a great nester, but we had had very little from which to construct this nest. We had been hard-pressed for rent money. An ad in the paper had brought us someone to share it—Ann Pelc, a Canadian, who had been unable to afford her abode when her friend moved out. Ann had chosen to stay on in the apartment after our departure to Atlanta. On our return, she was still there.

The only certain purpose we had in coming back to Chicago was completing my dissertation. Once again, Len's job would have to provide the necessary financial resources. My job future was uncertain, but it was now a seeker's market. Headhunting deans had been passing through the University of Chicago campus all summer. Several asked that I get in touch during the spring when I would be closer to getting the degree. More conservatively, the two from midwestern Canadian universities suggested that I call or write after I had completed a couple of years of teaching the higher learning. Their staffing problems had not yet become severe.

I was annoyed by the insensitivity of several deans in public institutions who recommended that I seek citizenship immediately so as to be employable. They made it sound as though giving up one's citizenship for another is as easy a decision as moving from one house to another. They probably caused me to delay applying for citizenship for several more years.

The clouds cleared away not long after we returned to Chicago. The search to replace a retiring faculty member in the Division of Teacher Education at Emory had broken down. The retiree agreed to stay on but wanted to give up all but his favorite course in educational psychology just as soon as possible. Jordan's efforts on my behalf were very timely. John Dotson, who had replaced Larry Haskew as director the year before, called to say that a temporary appointment was open to me for up to a year, with a tenure-line position if my dissertation was completed within that time. Paradise beckoned. I accepted; we were to be there for the start of the winter quarter in January.

We worked long days throughout that fall quarter. I went to the university most days to write, with the library resources I needed close at hand. In the evenings, Len typed what I had written, Ann proofread, and I revised. By the end of the calendar year, the basic chapters were written. I needed now to process and analyze the data and then draw out conclusions and recommendations. As things turned out, that first step took a couple of months of computing the regression equation for each child. With today's technology, this would be accomplished in a few minutes.

We said goodbye to Ann Pelc on December 31 and spent New Year's Eve in a motel in Terre Haute, Indiana. We were reminded of that night in Ritzville, Washington, a little more than two years before. We had managed to find a parking space for the loaded car near the window of our room, but we worried much and slept little. The motel was in an area of celebration that continued most of the night, but the car went undisturbed.

We stayed with the Jordans for a couple of weeks while a semicircle of tiny houses for Emory faculty members was being finished. We were to have a little house of our own for a couple of years, then the expectation would be that we would move out to make room for incoming faculty members. This was our ninth move and seventh abode in three years and four months of marriage. We settled in. Len had a nest to furnish, admittedly with sparse resources. We had returned to friends, familiar surroundings, and places of former work: Len went back with the surgeon and colleagues where she had been employed before, and I returned to Emory University and the AATES. Home again, home again, Finnegan. Never again would an automobile be sufficient to transport the things that help make a house a home.

WORK OF A HYBRID GENRE

My time was to be divided among Emory University, Agnes Scott College, and the AATES. In the past, the all-female Agnes Scott College, located just a few miles from Emory in Decatur (a participating partner school district in the AATES) had met the state's teacher certification requirements by sending students to the all-male Emory University for classes not offered at the former. But some parents expressed discomfort over their daughters' being in the resulting coed domain. Recently, the two institutions had negotiated a joint teacher education program that brought instructors from Emory to teach these classes to the now-growing group of prospective teachers at Agnes Scott. I was to teach one of these undergraduate classes each quarter, graduate classes at Emory, and in-service courses in the AATES.

I soon realized that I was settling into a new career of teaching teachers of children and youths and not teaching the young directly. With the learning of students in primary and secondary, not tertiary, schools the ultimate end, were my romances with schools to be vicarious from now on? Or were my satisfactions to come from brokering the romances of others? Would such be adequately satisfying? Perhaps there were romances to be had with the schools of higher learning. The dissertation work that kept me busy on weekends and most evenings and a unique program with which the AATES was associated raised my hopes for satisfying experiences on both fronts.

Clear findings were emerging from analyses of my data, now carted back to Atlanta. Overall, the promoted cohort fared better than the nonpromoted in both the personal and social domains.[5] For example, the rather high patterns of friendship enjoyed by the nonpromoted near the beginning of the year had faded away by the end. The promoted cohort revealed fewer signs of personal stress and especially of severe emotional disturbance. But it was some of the specifics that attracted my special interest. For example, the sources of stress in the two groups appeared to be quite different—the promoted worrying about not meeting parental expectations and the nonpromoted connecting their failure to a low sense of worth. The promoted were reported by their teachers to have cheated more; the nonpromoted to have been sent more often to the principal's office for misbehavior.

Old impressions were confirmed. The considerable differences in the academic progress of children, apparent even early in their school careers, simply do not fit into the age-graded structure of our schools—never have and never will. The question of whether promotion or non-promotion more favors children's well-being is simply the wrong question. The right question pertains to how to organize a school so as to best foster the steady, continuous, satisfying progress of children in all areas of their development. This raises another question: How did we come to get locked, passionately and obstinately, into a silly debate over the well-being of the whole child versus that of an academic piece amputated, presumably bloodlessly, from the rest of his or her being? Learning—in all the mansions of the self—is in large measure what it means to be human. Yet, we conduct our schools in many ways that dehumanize.

An answer to the myriad ways that the age-graded structure of schooling dehumanizes—with its accompanying archaic practices of promotion and nonpromotion—had begun to come to me while exploring literature related to my dissertation. I found a report of experimentation with "ungraded" classes in elementary schools of the Milwaukee district. Reports of a few earlier studies of the promotion/nonpromotion dilemma added to my growing belief that the way to get rid of it was to get rid of the graded structure itself. I had more and more come to ignore it in my one-room eight-grade school. Later, Robert Anderson, a fellow student I had met during that wonderful year at the University of Chicago, and I came up with what we called the nongraded elementary school.[6] It was to provide an array of romances with schools through the vicarious medium of their teachers, romances that were to be enriched by my involvement through the AATES with the Prescott Child Study Program.

I had taken a course with Daniel Prescott who, when I was in residence at the University of Chicago, was attracting a student following. He was charismatic, exuding a life of varied interests and experiences. The story passed around was that he had, with others, been adrift on a life raft after the ship on which he served during the war was torpedoed. Prescott talked passionately about children sidelined in schools, their halting progress even documented year after year in teachers' reports without any accompanying evidence of diagnosis and remediation.[7]

One of his colleagues, Caroline Tryon, was then engaged with others in documenting a sequence of "developmental tasks" confronted by children and for which they needed help.[8] There was a near parallel here with the work of describing children's "persistent life situations," in which Florence Stratemeyer and her colleagues at Teachers College, Columbia University, were then engaged.[9] Children apparently were beginning to move up alongside subject matter as a guide to curriculum development and instruction in the study of schooling. I do not recall Prescott referring to his program of child study, then in its infancy but soon to involve teachers nationwide.

One of my colleagues in the offices of the AATES was Lynn "Pat" Shufelt. I had been too busy during that first year in Atlanta to get much involved in his work. On returning, I learned not only that Prescott was his doctoral adviser but also of Pat's dismay over Prescott's unanticipated move from the University of Chicago to the University of Maryland where he now directed his new Institute for Child Study. There, he was putting in place not only a three-year sequence of child study for teachers but also a layered approach to leadership used in a variety of human enterprises. Further, he had negotiated the establishment of centers for delivering his program to teachers in-service and was expanding the number of these nationwide. The AATES was one, with Pat Shufelt providing the necessary leadership.

Four months after our return to Atlanta, I mailed a draft of my dissertation to the members of the committee. A month later, I arranged an appointment with Ralph Tyler, reserved a room at International House on the University of Chicago campus, and departed by bus for Chicago. My expectation was of incorporating suggested revisions into a final draft to be left for committee members' review.

Tyler startled me, as Fred Tyler had done regarding the final draft of my master's thesis a little less than three years before. "How long will it take you to make whatever revisions are necessary?" he asked, after I had done the rounds of visiting the other committee members. "Perhaps a couple of days," I replied. It was, I think, a Monday. "Then let's try to arrange the oral examination for Friday. That should give everyone time to review whatever revisions you make." I was astounded. He did what I never could have accomplished. He assembled a committee on incredibly short notice. I called Len, and she agreed that we would splurge. I would eschew that uncomfortable bus ride, take my second trip on an airplane, and fly home on Saturday after the oral the day before.

We had purchased our first new automobile that spring. In August, we drove again to Chicago and the summer graduation exercises in Rockefeller Chapel. Only the doctoral candidates came to the platform to be hooded individually. I noticed in each brief ceremony that, even during the handshake, President Robert Maynard Hutchins's expression conveyed either utter boredom or his mind being elsewhere. Today, I can be sympathetic. He was nearing the end of a long tenure before heading for California and new ventures.

We toured New England, took in several plays and musicals in New York, and returned to Atlanta in September. The promised appointment had indeed been confirmed; I was a bona fide associate professor. A year later, again returning from a September vacation, there was a note on the door from John Dotson and a surprise in store. I called and he asked us to come by after getting settled. He announced that he was departing to be dean of the school of education at the University of Georgia. After congratulating him, I asked who would be my new boss. "You!" he replied. He said that, because I was the newest and youngest member of the faculty, it had been decided that the appointment for the first year would be as acting director. No recruitment effort would be mounted, and presumably, with my elders grown comfortable with my year-long role, "acting" would be removed from the title. Located only some sixty miles away, Dotson would visit me from time to time and would be on call as my mentor, should he be needed.

I learned a little about mentoring that next year. I was incredibly busy with my duties and a heavy load of teaching—too busy and loaded down with so many quick decisions to make that I never called him. When he came, I had no store of unresolved issues to share. We were both a little embarrassed and uncomfortable, and the planned relationship soon faded away.

At the end of the academic year, I became director of the division of teacher education at Emory and of the Agnes Scott–Emory teacher education program. And there was a startling surprise: a joint full professorship was conferred! In September, apprenticeship into the higher education side of my hybrid career sharply accelerated awareness of fundamental differences between the cultures of the lower schools and the schools of higher education.

I had by then been several times near the end of the faculty line in the processions that accompanied the beginning and ending of the academic year at Agnes Scott College. I had assumed that the prevailing arrangement simply placed officials at the head of the line, followed by faculty members in a descending order from those of longest to shortest service. Once again, I took my accustomed place, but there were whispered instructions to move forward. Soon, a marshal escorted me to a place shockingly near the head of the line. There were murmurs after we passed pair after pair of lesser mortals. The placement was according to a combination of faculty rank and years of service. And so I found myself at the end of a very small clutch of full professors.

Why so few, when a major challenge of colleges and universities, especially in times of slow growth, is to keep a balance of assistant, associate, and full professors? To my surprise, I learned that the college still followed the practice of a sole full professor in each department. What my appointment had done was to force two full professors into the department of education and psychology. Unknown to me, this break in precedent had been a subject of consternation and conversation that probably challenged the wisdom of the joint teacher education agreement. Some of the congratulations sounded a little hollow.

Much more then than today, but still very much alive, the caste system sets higher education apart from the people's common school. Regardless of the rhetoric of a desired, seamless K-16 system of schooling, the gulf is formidable and difficult to bridge. Yet, for schooling and teacher education to be robust and renewing, a positive symbiotic partnership of the two cultures is essential. Given the purpose of the AATES—to upgrade the quality of schoolteachers through commonly extending to them the intellectual resources of higher education—its role was essentially one of *noblesse oblige*. But the child study program conducted through it was much closer to the hybrid genre of educating required for dual institutional renewal.

THE PRESCOTT CHILD STUDY PROGRAM

There is little doubt that Daniel Prescott viewed the child to be at the heart of the educative process.[10] Consequently, he saw the child-teacher relationships as critical. There is only a hint in his work of school culture also being of great significance. And even this hint is one of childhood peer interactions. He saw the teacher blocked from seeing the child by a curricular screen, a kind of sieve through which to pass the stuff of school learning. The first task was for the teacher to engage in prolonged observation of one child: a single child as a functioning entity—the person learning.

The process of child study extended over three years, each adding more of the child's interactions to the recorded observations. Successive cohorts of teachers studying a child came together during each school year and a period of each summer for discussions guided by carefully worked out procedures following rather nondirective, nonjudgmental lines that they, in turn, were expected to use in their own classrooms.

There was a degree of cultishness in the observance of some unwritten rules of group dynamics, probably observed and passed along by facilitators now removed from "the master," imitating him in form but perhaps not always substance. Prescott was a compelling figure, exuding an ethos of layers of personality unpeeled. Even his habit of smoking—or, better said, burning—a cigarette was mimicked by his group leaders, some of whom might have taken up smoking or the appearance thereof in order to be the genuine thing. Prescott commonly held a small ashtray in one hand and a lighted cigarette in the other while lecturing in his casual fashion. Little by little, almost everyone's attention ultimately turned to the pillar of ash growing longer and longer until, when extended by about an inch, Prescott at the critical moment flicked it off into the ashtray only to begin the process over again. His disciples impeccably followed suit. I found the habit to be very distracting.

I sat with groups engaged in each year of the program. Pat Shufelt and I observed that those in the third year increasingly expressed frustration with regularities of their schools that appeared to get in the way of the teaching-learning situation thought best for the child, often extrapolating from one to the whole class. Teachers' study had indeed pulled away a screen that had blocked their view of the child, but now other screens stood between, and these were seen as beyond their span of educational control. Pat polled his third-year classes and found that some teachers among them, especially those who were themselves instructors of first- and second-year groups, were eager for a fourth year focused on using their child-centered insights in constructing better classroom and even school environments. Pat and I decided to offer what was essentially the addition of a fourth year in the child study program.

The experience was both dismaying and rewarding. There were a couple of principals in the group of fifteen or so. They listened, sometimes with embarrassment, to a litany of things in other schools that got in the way of these teachers doing what they now believed to be right—morally right—for their children. But teachers saw most of these circumstances as being in the domain and responsibilities of their principals. After four or five sessions of this, Pat and I were becoming increasingly depressed with the apparent unwillingness or inability of the teachers to address what at the outset was the stated goal: to draw from learned insights into child development implications for the ongoing curriculum and daily pedagogy. The decks apparently had to be first cleared of debris that only the principal could (and should) remove. It was a very disturbing conclusion.

Very little of the complaining had come from the several teachers in the two schools that were represented also by their principals. One of these principals had gone through the three-year sequence with members of her faculty. The other had followed the work of teams of her colleagues as they went through the program and had managed to sit in as a guest several times. Both, very different personalities, met regularly throughout the year with their entire faculties, all inquiring into where they were headed as a school, what appeared to be working well and what not. There was no sharp line dividing principals' and teachers' responsibilities; they were involved together in improving the culture of their schools. The impression that emerged regarding the several other schools represented was of a bifurcation, with teachers' roles defined for one part, principals' for the other, and considerable fuzziness at some of the places where the two abutted.

One teacher represented a school that was highly regarded in the area, with credit for it commonly bestowed on the principal. She was enthusiastic about the child study program but in sharp disagreement with the idea of teachers assuming greater responsibility for the school as a whole. This would take time away from the classroom and the children, she said. Other teachers in the group supported her point of view; some spoke highly of her school and its principal.

I was by now regularly invited into schools and took advantage of invitations to visit the three schools lauded by their teachers—the two with both principals and teachers participating in our fourth year of the child study program (schools X and Y) and the one represented by the lone teacher (school Z). They turned out to be very much as described. But I found interesting differences. School X was located in one of the most impoverished (segregated white) areas of the city. The principal had been only a visitor to school study sessions but vigorously supported the program, dividing her time between the school and the community it served. She led the faculty meeting discussions and used them as a way of having everyone review what they were doing—and, clearly, as one of several techniques she used to be sure her absences were not causing problems. Everywhere she went, she was a vigorous spokesperson for the school, its children, its teachers, and its parents. The school was closely linked to an array of community services.

Schools Y and Z were in two of the more affluent areas of the city (again, segregated white). The principal of Y was quietly near invisible, more questioning than leading in the faculty discussions but very visible in classrooms and on the playgrounds. There was little sign of schoolwide rules and regulations; rather, the atmosphere was informal and familylike. Yet, there were no signs of disorder.

School Z would have delighted antiprogressives. The principal ran a tight ship. There were few faculty meetings; those that occurred dealt only with business matters and were short. The teachers liked this. It was a well-run, orderly, traditional place, one that many adults would recognize as "school." Unlike the other two, there was no sign here of an awareness of things that perhaps should and could be changed.

All three schools appeared to me to be safe and caring, but the leadership styles of the principals and the cultures differed. Schools X and Y appeared to be places where schools could and did change; school Z appeared to be a place of things thought to be as they should be. Clearly, each principal's departure would be a source of deep regret on the part of colleagues, central administrators, and, I think, children and parents. But which would then have the more problematic future?

I had an ideological bias that produced an ideological working hypothesis, one that I would pursue for years to follow. My worries about this bias were lessened when I read what James B. Conant, distinguished for his educational leadership as well as his scientific research, had to say about "a scientist's conviction that a working hypothesis is far more than a hypothesis—that it is a principle, that it is correct. Unless he is armed with such a conviction, he will not proceed with the laborious testing of the deductions from the generalization."[11]

My developing hypothesis was about the power of the culture of the school for educating and as the medium for educational change. And it was not the only hypothesis with which I would have romances for years to come. My conscience about these embryonic hypotheses being ideological is eased by adding just one letter so that the word becomes IDEAOLOGICAL.

Chapter 9

Renewing School Cultures

*The attitude toward change that we looked for could best be called
responsibility to change, and our image of it was a school in which
the staff regularly faced up to who they were, what they had, and
what they wanted, and, in figuring out how to get from here to
there, would seriously consider paths that they had never traveled
as well as paths they knew.*

MARY M. BENTZEN[1]

The Atlanta Area Teacher Education Service kept me close to
experienced teachers, administrators, and a diverse array of urban, suburban, and near-rural schools. My responsibilities as director of Emory
University's division of teacher education and of the Agnes Scott–
Emory Teacher Education Program brought me into the heart of the
culture of two different institutions of higher education and the preservice
education of those who soon would be new teachers and administrators
in schools.

It had begun to dawn on me that the culture of higher learning in
which colleagues and I were immersed was doing more to shape the
teaching and learning environments of the stewards of schools in
the area than was our pedagogy. I also began to realize that what we
were doing in the AATES classes taught in school settings was simply
giving closer geographic access to the same fare we were providing in
the regular in-service classes taught on our own campuses. Clearly, we
were conveniencing the AATES enrollees in getting their degrees. But
were we adding any value to their daily functioning in school and classroom simply by teaching most of these classes late in the afternoon in

the schools that were then largely empty of students and teachers? "Getting out into the schools" can mean many different things.

My experience with the culture of higher education was still quite new and limited. My mind stirred few budding hypotheses regarding what needed to be changed in order to better serve the education of educators. It seemed to me to be a little odd for the culture of the university to be so dominant in teacher education when the end goal is the education of boys and girls in elementary and secondary schools. My daily work was bringing me into the logistics and problems of joining two quite different cultures in the work of educating teachers.

I do not think I was aware then of the complexities inherent in this joining. School-university partnerships are today virtually a cliché of educational policy, but practice falls far short of rhetorical promise, largely because this complexity is so underestimated. Nonetheless, I was giving a lot of thought to my hybrid professional existence and the functioning in these differing cultures that accompanied it. My memory of how much I thought about a necessary relationship between institutions of higher education and schools in the health of teacher education is cluttered by more recent years of attempting to effect this relationship.

But the mind is a fascinating thing. My daily work may have been stirring more synapses than I was aware of. Recently, I looked up the word *hybrid* in *Webster's Third New International Dictionary*. One definition reads as follows: "having characteristics resulting from the blending of two diverse cultures or traditions." Perhaps, more than I knew, my hybrid experiences were creating for exploration some of the hypotheses that captured the attention of colleagues and me years later.

THE ENGLEWOOD PROJECT

I was ready for the phone call that came from my good friend, Bob Anderson. We had come together with common interests at the University of Chicago and stayed in touch. On completing his doctorate, Bob had become superintendent of a yet-to-be school district in a yet-to-be community on the outskirts of Chicago. Here he saw to the building of schools and hiring of staff while somehow managing to meet each family as it came to enroll children. Now, however, he was a faculty member in Harvard's Graduate School of Education.

Bob had become associated with the Englewood School, the southern-most in Sarasota County, Florida. Mr. and Mrs. William Vanderbilt had discovered and became enchanted with Manasota Key, just offshore from Englewood. They had built a vacation home there, purchased a large tract of land a little further south for development, and enrolled their nine-year-old son, Billy, in the school. Their enchantment did not spill over to include this little school. They visited with the county school superintendent with an offer to provide some supplementary financial support to upgrade it. Bob was brought in to give direction to this venture.

Prior to his call, he had completed a report and provided a set of recommendations that included sweeping changes in personnel. How-ever, he viewed the distance from Harvard to Englewood as limiting the services he could provide. Would I take on the directorship of the project? I would have full authority over the school and the additional funds granted by the Vanderbilts and would report directly to them and the superintendent. I think I had made up my mind before his call ended. But I still needed to add up the pros and cons.

I was on a plane to Tampa the following week where I met the pilot of a small charter plane that would take me the rest of the way. The wheels were almost touching the ground before I realized that there was, just below, a grass-covered, bumpy landing strip. A driver in a some-what beat-up Chrysler waited at the end of the field. He wore a rancher's hat curled up at the sides, a denim shirt, jeans, and loafers. His teeth were markedly tobacco stained. We were almost to the Vanderbilt home sev-eral miles away before I realized that I was in the company of Bill, former governor of Rhode Island, and a member of THE Vanderbilt family.

I spent a couple of delightful evenings with Anne and Bill, taking in as much as I could of the glorious sandy beach and the waves crashing on the bar a hundred yards beyond in the waters of the Gulf of Mexico.

The beauty and the grandeur faded on crossing the bridge back to the mainland. The main highway was eight miles inland, and the sign at the entry to the road to Englewood attracted few travelers. The tiny Englewood community was an isolated sliver of civilization known only to those who happened there seeking solace and that special breed of snowbirds who seek out the solitude that places like this provide in abundance. The condos and luxury hotels that were lining the shores northward from Miami had not yet found their way to Englewood and Manasota Key. There was a small market with a gas pump, a couple of less-than-inviting cafés, a makeshift marina that rented out small boats and a cruiser-for-charter, real estate offices, and the major gathering place, the post office. No movie theater, no bowling lanes, no ballpark, no library, no art gallery, no . . . Venice, a dozen miles to the north, provided a smattering of these, and Sarasota, still farther north, a great deal more.

The school fit. Rain had fallen heavily prior to my arrival, and the resulting lakes over the playgrounds had not yet subsided. I met the teachers, individually and then as a group. They were hospitable but cool. I could hardly blame them. They probably had not seen Bob's report but undoubtedly were aware of the recommendation that most applied to them: all but Frances should be terminated at the end of the school year. He had some good things to say about one of the other five who, with Frances, taught the six grades. He had no specific criticisms of the principal but thought it best that she move on, given the new expectations for Englewood School. Not an auspicious start for what became known as the Englewood Project![2]

During the concluding evening of the three nights I stayed with Anne and Bill Vanderbilt, I agreed to direct the project—in a role I later dubbed "the alternative drummer." They urged me to replace all members of the staff except Frances and to search the country for creative teachers. The Vanderbilt supplement to the school budget was sufficient to bring salaries up to those of the top districts in Florida and to compete with many elsewhere.

I had seen and heard enough to have something else in mind: We needed tough, spirited Jeeps, not top-of-the-line Cadillacs that would get stuck in the sand. I believed that the present teachers would either rise to the challenge and work of renewal or move on. There was no need, I thought, either to lower their sense of worth or to stir a tempest of community support for the teachers' appearing to have been treated unfairly. I would have plenty of time to build a list of potential replacements for normal turnover. These were thoughts I kept to myself.

I could understand the Vanderbilts' image of parachuting in a group of hotshot teachers and the essential materials for creating a school like the private one in a suburb of Boston that Billy would later attend. But I knew that this would be folly. I had prowled around enough before I left to sense a good deal of local uneasiness rising out of the little yet known about the Vanderbilt intervention.

Anne and Bill were right about the school's present lack of readiness to effect change; they had Bob's report to back up that perception. The school was like a six-room apartment complex, each a unit unto itself— four in the main building and two in adjacent temporary structures. The teachers greeted each other on coming and going and had occasional chats during the day. In conversations with them, I could not get any sense of planned change under way. They complained of isolation from the rest of the district and of intended delivery of essential supplies often getting no farther south than Venice. Their classrooms were devoid of adornment other than surprisingly little display of children's work. The rooms of Frances and another young teacher were exceptions—not only aesthetically, but in attention to pupils' learning.

I was astonished that a school of this size had a full-time principal. I concluded that Bob had been right in his appraisal. She had a good grasp of the basic routines of managing a school, but her conception of leadership did not include taking the school from where it was to where the staff, parents, children, and community might want to go over a period of years.

My romance with the Englewood School was intense for about six years, during which time we spent four in Chicago before moving to the Los Angeles area, a move that necessitated phasing out the relationship. The interplay of bringing two children into our daily lives, major geographic moves and changes in our living condition, and my hybrid career complicate accurate recall of this romance, particularly in regard to its chronology. The major purpose of this recall is to illustrate the importance of both creating a renewing school culture and of connecting it to the cultural context of the community if the intended bottom line is significant educational renewal. I choose to select out of the cluttered narrative of memory the stewardship of two successive principals.

The principal referred to above is not one of these; she was there for only a short time after my initial involvement. Prior to my first visit in the role of alternative drummer, I had informed her of some of my expectations for the next visit that included visiting classes, talking individually with each teacher, meeting with them all as a group, and scheduling a public session. Frances sent me a list of concerns about her social studies program and asked for an extended observation of her teaching to be followed by a conference. I did not hear from the others but visited their classes anyway. My general impressions were close to those reported by Bob Anderson. I saw nothing to suggest harm to or lack of concern for the children. There simply was a flatness in tone, a narrow range of institutional routine, an absence of laughter—much as I later described life behind the classroom doors of schools in my book, *A Place Called School*.

The session with the small group of parents (fewer than twenty, I recall) who responded to the invitation is memorable. The principal and five teachers arrived in two automobiles precisely at 7:25 for the 7:30 p.m. beginning. (Frances lived further away and had stayed in her classroom.) Six-strong, they formed a kind of phalanx, walked together to the school door, and sat together in the classroom where we would meet. The session did not last very long. I delivered a short message of steady school improvement, stressing the only programmatic need expressed to me by the teachers—strengthening the language arts program in reading and writing. I remembered inspector Calvert's words about ensuring that my pupils did well in arithmetic. But this was now the 1950s, and it was improvement in reading that was on the public school reform agenda. The questions were few and did not pertain to my short speech. They wanted to know about the Vanderbilts' role and their grant.

We followed roughly the same schedule for each of my three-day visits throughout the year, these occurring at four- to six-week intervals. Attendance at the evening public meetings roughly doubled from visit to visit, increasingly adding nonparents to the dominant parent group. My observations in classrooms made the teachers nervous, but invitations to do so and requests for conferences did increase. What encouraged me most was a request for more time to be added to the total staff meetings. A kind of camaraderie began to emerge, along with a growing enjoyment in discussing ideas. An exchange of readings began to occur.

A key visit for the year took place in January when school enrollment was growing daily because of the influx of snowbirds. This time, the incoming children were affecting class enrollments more disproportionately than in the past. Indeed, of the five who arrived on Monday and Tuesday of that week, four were declared by their parents to be in the fifth grade. This annual event was on the front burner of what we talked about at the extended staff meeting. But the tone was one of a condition to be unhappily tolerated, like the drainage situation and the nondelivery of supplies. The only solution put forward was the addition of another temporary classroom. But, clearly, this would not address the problem of the temporary winter surge of newcomers and their uneven distribution in the graded classes.

I returned at the time the spring trek back to northern states was about over, but the proportion of families leaving was sharply lower than before. The nationwide economic upturn was beginning to find its way to Englewood. There were stirrings in the real estate market and evidence of new business enterprises on the way. The well-attended public meeting brought forth questions and discussion to suggest that there were people settling in the area who expected more than a sluggish school culture. People residing for just a few winter months were less likely to get involved in school affairs. The schools of their higher expectations were back home.

I will not detail here the slowly improving quality of my subsequent meetings with the staff. It became clear that what the teachers feared most was split-grade classes that assuredly would accompany adding a seventh classroom. They wondered who among them would experience such a fate and then gradually moved to the conclusion that probably everyone would. I suggested an alternative that I knew would be only temporary but might give us a year to prepare ourselves and the parents for the anticipated calamity.

Clearly, a seventh teacher was now justified. Why not absorb the increased number of students into just six classes and have one teacher float as a helping teacher all fall and then take the newcomers into one multigraded class as they arrived? Enrollment in the six single-grade classes would be higher than normal throughout the year, but none would be disrupted during the winter months. Reasons opposing this idea came quickly, but the idea was not rejected.

During later visits of the year, I introduced both teachers and parents to some of our knowledge about the misleading message of the long-standing, traditional age-graded class. They were startled by my statement that there is no such thing as a graded class other than in name. Indeed, one would need a great many so-called fourth- or fifth-graders from whom to select twenty-five children achieving precisely at grade-level in tests to warrant a single grade designation. Individual and collective performance in an age-graded class is spread across many grade levels. Deliberately creating split-grade classes would serve to remind teachers of these individual differences.

Changing schools is a little like reducing weight. Weight taken off slowly by changes in diet and regular exercise tends to stay off. Weight taken off quickly by short-term, quick-reduction fads tends to come back. If you skip the time-consuming processes of involving the people who have a stake in a school, the first-level changes quickly attained fade, often strengthening the hold of the deep structure that continues to prevail.

Coping with Changing Circumstances

By May of that year, we were busily planning at Emory University for another round of the five-week summer workshop that had been created close to the time of launching the AATES. The "workshop way of learning" was a blossoming innovation in many parts of the country.[3] We were once more bringing in a superb staff from universities and school districts in several states who, in turn, attracted enrollees from afar who helped diversify the largely local in-service group of teachers and administrators.

A call from Tom, the supportive Sarasota County school district super-intendent, gave me additional things to worry about. He had decided to appoint Jean, the principal of Englewood School, to a supervisory position and had learned that two of the teachers probably were moving on. I called Jean to congratulate her and to learn more about the pending departures.

I had seen the resignations coming. There had been a growing readi-ness to discuss in our meetings quite significant ideas for change, but there had been a kind of drawing back from planning implementation. That would be for others to worry about. Two were indeed leaving—one to another district and one to full-time graduate study. And another was likely to leave.

By now, I was gaining a modest reputation as an innovator—enough to bring inquiries from educators interested in the Englewood Project, some recommended by professional colleagues. They fell roughly into two groups: the educational discontents and the educationally chal-lenged. Some in the first group reminded me of the old story of the traveler stopping for gasoline on the outskirts of a small Midwest town. "What sort of people live here?" he asked the attendant. "What sort of people live where you come from?" came the response. "An unfriendly, dishonest lot for the most part," said the traveler. "Well," observed the local resident, "I figure that's about the sort of folks you'd find here too." I figured that the discontents who saw others as getting in the way of their aspirations ultimately would view people in Englewood and the school in about the same way.

The people I was looking for had to be comfortable with themselves to the point of enjoying being alone with their thoughts and activities for a considerable amount of time. Yet, they also needed to enjoy being with others of quite different interests and beliefs. Above all, they had to be both individual and team inquirers and take pleasure from processes of learning—their own, their colleagues', and the children's. Englewood School needed cultural renewal, not infusions of reform. The necessary curricular and pedagogical changes would come in with it, not the other way around.

My thoughts kept turning to a young woman from Illinois, Lee Zimmerman, who had been on the staff of our Emory workshop the previous summer. I remembered her friendly greetings and smile, the slight lisp to her soft speech, enthusiasm, joy of life, and comfort with fresh ideas. The Englewood School had entered into our occasional conversations, and she had expressed great interest.

I called to ask if she might be interested in the principalship. She had never been a principal; she currently served in some kind of counseling supervisory role in a highly regarded school district just west of Chicago. Could I, would I, hold back on looking elsewhere until she and her fiancé visited Englewood at the close of her school year? I could and I did. My attention turned to recruiting these new teachers. If Lee said no, I would seek other suggestions from the well-connected colleagues who would be joining us for the summer workshops.

Lee and Bob Howard, a writer, were as enchanted with Manasota Key as I was: the long stretches of sandy beach, almost unpopulated except for the birds, scattered with shells of many colors and an astonishing supply of sharks teeth worn smooth by the sea. Yes, the "town" was bereft of enticement; yes, she had talked with some interesting residents; and yes, the school was gloomy and housing prospects not good. Yes, she would accept the offer and help me fill the teaching positions still open.

Lee stayed for only a couple of years, but the expectations I had for the relatively early future were more than fulfilled. She visited our summer workshop for several days, and we had long talks about Englewood, the school, procedures we had been following, the remaining teachers, the sand traps, and more. Consequently, I did not feel guilty about deliberately not being in Englewood for the first days of school and her first open public meeting. I heard good reports of her friendliness, enthusiasm, and rapport with children, parents, and teachers.[4]

On my first visit soon after, I found the tone of the school and our several meetings to be very different from what I had encountered during those initial visits. But the schoolhouse was still the bleak physical presence it had been for years. There had been rain again, and the resulting lakes had not yet subsided.

Lee was a little apprehensive about the parents and other residents. They appeared to be waiting and watching, spectators but not participants. This came to me as no surprise. I noticed that Lee followed the old custom of sending one of the older boys to pick up the mail each day. I suggested that she pick up the mail herself. "But I might get stuck for an hour or so each day," she protested. "Everyone gathers there." "That's the point," I replied. "You'll get to know them and they you. Can you think of any better forum for spreading the good word regarding the school?"

When I returned the next time, she was ecstatic. "I've even been invited for dinner at the Clarks." Mr. and Mrs. Clark, both artists, were magnets for malcontents whose discontent was directed to the school as well as to other things. "They would like you to join them and friends some evening," Lee said. I did. I do not think the Clarks became strong advocates of the school, but they quit knocking it.

Lee was a warm, caring, competent presence within the school and its ambassador beyond—not just with parents and the general public in Englewood but with other principals and district officials. She possessed a keen sense of how the ground had to be prepared for seeds of change. School change is not something delivered in packages by UPS.

In the district offices, Lee got the drainage problem moved up on the maintenance schedule. She met the chairman of the board of education, an architect, and reminded him that it was time for the postponement of a new school building for Englewood to be reconsidered in the light of predicted increasing enrollment. I went with her to pick up the mail. She greeted almost everyone by first name and introduced herself to those she had not met earlier. She persuaded the teachers to hold short, open meetings for parents of children in their classes to follow immediately after the close of the regularly scheduled public sessions. And, instead of my extended meetings with the faculty taking place in a classroom, each was shifted to her domicile or that of a teacher. On the warm evenings of fall and spring, we usually went for a swim before supper.

Late in the year, Lee managed a stop over in Columbus, Ohio, on her way back from a professional meeting. There, she talked with members of that stellar faculty in the arts and arts education at The Ohio State University regarding how best to promote the arts in the elementary school. When school opened for the following fall, there was in each classroom a print of a painting by a noted artist. Some parents complained that this would stifle children's creativity; they would simply try to copy what they saw. Lee put the topic on the agenda of the first public gathering of the year. The children did not copy. Rather, their own work was influenced and enriched.

The teachers had come to agree the previous year that the "floating teacher" concept was the best of the several alternatives they saw as a short-term answer to the enrollment problem. But now they were into further pupil population growth and multigrades. Lee's counseling background strengthened her leadership role in addressing the problem of increasingly apparent years of individual differences in academic achievement characterizing classes even of only one or two designated grade levels. The lack of instructional materials became a major problem, especially in the teaching of reading.

Lee and a couple of teachers opened up an old cloakroom no longer used for its original purpose where, over the years, graded readers replaced by new editions had been stored. They sorted them into clusters so that books labeled for the second grade, for example, were side by side with some labeled for the third and fourth. They then marked each cluster to make it easily accessible to a teacher in search of something reasonably appropriate for a given child.

This solution was far from ideal. Graded reading texts are not my idea of magnets to attract and develop children's reading interests and skills, but it was a beginning. And it gave some stimulus and direction to the little school-community library and to parents for the purchase of children's books. Since then, I have been in schools where there was on hand, carefully catalogued, a wide range of reading materials classi-fied by topics such as the oceans, outer space, ships and shipping, insects, and more.

By that stage of my hybrid career, I had rejected the popular idea of there being a set of generic characteristics to describe the ideal school principal—or any other educational leader. The ideal, rather, is the good fit of person and context, a fit that often changes over time. In one of her books, Sara Lawrence-Lightfoot describes the good fit of a trou-bled school and the new principal who guided it through early stages of renewal. But the principal had the wisdom to realize that he was not the person to guide it through the necessary next stage. He and the superintendent agreed, and this wise man took on the early renewing process of a second troubled school. Things and people change, but not always together.[5]

Although Lee did not talk with me directly about the school being ready for someone else, I think she sensed it. Increasingly, she spoke of how much she enjoyed working through a problem with others, but also of often coming to the end of feeling prepared to provide guidance. Since then, I have frequently encountered this fascinating phenomenon that drives people to more intensive periods of learning. I was disappointed but not surprised when Lee told me that she wanted to dig intellectually more deeply into some things and perhaps study for the doctorate. I watched this bug catch up later on with Frances and, eventually, almost all of the new people who joined us in Englewood.

REFINING SCHOOL RENEWAL

By the beginning of Lee's second year, Len and I were once more in Chicago where I was now a professor and director of the Center for Teacher Education at the university. This time, however, we brought along a three-year-old son and a one-year-old daughter—nice, but not accompaniments fitting neatly into the context of a third-floor, walk-up apartment, especially during Chicago's winters. We had left our first entry into home-owning—a comfortable little bungalow in a large treed yard. Where would we send little ones to play now? During the snowy months, by the time both were bundled up for the cold and taken downstairs, one or the other was asking to go back up to the bathroom. They never tired of watching the chicks break out of their shells and the electric model trains threading their way through tunnels and mountain passes at the Museum of Science and Industry, but Len's enthusiasm for these visits began, over time, to wear a little thin.

We would not have returned to Chicago at that time—perhaps not ever—had an episode during my final year at Emory turned out differently.

Early on in that year, the librarian, whom I had come to know and like, invited me to address a group of women whose Saturday Morning Club met monthly on that day of the week. She had requested that I talk about the changing role of children over the last couple of centuries. This I did after an hour of informal conversation spiked with sherry and fruitcake.

Soon after, one of these women, aided by a cane, slipped quietly into my office late in the afternoon. She was, I recall, the last surviving direct descendant of the family that owned Fernbank Forest—a beautifully wooded acreage just a few miles from the campus. Would I like to have its use for implementing the concept with which I had concluded my remarks—a twenty-four-hour-a-day center for family educational, health, and other human services? I would.

Thanks to her, I soon found myself discussing logistics with a much-respected member of, I believe, the university's Board of Trustees whose additional connections to the Coca-Cola Company gave promise of securing at least part of the necessary financial resources. A gratifying chemistry between us arose quickly, even before I became aware that he was very ill. He lived only a few weeks after I delivered to his home (where I was not able to speak with him) a fifty-page manuscript detailing concepts and strategies. His death was a great personal and professional loss.

At his suggestion, I had delivered simultaneously a copy to President Goodrich White. Several months passed, and I had received no reply. Then, I told both of the deans to whom I reported—by now good friends and colleagues—Judson (Jake) Ward of the College of Arts and Sciences and Leroy Loemker of the Graduate School—that I had been approached by three major universities in the North regarding my possible interest in appointments there. I subsequently decided against two of the offers and doubted I would accept the third.

Then a short letter came from President White to the effect that Emory was not at the time ready for what I had proposed. The next day, I miserably played the usual monthly game of golf with three colleagues. If my career was going to be heavily weighted on the side of higher education, with the Englewood Project offering occasional deep immersion into a school for the young, perhaps I should accept the offer from an institution where I could drink daily from one of the deepest intellectual wells in academe.

President White, on learning that I might leave, asked Jake Ward what it was I wanted and countered with the conventional solution—a significant increase in salary. He just didn't understand. Given the daily environment of *his* calling, how could I have expected otherwise? At the end of September, we, in our Chevy station wagon with our worldly belongings in a moving van, were en route to Chicago one more time, for what we thought would be a long stay.

The university's policy provided a twelve-month salary for three quarters of service. The fourth was to ensure a concentrated period of research. I chose fall, winter, and summer; spring would find us in Englewood. The publication of two coauthored books cleared the decks for concentration on the project there. Increasing enrollment would bring not only the addition of a building but the necessity for all classes to have a mix of grades. The concept of nongrading that had emerged during the writing of my dissertation was once more on the horizon of my mind.

Early in that first winter of our return to Chicago, Lee told me that she would like to enter once more into graduate studies within a year or two. Her timing would depend on securing some financial assistance. I was to be once again engaged in a search for a principal, but for a context that would be in significant ways different from what it had been when Lee began her good work in Englewood. Leadership is not a one-model-fits-all concept.

Each winter, I taught the course earlier taught by that superb mentor I first encountered at the university, Ralph Tyler, whose friendship I enjoyed and advice I appreciated up to his death in the early 1990s. My attention was drawn to John Bahner, who had been a school counselor in Ohio and was recently recruited to a fellowship in the program of the university's Midwest Center for Educational Administration. After learning more and talking with him, I concluded that he would be a good fit for the changing context of Englewood and its school. I also learned that he was being encouraged by the center's director to get some administrative experience. By the following late summer, he, Ruth, and their young daughters were residents of Englewood. I recommended Lee Zimmerman for a teaching assistantship in the university, and by fall she was working and studying where John had recently been.

John Bahner did not come with a preconceived list of school needs and proposed changes. Nor had I expected him to. Instead, he brought a disciplined focus, a keen mind, and patience to the central business of schooling: purpose, structure, curriculum, teaching, pupils' progress and well-being, parent role, district relationships, etc. His "what" questions were almost invariably followed by "why" questions. John revealed excellent peripheral vision that took in a good many things at once, and these quickly became context for his ability to sustain focus on one important matter until it achieved a near self-sustaining trajectory. He then brought another piece of the whole to the forefront. This mode required careful public explanations to ensure that those not directly involved understood and were brought along. Lee Zimmerman had gone a long way toward establishing a solid foundation for this.

John Bahner took over a school that was expanding rapidly in a community context that was changing at an accelerating pace. Over a two-year period, small businesses increased multifold—three supermarkets were built, a bank was established, and two physicians and a dentist began practice. Nationally known authors and artists became full- or part-time residents. But recreation and entertainment remained as before—entirely up to individual and small-group creativity.

The faculty of Englewood School grew in size each year. Even though intellectually aware of the social context prior to coming, some found adjusting to the limitations to be difficult. Paradise may beckon, but it rarely awaits. The teachers came from many different places and backgrounds. The largely self-contained social unit they sustained was not without tensions. For me, coming in only to work and play with them always was a richly rewarding experience.

Englewood School was a difficult place in which to teach, especially when teachers came with high individual expectations that fueled collective high expectations. The pupils came from all walks of life, ranging from the lowest category on any scale designed to measure cultural, intellectual, and socioeconomic traits to the highest category. There was still a good deal of community apathy toward education. Some of the faculty had never worked with children as deprived as many were. Their interest in and concern for all was palpable. Parents needed no "clearance" by the principal to join their children in classrooms.

The opening of the new school building at the beginning of John Bahner's second year could have been a disastrous event rather than merely a bumpy one had it not been for his encompassing span of administrative management, the prior planning that went into it, and the inordinate flexibility and commitment of the teachers. The weekly two-hour group sessions, now the norm, had prepared for full implementation of multiaged classes of children in a building designed for both self-contained classrooms and team-taught combinations. They had worked closely with the architect in seeking to ensure flexible-use space to connect with a flexible concept of pupil placement and upward progression. Many things had to come together at the outset.

But well-laid plans often go awry. The builders worked through the Labor Day weekend to get four of the nine classrooms ready for occupancy on Tuesday. Furniture was moved in on Labor Day and through most of the night. Three weeks later, the other classrooms were ready for occupancy. Providing for the overflow of more than a hundred children in a combination of the old and the new structures challenged the teachers' patience and ingenuity. Heavy rainfall did not help.

The precarious opening weeks of the new school year slowed but did not stop progress of the faculty through an agenda of business that had arisen in part out of the previous year's weekly meetings. Twenty-six topics were of the kind any elementary school might encounter. But several others were boundary breaking: modification of the age-graded structure, deployment of teachers in the flexible space of the new building, adapting curricula and pedagogy to the individual learning trajectory of each child—sometimes one-on-one and sometimes in clusters—and bringing parents to a level of understanding the reasons behind what the teachers were endeavoring to do.

A subtle shift in my role occurred. I became less of a different drummer and more of a friendly critic. By now, Bob Anderson and I were getting into the writing of our book, *The Nongraded Elementary School*, published in 1959.[6] The USSR's Sputnik, circling the globe in 1957, had frightened the American people and stirred a flurry of concern over their schools very similar to that later one stimulated by the report, *A Nation at Risk* (1983). It fascinated me, years before the information age put happenings and ideas only seconds away, how people sometimes appear to come simultaneously to a common awareness not yet appearing to be part of the conventional wisdom.

I had given no presentation on nongrading in sessions with the total staff. In the steady progress toward multiage, multigraded classes that had begun with the snowbird crisis several years earlier, I had not pushed for abandoning grade designations. We would need to prepare both ourselves and the parents for what would otherwise be a disturbing and perhaps disastrous move. But these teachers were now so far into aligning daily activity with the interests and progress of their pupils that graded designations were recognized as fiction.

A major problem arose. Teachers receiving children into their classes who had been with other teachers the previous year wanted to avoid curricular duplication. They could no longer assume that fourth- or fifth-grade subjects and tests had been part of their charges' learning experiences. We talked the problem through and came to the conclusion that the curriculum of Englewood School was made up of the paths already walked, not those ahead. The demanding task now posed for the teachers was that of maintaining careful records of what had been encountered along the way.

How today's computer-rich advancements would have helped us! We did the best we could with handwritten pages of information filed in the school's growing curricular data bank. Today, I look in puzzled wonderment at the relatively mundane use of the wonderful technology that has been employed so little to bring nineteenth-century educational practices beyond twenty-first century encasement in concrete.

By the end of the 1958–59 academic year, Englewood School was as close to Bob Anderson's and my conception of nongrading, organizationally and philosophically, as any school claiming such that I have seen.* What remained was to designate it as such. This the faculty decided to do in the spring of 1960. By then, all pupils were in classes embracing at least a three-year age span. But none was in a class with a wider academic achievement span than characterizes the typical "single grade" of the traditional school. John Bahner captures in his doctoral dissertation a sense of the careful in-school and out-of-school preparation for this transition. His letter, attached to all report cards at the end of the 1958–59 school year, contained the following paragraphs:

> Most of the parents of Englewood School pupils realize that their own child does not perform at the same level in all subjects. They also realize that within any one classroom there will be students who are achieving in reading, for instance, on several different grade levels. Therefore, calling a group of about 30 children "third graders" does not mean that every child in the room is achieving on a third grade level in all areas.
>
> When these facts are considered, it can be easily understood that there is no such thing as promotion at the end of the year in Englewood School. Our pupils are progressing at various speeds and in several different groups throughout the year. In June we merely re-arrange the pupils into groups which the teacher feels will provide the best stimulation for each individual child and which will allow the child to continue his development at his own speed. As far as "promotion" is concerned, the vacation period between June and September is no different than Christmas vacation—although the period is longer and the children are most likely to have a new teacher upon their return.[7]

The report cards sent home at the end of the 1959–60 school year were accompanied by a similar letter, but this time, no grade-level designations

---

*So far as Bob and I have been able to determine, this was one of the first two team-taught, nongraded schools in the United States, the other having emerged at about the same time in a similar step-by-step process of renewal in Massachusetts under his caring guidance as alternative drummer and critical friend.

appeared. Classes were now known by the names of the responsible teachers or by room numbers. It was still necessary, however, to provide grade classifications for all children in district-required records. Nonetheless, as John notes in his manuscript, the transition of the Englewood School to a nongraded structure had taken place. Refinement of it would continue to be a work-in-progress.

CALIFORNIA BOUND

It was not a sense of completion that drew me away from Englewood and its school. Englewood and its people remain among those time-defying knots of memory from which I still draw nurturance. Nearly all of the teachers that Lee, John, and I recruited were bitten hard by the learning bug and went on to doctoral-level studies. Several with whom I shared romances with Englewood School have been long-term friends and professional colleagues.

Our son, Stephen, had not taken well to Chicago's winters. The humidifier beside his bed each night eased his breathing but curled the wallpaper. We were told by the pediatrician that a warmer climate might help, but this was far from certain.

Largely out of courtesy, I accepted an invitation to go to lunch with a visitor, Howard Wilson, dean of UCLA's School of Education. He brought with him a comprehensive report, prepared a couple of years earlier, on the famed laboratory school there. It had been precipitated by the retirement of its founder and long-time principal, Corinne A. Seeds.

A major recommendation was that a director be appointed to whom the principal would report for the school's daily operation. A major role of the director would be to connect the University Elementary School (UES) more closely than it had been before to faculty members' research interests campuswide. The capable young man appointed at the assistant professor level simply could not fulfill both these functions and the scholarly requirements for his promotion. Needed was a full professor with a record of school-based educational research, development, and innovation. Wilson admitted also that such an appointment might put to rest parental fears that the progressive educational ideas of Miss Seeds for which the school was known were now in danger.* Might I be interested in the position?

It proved to be another of those decisions that gnawed away at us for quite some time. Stephen's health always rose above all else. But the reputation of Los Angeles for smog gave us pause. Then we learned that it was considerably reduced on the west side where UCLA is located and where we might live. Since UCLA was not then in the top ranks of the nation's universities, Frank Chase, chairman of the University of Chicago's department of education, thought that I would not consider seriously the prospect of going there. I called Ralph Tyler. He thought that UCLA's time was come; that it was a rising star of coming decades. Chase said that, if it was the laboratory school there that most attracted me, I should know that the directorship of Chicago's was open to me. For reasons not clear, I had developed no romantic inclinations toward it.

I knew that leaving the home in which we had invested and lived for the previous three years would be very painful for Len. Late in that first winter of living in the walk-up apartment, she had taken to driving south or southwest until the snow on the roadside was no longer black, and there her house-hunting began. After weeks of discouragement, she found it—her dream nest. She had stopped to admire it when she noticed an inconspicuous "for sale" sign almost obscured by some bushes.

It was a lovely Tudor with a Vermont slate roof, solidly constructed in 1928 just before the financial collapse of 1929. The couple for whom it had been built lived and raised a family there during the many intervening years. But could we afford it?

We didn't get to make the very few changes, such as replacing the well-worn carpeting in the living room, we couldn't subsequently afford. We went to California, the sunny mirage of my childhood dreaming. I later learned that Len had cried while our belongings were being loaded into the moving truck. I was in Washington, D.C., at the time. The family picked me up in our station wagon at the Kansas City airport for the rest of the trip westward. This ill-timed disjuncture is

---

*In all of my years at UCLA, I never heard anyone refer to Corinne Seeds as anything other than Miss Seeds.

underlined in red on a debit page of our family history. As observed in a newspaper comic strip, "Husbands are a sorry lot."

There had been, four years earlier, a full-page story on my arrival in the University of Chicago's campus daily. There was no mention of my departure. Presumably, full professors there never left; they just faded away. I still remember what was said about faculty members who went elsewhere: both institutions would be improved. Perhaps this is said about all professors who depart from major universities while in mid-career. I have often wondered what was said of me.

THE UNIVERSITY ELEMENTARY SCHOOL

Len had her sights on our living in one of the many old Mediterranean-style houses near UCLA. What we had in the bank from the sale of our Tudor in Illinois suddenly looked puny. We looked further westward, rented a house in Pacific Palisades, and she set out once more looking for a nest. The four of us went regularly to Santa Monica pier for fresh seafood and to smell the salt air and seaweed. Home again, home again, Finnegan.

Given what Los Angeles and UCLA are today, they are best described as adolescent at the time of our arrival. The several campuses of the University of California, Stanford University, and other universities and colleges were soon to provide balance on the West Coast for the long dominance of the East Coast in higher education. I missed the ready-made intellectual climate of the University of Chicago that was to come later at UCLA under the leadership of Clark Kerr, president of the University of California, and Franklin Murphy, chancellor of its Los Angeles campus. The near-quarter century of our residency in southern California was a tumultuous period in the history of the United States and a wonderful time to be an educator, especially in that dynamic educational context.[8]

Since for all those years I was director of what is now the Corinne A. Seeds University Elementary School, this romance might better be referred to as a marriage. I guess I became a bigamist in adding to this post after seven years the deanship of the Graduate School of Education.

Both cultures probably suffered from the demands of this hybrid relationship.

Early on, I recalled some conversations with colleagues at the University of Chicago regarding what they thought would present greater difficulty than in Englewood—to effect similar changes in middle-class communities where parental expectations for their children's success in school and access to college would be higher. I had not been convinced. But I was confident that there would be some quite different challenges calling for quite different strategies. It would be fun to find out.

The teachers came a week before arrival of the children. I had met most of them socially before the summer break. Acting principal Margaret Mathews called them together for the first total staff meeting of the year. Several came with a copy of *The Nongraded Elementary School*; most with pads and pencils. Did they really think that I was going to mandate nongrading? I thought it best to disabuse them of the idea at the outset. I wanted to know a lot more about the school— what they were doing, wanted to do, and why—and told them that I would set up a schedule to meet with each of them individually for at least an hour over the next month.

I waited a week for everyone to settle in before I began to browse. The setting contrasted sharply with the conventional image of an austere school building surrounded by treeless flat ground. The UES had received architectural recognition for its blend of connected, cottage-like sections; appropriate open space adjacent to each; and an interesting mix of large and small trees, shrubs, and colorful ground cover. A small stream, running much of the year, traversed the whole and was bridged, cemented, and fenced off for foot traffic and safety.

There had been some interesting additions such as a kiva to accommodate the curricular unit on a pueblo culture. I had been impressed during that first week of children in attendance with the easy access of all sections to the library and the way in which the teachers began to prepare the littlest newcomers for their independent use of it. It was amazing to see the ease with which any classroom group gained access to play space without bothering other classes.[9]

The UES was and is to considerable degree a place of and for children that so far has managed to resist the resolve of some within UCLA to move it to a neighboring school district to make room for academic activities of their higher priority. I do not remember how many times I had to explain and defend the education of children in the budget-making deliberations of the University of California. Governor Reagan blue-penciled the UES along with the several remaining laboratory schools of the California State University system, but thanks to a friend of his and the school's, it alone was spared. My point here is not to defend university-based laboratory schools. I think there are better alternatives. But where there exists a school designed and conducted to be a good place for children that serves the public purpose of education in a democracy, we would be well advised to leave it be, just as we seek to maintain other national treasures. All schools should be such places.

The responses to my "what" and "why" questions were troubling. I learned some useful things about the teachers in our one-on-one conferences but little about what they would like to do beyond what they were now doing. They had some gripes and wants akin to those a tenant might convey to the landlord, little of substance to be studied or changed. I asked most of the "why" questions during my classroom browsing.

I was curious about the construction work that Miss Seeds had introduced years ago, which was of much interest to visitors. A storage building was well stocked with thin boards that could be easily sawed and shaped. The children cut, hammered, and built all manner of things. But the teachers could not give me any reasons beyond the obvious one of learning potentially useful skills. The possible benefits of adding the kinesthetic to enrich and supplement other modes of learning were mentioned by only one teacher, who did not go further than what I am now writing by way of justification and explanation.

The four teachers in the early childhood wing of the school—nursery school and kindergarten—had a shorter teaching day and welcomed the opportunity this provided to meet with me regularly as a group. They were all experienced, superb teachers with considerable study of child development in their backgrounds. I pushed them hard, especially in regard to the presence of bantams, balancing boards, tricycles, building blocks, and other "materials" of instruction in the play yards—which, too, were a significant part of the learning milieu.

They gave me good answers, but their occasional annoyance suggested wonderment about how one so ignorant about good educational practices had been appointed director of the school. However, when I pushed beyond what they saw as obvious, into such questions as how the children were reacting to this educative milieu, they began to understand what I was driving at and to push back at me. They admitted to wondering about which children were and were not thriving in the school's environment. A professional colleague, Louise Tyler, joined us in an inquiry into what we should be trying to accomplish, how we might find out the degree to which we were accomplishing this, the development of an instrument that proved to be gratifyingly accurate in sorting out the progress of each child, and a process for addressing the problems of individual children.

My inquiries into the work of clusters of children beyond the nursery school and kindergarten were much less rewarding. The morning routines of mathematics, reading, spelling, and other subjects were very much like what I would have found in grades one through six of neighboring schools but, overall, better carried out than in most. The afternoons were quite different. The integrated-project method took over. The social studies provided the core; visual arts, music, and the language arts were built into it. A carefully designed unit provided a comprehensive curricular organizing center for each grade level: transportation, the westward movement of the nation's pioneers, the pueblo, and finally, the United Nations in the sixth grade. Children, teachers, and parents knew what would come next in the sequence.

The teachers were patient with my questions, but most regarded them as for my informational repertoire only. My "why" commonly brought forth only more detailed descriptions of the "what." The curriculum was a given. Many of the ways of carrying it out were, indeed, interesting. For example, the little stream had been partially dammed to create the Pacific Ocean, a local harbor, and far-distant ones, connected at the shores to train terminals, for purposes of facilitating learning in the transportation unit. There were similarly appropriate provisions for the other units. Needless to say, the UES was a great place for both future and experienced teachers to get beyond the textbook regarding the project method in progressive education. I would have enjoyed visiting it when I attended normal school.

The UES was a veritable oasis and would be even more markedly such in today's desert of mandated schooling. But some things disturbed me, nonetheless. There was in many classrooms a kind of abstract didactics, suggesting more the form than the substance of progressive education. The teachers demonstrated almost daily for visitors what was outside the box of conventional public schooling. The parents defended and bragged about the UES just as most parents defend their local school. Since getting a child into it was on a par with getting offspring into the medical school, they were not likely to knock its practices.

Nonetheless, the school was crippled in its functioning in more subtle ways. Its reputation for programs in reading, writing, and arithmetic was not what attracted parents to it. The beacon was the departure from the norm and the accompanying satisfaction of their children. Now, with Corinne Seeds no longer at the helm, more than a few parents saw themselves as navigators to keep the ship on course. The words of colleagues at the University of Chicago about the difficulties of changing a school with an education-intensive parent body came back to me.

Perhaps even more threatening to the school's functioning as a laboratory was parental fear that the progressive rather than traditional grounding their children were enjoying would not prepare them for academic success in secondary schools and, ultimately, top universities. They were not fully persuaded by the testimonials of UES graduates who had distinguished themselves academically. They wanted to be sure their children were getting at UES what others were getting in nearby schools. And so, a high percentage had their children tutored, especially in mathematics and reading. This virtually removed the obvious research category of comparing UES pupils' academic progress with that of control groups elsewhere and our ability to defend the school on conventional criteria. Of course, a similar problem exists in comparisons of public schools. Even if affluent parents do not have their children tutored, the resources they are able to provide in the home environment invalidate many of the rankings for excellence attributed to some of today's schools.

It became clear to me that renewal at the UES had declined somewhat proportionately with the rise in its reputation. It had "arrived." It also was clear to me that it still retained in its deep structure some of the anachronisms hobbling schooling in general—practices in organization, curriculum, and pedagogy now out of sync with the implications of relevant knowledge. It became especially clear to me that effecting significant change would have to be orchestrated very carefully. Formulas for educational change abound, but school renewal is context specific.

In retrospect, I realize the degree to which the UES was delicately oriented toward change at the time of our coming. On one hand, there was the immediate parental fear of losing what Miss Seeds had created. On the other, there was the long-time concern over whether the school she had built prepared their children well for the higher learning. Parents looked anxiously for signals regarding what the new person in charge had in mind. After considerable pondering, Len and I had made a decision before our arrival that sent a powerful signal.

John Bahner had told me that our spending a couple of months each year in Englewood and then, when Stephen was five, enrolling him for these two months in the kindergarten had contributed significantly to parental confidence in what we were doing in the school. But the UES situation created a dilemma for us. Chancellor Murphy had made it clear to me that the pressures to let children into the school were mine to handle, even those from deans seeking to use promises of admission as an added inducement in seeking to recruit new faculty members with children. "When I get pressured regarding admission to the UES, I'll simply tell the interested party to talk to you," he said, with accompaniment of his charming, somewhat mischievous smile. Dare we take up two precious places in the UES by enrolling Stephen and Paula? We were not sure we even wanted to, given the transportation problem and our reluctance to send them to a school out of the neighborhood in which we would be living.

Nonetheless, we decided that neither we nor the school could afford not to enroll our own children. It was impossible to determine the full impact of our decision. But I am sure the occasional criticism was far outweighed by the confidence engendered in the uneasy parent body.

An Agenda of Renewal

Some of the teachers were becoming aware that I did have an agenda, but of an unusual kind. Let's just call it an agenda of renewal that inquired into our mission, practices relevant and not relevant to it, and strategies for moving from where we thought we were to where we thought we wanted to go. This was a relief to these teachers because they appeared to me to be those most aware that the school was resting on a plateau of earlier accomplishment.

They were right. There was not any ongoing discussion of mission, let alone inquiry into it. There was a deeply ingrained valuing of children but no separating out, for purposes of learning, cultural assets to be cultivated through the school's functioning and liabilities to be dropped from it.[10] My questioning was producing an agenda of catch-hold points for regular faculty meetings: Why did the UES have hands-on construction activities, the simulated harbors and ocean, the kiva, the unit on the United Nations—each extending over six weeks or so—classes divided into A and B (2A and B, 5A and B, etc.) with semiannual promotions or retentions, and more? Two teachers there from the early beginnings filled in some of the historical—but much less of the philosophical—underpinnings.

The pattern of in-service education had been that of learning to do better what the rhetoric of UES functioning said the school stood for. Teachers were recruited because they did the conventional well; very few had experience in the unconventional. Corinne Seeds assumed responsibility for the necessary apprenticeship of all but the teachers in the school's early childhood unit. Margaret Mathews explained to me that Miss Seeds paid much less attention to the practices there. Her perspective was that nursery school and kindergarten were largely for play. School learning, especially in reading, began in the first grade. It was from here on up that she shaped the models. This information helped me enormously to understand the cultural divide between the early childhood education unit and some other segments of the school.

Corinne Seeds and Helen Heffernan, the state director of elementary education, had enjoyed a long personal and professional relationship. The latter used the UES a good deal for in-service teacher education, particularly involving the large corps of district supervisors then characteristic of California. She had heard about our not holding back on some children's learning to read before the first grade; she requested and we approved a visit of several supervisors who wished to observe. Three came, dressed in black, and sat all morning observing, but scarcely saying a word and occasionally frowning. Clearly, they disapproved of the environmental cultivation of children's interest in and ability to read. Nursery school and kindergarten were for play. Reading was something to be left for the first grade.

Ironically, I was then speaking out in opposition to the drive in the Los Angeles Unified School District for more of what were traditionally "first-grade expectations" to be pushed down into the kindergarten. When will we ever begin to respond appropriately to the facts of children's profound differences in learning and most everything else?

My raising of "why" questions stimulated many informal conversations among pairs and larger clusters of teachers. I sought to move these conversations into the more formal processes of our regular faculty meetings. We shifted all but a few business matters to notices and memos in teachers' in-boxes and elevated the importance of checking on these at least once daily. This left us with all but ten or fifteen minutes taken out of each two-hour session of addressing three guiding questions: What do we like that we want to keep and strengthen? What do we not like that can be quickly changed and what do we recommend? What do we not like that will require long-term study and change and what procedures appear to be useful? We then organized into working groups of common interests. A large number of the total staff meetings were subsequently devoted to progress reports from the groups, discussion, and suggestions for next steps.

Ultimately, the work of these groups was virtually to take the school apart conceptually and put it back together again, both conceptually and in practices. The understanding that steadily grew stronger was that the same questions asked about what was changed would later be applied to the changes made. As the teachers became increasingly aware that practices once innovative had become over the years sacred, they also began to realize the dangers of passing along to visitors UES practices now frozen in place. By the end of our first year together, we had before us an agenda of process and substance that evolved over time. Renewal is never finished.

By the end of that year, the Goodlad family was getting settled in for what turned out to be a long stay. We bought a house farther west on the lower slopes of the Santa Monica range of mountains in Malibu. The longer trip to the UES was somewhat relieved by a schedule of sharing the commute with other parents who had children there. But we rolled up the car mileage nonetheless. Not attending local schools deprived Paula and Stephen of playmates for several years but brought them together in dependence on one another.

Occasional encounters with rattlesnakes were a minor threat compared to the big three: mudslide, earthquake, and brush fire. We met people whose habitat, or at least part of it, had been swept away, sometimes more than once. Not envisioning a better place to live anywhere on earth, they simply rebuilt. The spirit of renewal often runs deep.

CATCH-HOLD CENTERS FOR SIGNIFICANT CHANGE

In seeking school renewal, it is important to be alert for opportunities that arise out of commonplace routines and offer entry into practices encased in amber. In the Englewood Project, it was the winter migration of the snowbird families that opened up entry into the deep structure of schooling. Routines common to all schools were the serendipitous catalysts in my romances with the UES. What follows is a brief story of several that brought both the conventional frozen and, ultimately, the innovative sacred characteristics of the school into the net of renewal.

Routine happenings over a period of several months accelerated the urgency of addressing one of the problem areas that had found its way to our agenda—that of the B and A half-grade structure and the semiannual promotion/nonpromotion regimen resulting from it. This already had stimulated intense discussion of children's individual differences and their implications not only for school organization but also for curricula and pedagogy. Although tests of various kinds were used from time to time by professors whose research projects we had approved, administering standardized achievement tests was not part of the UES culture. I asked Sterling Stott, our guidance counselor, to administer achievement tests in two classes—one from the so-called second grade and one from the fifth—and assemble the resulting data to reveal the spread as Bob Anderson and I had done in *The Nongraded Elementary School*.

The results were as anticipated—a spread of several grade levels for most children individually and, of course, for each class as a whole. As the implications dawned, teacher distress increased. One of the two who was part of the entire history of the UES, Cynthiana (who later became a strong advocate of the changes we made), was particularly upset. She was much respected by parents and colleagues, largely because of her caring and devoted attention to her first-grade children. She did not expect children to be reading when they came to her, but she did expect them to be ready and to be reading when her year with them came to a close. She viewed our data as representing a giving-in to these individual differences rather than a challenge to address them—a legitimate concern up to a point. What we had not yet gotten into was the power of good teaching and appropriate curricula to move everyone along to higher levels of performance that would not, however, result in everyone achieving at the same grade level.

At about the high point of these total faculty discussions, the work of the early childhood group with Louise Tyler and me had brought out deep concern with the kind of expectations expressed by Cynthiana. From our studies of children's apparent degrees of "fit" with the educational environment being provided, the teachers had concluded that simply promoting children into the first grade and its predetermined expectations was not good enough. Surely the teachers sending children on and those receiving them could work together toward the design of alternative placements. The teachers of the early childhood unit recommended the institution of a process toward the end of each school year during which they would share their extensive information about each child with the receiving teachers. They were frustrated, however, by the existing school structure and did not see how it might be changed so that the fit between children's characteristics and the class milieu might be improved.

I did not realize at the time how much the consequences of Peg's decision to retire would help to solve this problem. Peg had been a kindergarten teacher at the UES for many years. She informed me of her decision months in advance so that I would have plenty of time to find a suitable replacement. I was very sorry. Peg was a superb teacher and colleague; I appreciated her thoughtfulness. And then I sought out Edie, the other kindergarten teacher.

I asked her what she thought we should do about Peg's pending departure. Edie was startled by my question and quickly responded, "Why, find a first-rate teacher, of course." "That's an alternative," I replied, "but there is no mandate compelling us to fill a full-time position with just one person. We could hire two or ten and split the available salary into halves or tenths." Edie's blue eyes opened wide. "Give me a little time to think about it," she said.

She was back within a few days, bursting with enthusiasm. I had embellished my comment with the observation that, should we employ two or more part-time people, Edie would chair the team. She now wanted to split Peg's position into two, but there was a condition. The two kindergarten rooms shared side-by-side lavatories. Since each lavatory had its own door, could we open up the access corridor to provide easy passage of teachers and children from classroom to classroom? I said that we could if the wall in question was not a bearing one. When school opened in the fall, three teachers on a budget for two shared the two rooms, now partly open to each other.

During the next year, the egg-crate of age-graded, single-teacher classes simply fell apart. Readers should not conclude that I had this eventuality in mind all along. I did not. By being able to stand back as a drummer for alternatives, I was able to see the degree to which long-standing conventions of the way schools are need not and should not be. I was more sensitive than the close-to-the-scene teachers could be to opportunities for change that arise serendipitously out of some routine events.

Good teachers are a necessary condition of good schools, but the demanding nature of their work is such that someone a little removed often is the necessary catalyst for effecting changes in the restrictive deep structure of schooling. Is this a potential role and responsibility of principals? I think so, but they currently receive little preparation for such. In spite of its rhetoric of leadership, the current era of school reform offers little hope for change.

There was declining need for me on this front, given the arrival of Frances and, later, Jimmy from Englewood to teach at the UES and pursue their doctorates in UCLA's Graduate School of Education. The structural clustering of classrooms lent itself nicely to the organization of teaching teams. I was able to secure financial support for getting rid of parts of nonstructural walls; this eased staff communication and team teaching. The teacher turnover was modest, but enough to enable more splitting of full-time positions into equivalent combinations of part-time people so that, within a few years, the budgetary allocation of about twenty-two FTE (full-time equivalents) often covered as many as forty people of varying percentages of employment. Not surprisingly, most contributed, out of interest, more than was expected of them, and of course, it was not uncommon for full-time team leaders to be recruited out of the part-time workforce.

We worked deliberately toward the creation of at least three somewhat different class cultures in which to place children leaving a team cluster at the end of a given year. Characteristics of the receiving teachers ranked high as a criterion. We left open the option of a full-time teacher conducting his or her largely self-contained class of either a single- or multiple-age group of pupils. Cynthiana opted for a single-age, self-contained class before she later became an enthusiast for alternatives. After a year of teaching children in the early childhood unit, Jimmy proposed, and we approved, what we came to call a "banana group"—a class with an age spread nearly that of a one-room, six-grade school. In effect, the class's enrollment was drawn vertically from several age levels, such as among the siblings of a family, rather than horizontally from only one.

The matter of moving children upward was now no longer one of routine promotions from grade to grade. For example, when teachers of the early childhood unit met with potential receiving teachers, there were several alternatives: Cynthiana's class of six-year-olds, Debbie's class of six- and seven-year-olds, and Jimmy's class of five- to eleven-year-olds. An exceedingly fast-moving youngster who might be bored in most first-grade classes probably would be assigned to Jimmy's banana group where she would not bump her head on any graded ceiling. However, if this child was thought to require, for her social development, continued association with more age peers, the likely decision was that she would be with Debbie. As with the Englewood Project, we made no effort to change the traditional graded language to nongraded. From the parental perspective, all of the children moving up were going into the first grade. And, again, as at the Englewood School, the non-graded concepts and wording gradually crept into the culture of the UES.

The most critical questions arose as, increasingly, parents discovered that the children of other UES parents, thought to be in the same grade, were engaged with different topics or materials of learning. I asked one of our teachers who was well versed in the use of audiovisual aids in his teaching to develop a short demonstration of two children of the same age reading or attempting to read the same book—a little girl who could skim through it and a little boy who struggled with it. Indeed, his suffering was palpable. Parents suffered, too, when at one of our regular overcrowded meetings, we presented what two cameras had filmed—one focused on the faces and upper bodies of both children and the other on the printed page. Mary's voice soared without hesitation, with all the appropriate pauses and enunciation. She quickly turned to the next page. Arthur was still moving a finger hesitatingly along the fourth line, stumbling and halting over each word of two or more syllables. But it was the contortions of his body and face that so pained our audience. We no longer needed words to explain a popular expression, "Different strokes for different folks."

The discussions of teams sending and teams receiving children were no longer confined to the concluding weeks of a school year. We developed with all team clusters and individual teachers a mode of watching carefully for children appearing to fall through the cracks. All teachers coming in contact with each such child then met with Sterling Stott to share information, adopt a hypothesis of needed action, and come together weeks later to reassess and agree to continue or adopt a new course of action. If placement with a different team appeared to be a viable option or was anticipated for the following year, a teacher or teachers from this other team joined in the discussion. And placement decisions at the end of each year always involved both the sending and the receiving teachers.

This was a time-consuming process of a kind featured especially in family medicine. The payoff for learning, instruction, teachers, parents, children, and home-school relationships was enormous. I shall always remember our documentary film of Sharon. Sharon was a little girl in kindergarten who virtually recoiled on coming in contact with another child. She would not join with others in taking turns down the slide or on the playground; indeed, she cried on being encouraged to climb the short ladder to the top of the slide.

Sterling and the teacher-stewards of Sharon's group of children developed a plan and revised it over a period of two or three months. Sharon was introduced slowly and carefully into nonthreatening associations with classmates. The concluding picture of Sharon laughingly pushing and jostling others after coming down the slide hands-free caused me to wonder if she now needed some guidance in the control of aggression.

CURRICULAR FRUSTRATIONS

The journey toward giving greater attention to the individual child and providing for children's individual differences was, of course, marked by a good deal of turbulence. Faculty meetings were rarely marked by smooth transitions from dialogue about a problem to determination of a course of action to, later, evaluation of the actions taken. When we got into curricular matters, where profound changes from the traditional had been made years before and from which the UES had primarily established its considerable reputation, the going was particularly rough.

My "why" questions produced a good deal of progress in seeking reasons for the afternoon program of integrating subjects into the essentially social studies units of work, each extending over a period of several weeks. Although claims were made for including the arts and written language, it appeared to me that the attention given them was casual and incidental. I was not satisfied with the improvements in visual arts products and paragraph writing that occurred over a period of years. Most of the teachers were obviously interested and competent in the social studies, but less so in the other fields, especially the arts.

The solution sought created a problem that appears to me to be virtually endemic to elementary schools. The breakup of the standard pattern of one teacher to each salaried position enabled us to employ part-time and often short-term specialists to supplement our teaching resources. The idea was that they would join the generalists in their classrooms for purposes of both enriching the education of children and strengthening the competence of teachers in areas of their respective weaknesses.

Achieving these purposes turned out to be an uphill struggle. Most of the time, we achieved disappointing plateaus. Commonly, the specialists had little patience with both the shortcomings of their peers and what appeared to them to be a secondary role. If, for example, music was their thing, they "graciously" encouraged the regular teacher to take a break. Given the demands of teaching at the UES, it was hard to resist. The desired team teaching and curricular integration remained somewhat chimeric.

Neglect of the arts in schooling is a common complaint of both parents and teachers and is commonly blamed on district priorities. Part of the answer lies in teacher education, both preservice and inservice. One way to bring the arts into the general education of the young is through greater integration of arts specialists into the regular classroom. In so doing, specialists would build a constituency of peer support now largely lacking. What I learned about the problem helped me with it only after I had left UCLA and gone on to other endeavors.

SCALING UP

There is now a substantial literature describing sustained efforts to significantly change individual schools, much of the work supported by private philanthropy. Politically driven school reform has expectations for changing whole systems of schools, and ultimately, philanthropic foundations want to scale up what they observe to be good in innovative schools. But both groups commonly become disenchanted with the apparent difficulties and disappointing results. Improving both schools and teacher education then tends to go out of fashion for a time.

For each of several years from the mid-1960s into the early 1970s, the UES was host to more than five thousand visitors. They came by the busload or by plane, train, and carpool. Over these years, I met often with groups at the end of their day. Most were both impressed and overwhelmed by what they had observed; many had taken copious notes. Some passed off our work as what might be expected in a university-based laboratory school. The most common reaction, however, was that much of what they saw would be impossible to bring off in their home settings. I pushed hard for "why."

The answer, variously worded, almost always boiled down to the same theme: there was no infrastructure in the school and district for effecting change. "Indeed," said many, "there is no mechanism in my school even for reporting and discussing what I have experienced here. There will be some casual questions but no conversations with colleagues."

Although I visited in schools regularly, I rarely probed into their infrastructure. Nearly all conducted faculty meetings of one kind or another, but it had never dawned on me that these dealt mostly with relatively routine matters of business and management. For most, introducing the kind of discussions leading to the actions we conducted in the Englewood School and the UES would have been a significant innovation. What I was now hearing from these visitors was profoundly shocking to me and provoked a series of responses.

First, we instituted the requirement that visitors come in teams that included the school principal. This added the benefit of cutting down on the visitation schedule, which we later managed to reduce even more. Second, we decided that we needed to know more about the school contexts from which people came in order to serve them better. I secured a small grant from the Ford Foundation, and several of us went on the road to learn. Our findings provided much of the motivation for later conducting a much more comprehensive study of schooling and then of the education of educators. Third, I took special care to meet with teams of visitors from schools in southern California and to talk about their interests in effecting change and how we might help. From this activity was hatched the League of Cooperating Schools and the accompanying Study of Educational Change and School Improvement. These inquiries constitute much of the backdrop for my effort in Chapter 10 to tidy my mind somewhat regarding the untidy world of schooling.

Several of the major "whys" cluttering my mind at the time are summarized in our report on those visits to schools of more than three decades ago:

. . . why truly exciting proposals conceived and even developed by project staffs appear to lose much of their innovative character in any broad-scale attempt to implement them; why the form and not the substance of seemingly powerful proposals for change is what the schools embrace; and why the heat of educational change is so puny in comparison with the smoke.

Perhaps the most telling observation about our educational system is that there is not, below the level of intense criticism and endless recommendations for improvement, any effective structure by means of which countervailing ideas and models may be pumped in and developed to the point of becoming real alternatives. Stated conversely, the system is geared to self-preservation.[11]

What the later tidying of the mind confirmed for me is the hopelessness and incredible cost in human time and dollars of large-scale efforts to dot the landscape with schools made excellent by precooked reforms, whether mandated or parachuted in from their origins. For schools to become good, the entire culture of each must be renewed through an intensive process of inquiry. The challenge is how to make this uncommon process common—in other words, how to scale it up without flattening it out to the near level of the conventional.

Chapter 10

Nourishing Educational Belief

It is our customary and unexamined way of thinking about education, our subliminal assumptions, that must be put in question, if significant modifications of practice are to ensue.

DAVID SOLWAY[1]

There is no sure way of knowing what thoughts and whorls of memory one will carry into a new place. New places bring new thoughts and stir old, renewing and replacing some. Los Angeles is a very different place from Chicago. We were to enjoy its robust ambience for a quarter of a century.

LEARNING FROM EXPERIENCES

I had settled into the academic life of UCLA thirty-four years after running away from my first encounter with a place called school that was named after a star. Now here I was at a school that was soon to shine brightly in the terrestrial firmament of higher education. I came with mental space crowded with hypotheses gleaned from years of romances with the so-called lower schools that were approaching the level of theories and beliefs. Schools of the higher learning and their connection to the lower were far more theoretical, in the conventional sense of that word. Little did I realize how much the former would be strengthened and the latter shaped during the years the Golden State would be our home. The renewing ecology of my educational belief increasingly served as a kind of filter for retaining, rejecting, or recycling the buzzing, ubiquitous teaching of my daily surround.

I look back in awe and wonderment at the cacophony of this teaching that was to bombard my mind over those years. Refinement in the process of filtering provided a guiding credo for assessing both the familiar and the unfamiliar in the existing regularities and systemics of schooling and repeated proposals for change that had remained remarkably the same over the preceding thirty-four years and were intensely revisited over the succeeding twenty-five. Had Rip Van Winkle been an "education governor" and awakened circa 1965, after his legendary nap, he might well have dusted off his earlier platform and campaigned again on the same agenda of school reform. And, of course, he might well have dozed off again to awaken today and been right at home in repeating his message.

Deeply embedded in my mind is the realization that today's educational problems and issues are much the same as they were when I entered the first grade and, thirteen years later, began teaching in a one-room school. And the largely politically driven remedies have been recycled during reform eras of the last fifty of these years. Ironically, the proposals for change based on reflective experience and inquiry that have surfaced during these years—many of them endorsing oft-confirmed educational principles—have been largely ignored.

I know these things because I have experienced and inquired into them not only during these years but also during the many more that have transpired since. They have nurtured educational belief that now guides my thinking regarding good educational work. I am reminded of environmental principles and concepts honed by those who work the soil and tend to the crops. Long intimacy with the phenomena informs their opinions, as Wendell Berry so eloquently claims for his views on our responsibility to the land: He now walks hand in hand with his grandson over the land he once walked with his grandfather. "We are part of a long procession, five generations of which I have seen, issuing out of generations lost to memory, going back, for all I know, across previous landscapes and the whole history of farming."[2]

The cognitive psychologist Howard Gardner makes similar claims for the groups of teachers who hone the practices of the educational institutions to which he would comfortably send his toddler, elementary school child, high schooler, or college-age offspring. He then goes on to propose that every researcher wishing to explore the field of education be required to immerse herself or himself in the work of educational institutions and practitioners—in effect, the culture of schools and teaching.[3]

Reflecting on this perspective in the misguided era of school reform that marks the beginning of the twenty-first century, I am shocked and pained by the nonsensical policy stances of our present federal department of education: "Scientific research"—and only scientific research—is to be the authorizing criterion in judging educational practice and proposals for change. The reflective experience of practitioners, the documented observations of scholars, the investigative reporting of journalists, and the memories and case studies of an array of inquirers are to be ignored. Such nonsense! Apply this same criterion to the fields of medicine, law, engineering, oceanography, and the space sciences, and this house of cards will quickly come tumbling down.

The perspective I have endeavored to sustain throughout the foregoing years is that of romantic engagement with the culture of my daily work—that work including years of required attendance at school. The meanings of these engagements were relatively easy to unravel when—as pupil and teacher—I was confined to a single, rather consistent culture. But when the conduct of daily work slides over into a second and perhaps even a third culture and these, conceivably, are not in harmony, the probability of filtering the messages into a guiding ecology of educational belief is at risk, as are the prospects of engaging romances.[4]

Thoughts pertaining to my new work that I knew had come with me had to do with the quite different cultures of our elementary and secondary schools and our institutions of higher education, and the missing connections between the two. There was much less in my mind about relationships to their social and political context. Nonetheless, I carried with me from Atlanta and Chicago to Los Angeles seeds that soon would be nourished.

These seeds came from two sets of experiences. One was part of our daily lives—racial tensions and their intensification after the Supreme Court *Brown* decision of 1954. With two children to raise, they took on increased significance. We were acutely aware of the problems that the outspoken daughter of an even more outspoken colleague (members of a family recently arrived from Montana) was having with her peers in the high school our children would probably attend. But we thought we could handle whatever might lie ahead. Then, an episode close to my professional interests, mentioned in Chapter 9, clinched our difficult decision to leave Atlanta and the lifelong friends we had made there.

I have referred only briefly to our encounters with racial prejudice and intolerance in both the North and the South. In the North, it was sharply evident in the segregated zones of housing. In the South, prior to the Supreme Court decision of 1954, segregation in physical space was a given; interpersonal prejudice was commonly wrapped in subtlety. On probing into my institutional experiences in classrooms and our social experiences beyond, another manuscript began to emerge that complicated the themes of this one, and so I backed off. But my mind began to reserve space for thoughts about humankind, what it means to be human, and how to make the world a home for everyone, whatever their color, language, religion, cultural habits, or lifestyles.

We are all one people, Len and I believed, and the broadening of experience from Canada to the North and South of the United States strengthened this belief. There were, when we came to California, experiences behind us and experiences to come that jarred but strengthened this belief. Len never will forget the day in Atlanta when she was rudely ordered out of a public carrier for protesting the driver's putting a black man off the bus "because he smelled." She had suggested that the man probably did not have a place to wash. When we questioned differing views on race, we often were bluntly told that we simply didn't understand. When we replied to the question, "And what church do you belong to?" the subject was quickly changed. When professional acquaintances of friendly demeanor asked what college I had attended and I replied, "Correspondence courses and summer school at the University of British Columbia and a year of residence at the University of Chicago," their eyes glazed over in bewilderment. That was a question I enjoyed. What often causes us to reflect in wonderment is how two people who had grown up in such innocence were so immune to contrary beliefs and the informal teaching that sought to colonize our minds.[5]

What I chopped out of Chapter 9 and then, later, restored in a shorter version was a sequence of experiences that prepared me, I believe, for a later sequence that profoundly broadened my perception of the central mission of education in schools of all levels. A key episode is that of my plan, died aborning, to create a center of education, health, and human services in Atlanta's lovely Fernbank Forest. Troubled then by this nonevent, I am grateful for it now. Asked sometimes in interviews to recall some of the most fortuitous events or decisions in my life, the answer has been "the roads not taken."

Up to the Fernbank-related experiences, almost the whole of my educational attention focused on the commonplaces of learning, teaching, and learning-teaching relationships. These are, of course, central and must be ever kept in close range. But the mission and necessary conditions of the educational journey must be clear. John Steinbeck, in *East of Eden*, advised us to take a long look at where we are going and then to watch our feet, lest we stumble. The long look for me grew in part out of my serendipitous involvement in Chicago with the Council for the Study of Mankind during the year before we headed west.

It was, I think, *The Nongraded Elementary School* that brought Gerhard Hirschfeld to my office door. He had founded and brought together in the council a small group of leading scholars from such University of Chicago departments as anthropology, history, philosophy, and sociology, to which were invited from time to time equally visible scholars located elsewhere. Since some of these were women, it is rather strange that the key word in the council's name was not changed to "Humankind." I needed no persuasion to join the group. Our conversations elevated the concept of humankind from a secondary to a primary concern and sought its myriad meanings, implications, and relationships to concepts such as democracy, environment, and religion that usually take precedence.

While Gerhard was growing up in Berlin, his motivation for his later creation grew out of his literary encounters covering more than five thousand years of human struggle and thought. Then, World War I swept away his placid world, severely testing his dreams and ideals. Badly shaken by the experience of being witness to the massacre and his and his mother's grief over losing his two brothers, he determined to work for the abolition of war. When he and I came together, the conversations of council members were honing a comprehensive view of the conditions necessary to worldwide human well-being.

Once settled in Malibu, we were startled and pleased to learn that the Hirschfelds, too, had moved and were now our near neighbors in Santa Monica. Gerhard and I—he as founder and I as member and then chairman of the Council—managed its affairs for more than a decade. His charisma and passion took us only part way to securing the financial resources necessary for a robust program. When he and his wife, both aging, found it necessary to be with family members on the East Coast, we lost the Council's driving spirit. But not before producing several books that quietly added to the documented human story that had captured Gerhard's imagination in the first place. There was little readiness then and, it appears, little now for the message that must be converted into routine daily behavior if the world and its people are to survive the terrorizing and destruction of human beings and their habitat that history tells us are virtually a chronic malaise.

What have the immediately foregoing paragraphs to do with education and schooling? A very great deal; some would say "everything." What Gerhard Hirschfeld and members of the Council taught me and what the subsequent odyssey of educational inquiry and change added continues to renew educational belief that guides me daily.

THE CONTINUING ODYSSEY
OF EDUCATIONAL CHANGE

In retrospect, what I now realize was beginning to become clear to me by the time of our coming to California are the power and the necessity of renewal in the healthy continuity of individuals, institutions, and the social, political, and natural order in the well-being of humankind and planet earth. Renewal requires a sense of moral identity that consciously guides individual and collective transcendence from narcissism through tribalism to much broader intellectual, spiritual, and behavioral compass. Few of us make the journey without hurting someone or damaging something along the way. There is no beckoning goal of excellence or perfection to be attained even as one acquires pieces of parchment attesting to such along the journey. Helping the young to sense this moral identity and to engage in its strengthening through lifelong renewal is what makes teaching a moral endeavor, whether in home, school, or marketplace.

RENEWAL AT THE UES REVISITED

I had come to the UES with a good deal of experience regarding existing school practices that misaligned with knowledge of human cognition and development and both pupil and institutional renewal, as well as experience with nonexisting recommended practices that aligned. But I also came with awareness that the latter had to make enough sense to teachers and parents to transcend their commitment to what existed inside their school and, perhaps, long-established regularities in schools beyond.

One of my beliefs that was enormously strengthened is that educational change is not something to be dropped from a hovering helicopter, carted in during the dark of night, or imposed by administrative or imperial edict. These are the impositions of "reform," which I had seen demonstrated at Biscoq, that had a low success record in reducing recidivism. Wanting to change generates renewal. What then transpires is heavily dependent on the nature of the moral context. It is here that the role of the educator is vital. Since education is a neutral concept, the moral must be built into it.

Making changes similar to those effected in the Englewood School proved not to be the near impossibility predicted by several colleagues at the University of Chicago. There we faced a major problem of uninterest. Here, we had to deal with intense interest accompanied by the often-zealous belief that the UES was near perfection. But there was

also that nagging parental belief that traditional direct teaching pro-
duces academic results superior to the more nondirective teaching that
prevailed. A little more attention to rigor would help. We succeeded in
explaining and demonstrating how aligning pupil progress with learnings for which they were ready made more sense than attempting to
align it with the fiction of grade levels. The appointment of Madeline
Hunter as principal was timely.

Madeline had come on board a year after my arrival, while on a
leave-of-absence from a neighboring school district, to work on her
doctorate at UCLA. Drawing from behavioral psychology, her dissertation put forward an instructional model that attracted over later years
widespread attention. At the time of her coming to the UES, we had
not found in our first search a candidate for the principalship who met
our criteria. Madeline clearly was the best qualified among those we
considered in the second round of the search.

The UES position provided her with both a ready laboratory for testing and refining her model and a vehicle for extending its use beyond. She
fitted nicely into the school's renewing mode and added an important
component to our repertoire of educational exhibits and services. The
summer workshops that Madeline and I conducted together challenged
much of the existing apparatus of schooling and offered the children's
summer school as evidence of attainable alternatives.

Inside our school, we focused particularly on the challenge of fusing
theory and practice as a way of thinking and acting toward a unified
whole. I have met few educators equal to Madeline in conjuring up
word images that conveyed this necessary fusion. Her commanding
presence and ability to articulate this work with parents as well as teachers enabled us to make swift passage without crashing on the rocks that
so often block progress. The teachers, too, became increasingly adept
at both exhibiting and explaining what they were about. There were
many parallels here with the Englewood experiences in my evolving
ecology of educational belief.

Although only half of my time was budgeted to the UES, I had
decided at the beginning to serve for a while as much as possible in a
dual role of both director and principal. I had redefined the role of act-

ing principal Margaret Mathews to take full advantage of her gracious manner and long history with the school, emphasizing her visibility and availability, especially when I was in Moore Hall—the home of the School of Education—or elsewhere. Madeline's coming made it possible for me to back off quite a bit, especially in staff development, which I consider to be significantly in a principal's domain. I intensified attention to school culture, that powerful ubiquitous teacher to which I have implicitly and explicitly paid homage throughout this volume.

The faculty had grown accustomed to my seemingly casual reference to an idea my mind had been playing with, a practice I had seen or heard about, a book I had read—usually selected because of a concern, frustration, or need earlier expressed by a teacher. Sometimes the book was in my hand and headed for the library, or already there. Our professional collection was in the making. I was gratified by the frequency with which ideas were picked up, books read, and conversations kindled. I introduced the work of the Council for the Study of Mankind, invited Gerhard in to discuss it, and in 1964 brought in the Council's book published that year, *Education and the Idea of Mankind*, edited by Harvard philosopher Robert Ulich.[6]

The idea caught. It contributed to our decision to keep enrollment of UCLA faculty children to no more than 10 percent and to cease guaranteeing admission to siblings (a decision that triggered the necessity of bringing Chancellor Charles Young into the ensuing controversy) in order to increase enrollment diversity. Our discussions about there being only one people in the world and only one human conversation, with rich nuances of different languages, religions, colors, and cultures drew our attention to the school's curriculum. What were the children learning from the units on American native cultures and the United Nations they studied? What concepts and behaviors were they carrying home and into their daily lives?

Such questions brought on a summer experiment preceded by a period of intensive inquiry, both supported by a modest grant from the Ford Foundation. The first step was to extract educational implications of ideas and concepts about humankind from the works of the council. The second was to prepare a segment of curriculum for children. The third was to teach from a humankind perspective both a group of elementary school children and, paralleling this, a group of teachers. All three steps proved to be extraordinarily difficult, exceeding in magnitude even our own considerable trepidations about them.[7]

The experiences with the children supported what should be obvious: Moving talk of human virtue to the daily reality of interpersonal relationships is very difficult. It is folly to believe that high test scores on academics predict their transfer into behavior. Nonetheless, this belief appears to be the fantasy of many policymakers. Our summer school class of fourteen boys and ten girls voiced a high level of respect for human diversity in race, religion, and cultural norms. But this verbalization took on the characteristics of veneer during the first of several sessions in which they shared space, food, play, and academic learning with a group of all-minority children from a school in a low-income section of Los Angeles. They shared their mental processing of this, and if the shock and shame they expressed were supported in their home environments and beyond, perhaps some of their virtuous expressions of belief carried over into behavior then and later.

Perhaps the most significant outcome was the degree to which it turned teachers' attention to both the curricular sequences and the accompanying pedagogy that had been assumed to connect with the knowledge and attributes required for effective citizenship in a democratic society. We became more conscious, too, of the need to be ever-alert to our own functioning as colleagues and moral stewards of our school. There was in the ethos of our outward look toward school practices a hint of missionary zeal that, I feared, could lead to leaving the home gardens less well attended.

THE PERILS OF SCALING UP

The open-ended nature of the momentous Elementary and Secondary Education Act (ESEA) of 1965 invited and challenged educators to innovate. In the conference of its launching, Vice President Hubert Humphrey passionately and brilliantly tied education to the elimination of poverty, urban decay, crime and violence, illiteracy, and even war among nations and placed schools and universities in the drivers' seats. His speech was not about what schools should and must do for the nation but about what the nation should do for its schools so that they would have the capacity to serve the common good.

Educators nationwide took up the challenge. Thousands streamed to our UES classrooms for ideas. The worries I had on first coming began to creep back into my mind. Were we losing the momentum of renewal in part because of an excess of telling and demonstrating? This good little school had stalled on a plateau before. I was not about to let complacency with earlier accomplishments become the norm once more.

I was worried, too, about what these visitors took away in their heads and what they did with it back home. Together in our leadership roles, Madeline and I managed to maintain a balance between what visitors tended to focus on as form (teaching) and what they tended to ignore as ground (cultural context). But, as I have noted, what they were taking away was the former, to school gardens ill prepared for its nurturance. Many came back for more with the expectation, apparently, that additional seeds would increase the probability of some sprouting. Increasingly, they wanted us to deliver the sprouts directly to their own gardens.

It was this major difference in the ways our ecologies of educational belief filtered our respective experiences that led Madeline and me down quite different paths in the educational world beyond the UES. For her, the difficulty visitors experienced in doing back in their home schools what they saw at the UES was a teaching and learning problem. They needed to be taught to know and to do. For me, it was primarily a contextual problem that, in turn, called for a differing theory of pedagogy. The culture of the visitors' home schools massaged longstanding conventional practices that resisted entry of the new. The culture of each had to be prepared for new beliefs and practices to enter and flourish.

Madeline and the UES teachers she trained went on the road to teach others the theory and practice of a rigorous pedagogy. Colleagues and I set out to learn more about the resistance of school cultures to change and to seek their renewal. We did not disagree over the importance of addressing both pedagogy and context, but our entries into and subsequent involvement in the educational change process were quite different. Once again, an unexpected opportunity opened paths to assessing beliefs that had been strengthening in my mind.

During the year of congressional passage of the ESEA, two officers of the Charles F. Kettering Foundation came calling. We talked for hours. They were seeking to design a bold and constructive nationwide school improvement initiative. Their efforts over a period of several months shaped creation of the Institute for Development of Educational Activities (|I|D|E|A|) as the education arm of the foundation.

Subsequent agreements between the vice president of the foundation and the vice-chancellor of UCLA resulted in my directing the research division of |I|D|E|A|, one of three divisions in three different locations charged with responsibility for carrying out the institute's mission.[8] Although this research arm was to be conveniently located in offices adjacent to the UCLA campus, the addition of responsibility complicated my hybrid educational career. It became even more complicated when the deanship of the university's Graduate School of Education was added a couple of years later.

The Kettering Foundation bought into the concept of the League of Cooperating Schools that colleagues and I were in the process of creating and provided the money not only for its development, but also for the study accompanying it that came to be known as the Study of Educational Change and School Improvement (SECSI). Virgil Howes, the first person I employed for the work to come, and I cobbled the league together out of conversations with superintendents (and often their boards of trustees) over a period extending from May 1965 to January 1966. The document of agreement called for each district to join with the other seventeen participating districts in selecting one elementary school for membership in the proposed league network. The UES would be the representative school from UCLA. District rules appearing to block progress would be waived as thought necessary and appropriate. The eighteen schools were spread out in terrain stretching from San Diego to Santa Barbara and east to San Bernardino and Riverside.

The serendipitous entry of the Kettering Foundation into our plans and subsequent work saved me from what otherwise would have been an embarrassing series of nonevents and perhaps disasters. In spite of my awareness that cultural renewal is not a built-in characteristic of schooling and that serious collaboration with schools does not come comfortably into the ecosystem of higher education, I had far too rosily romantic expectations for the fruition of both in the league. Foundation money made it possible to recruit a dozen graduate assistants experienced in schooling, given their successful admission to studies at UCLA. Without them and the several full-time staff members who joined us, I would have been left trying to prop up eighteen schools in a near-solo stewardship of educational renewal. With this team, I came face-to-face with the realization that scaling up from one school to more necessitates developing in each school processes comparable to, but individually varying from, those of the Englewood and UES initiatives.

Success with these processes of cultural renewal requires, in turn, supportive conditions similar to, but rarely identical with, those accompanying these two initiatives. The intent and the conditions for this renewal seldom accompany the state, federal, or philanthropic dollars that bring initial enthusiasm to those seeking to effect school change. And therein lies a considerable part of the explanation for failed "reform" eras.

Even with the financial and human resources we had, the paths to change were bumpy. We counted primarily on the graduate assistants, all experienced teachers and administrators, for technical support to the schools and to be their alternative drummers and critical friends—but soon found that most of them were inexperienced in nondirective, helping roles. This intended function was further compounded by the expressed desire of many in the league schools to be told what to do—to be given answers to their problems. There was considerable ambiguity and variation in what was desired, however, for which we coined the descriptive sentence, "Tell *us* what to do, but don't tell *me* what to do."

We focused a good deal on the role of the eighteen principals who, viewing their schools as having been chosen and therefore to be already good, began with enthusiasm and expectations for great things about to happen. Actually, we had stressed with the superintendents not to select their schools of highest reputations; we sought and succeeded in putting together a quite diverse sample. There was little interest on the part of the principals in what was going on at the UES. They did not wish to replicate "models." But we soon discovered that only a couple of them ever led their faculties in serious discussions of either educational ideas or domains of needed change in their school practices. Most had little idea of how to carry on faculty meetings for any matters other than routine business. Several tried very hard to get the support persons from our staff to conduct faculty meetings during their visits.

We tackled this critical leadership problem in two ways. We were fortunate in having in our corps of mostly part-time personnel competent researchers from several relevant fields. At that time, universities rarely employed the spouses of professorial appointees; some had policies against it. We were able to offer interesting work, mostly to women who had accompanied their husbands to Los Angeles. We brought together a group of people qualified to be faculty members in almost any college or university. Observing what was happening and not happening in league schools, we came up with a problem-solving sequence for faculty groups that proved to be attractive and productive: *dialogue* about the problems or issues, *decisions* regarding courses of action, subsequent *action*, followed by *evaluation* of the entire process (DDAE). The result might be the establishment of a new school policy or practice or a decision to revisit the problem and repeat the sequence.

Second, we firmed up a schedule of regular meetings of all the principals for the first Monday of each month from October through May of each year that first took place in our conference room and later moved from school to school. The agenda for each meeting was set in advance. Depending on the topics scheduled and the schedule of their graduate classes, several of our school-connected personnel participated. Even though I had become dean of the Graduate School of Education by the time this procedure was initiated, I managed to be part of nearly all of these sessions throughout the six-year history of the league as an organized entity.

This combination of reflective experience and accompanying systematic research produced some interesting findings regarding our sample of schools, strengthened some of the hypotheses that had stimulated formation of the league in the first place, and produced some insights into schooling that provoked further inquiry. For me, the total array of experiences joined with others of this period of time in creating a kind of mental watershed from which flowed streams of thought too enticing to ignore.

The DDAE cycle may appear to be linear and straightforward, but in practice, it is not. The major difficulties arose out of the first step: dialogue to the point of reaching a "working" consensus. For total staff meetings, the principals were expected to take the lead. Most had difficulty sensing when a general agreement on the problem had been reached. At this point, they were expected to so declare, note the presence still of any disagreement, and then seek agreement on a course of action, making clear that the results would not be embedded in concrete but were always open to future reconsideration. Moving forward on the basis of general rather than complete agreement was troubling to some principals and, of course, those teachers who were not yet convinced. On the other hand, holding off on declaring a working consensus before the problem had been thoroughly discussed was difficult for some, particularly principals accustomed to making important decisions without consultation. These problems were far less present in the discussions of small groups of teachers subsequently engaged in moving forward with implementation of total staff decisions.

A significant lesson for researchers emerged from our inquiry into the DDAE process: Do not trust the validity of self-assessments. School faculties that went through the process superficially, without really identifying and tangling with the deep-seated issues of their schools, tended to rate themselves higher for accomplishment than did those that courageously tackled longstanding regularities likely to be controversial. In later work, with school-university partnerships, our close observations revealed that those most advanced tended to see much more to do and to rate themselves lower than faculties more casually engaged.

One of our most satisfying findings was the extent to which the ongoing work broke down the daily isolation of teachers from one another to which many researchers have referred—isolation that contributes to the longevity of anachronistic whole-school practices. It is interesting to note that, in their enthusiasm for working together on matters of mutual interest, some groups of teachers got ahead of the place where principals felt comfortable with change so that these designated leaders felt threatened in their leadership roles. I have sometimes wondered if the principals would have felt more secure if we had given more attention in the early years to ensuring the support of their districts' superintendents. We were so engaged early on with stimulating the renewal process in each school that we somewhat neglected the relationship with superintendents established in creating the league initially.

One of the most gratifying findings in our research was the significant improvement in the daily attendance at their schools of both teachers and pupils. The Monday and Friday morning calls of teachers who were claiming illness fell off markedly. Our evaluation also revealed growth in professional self-awareness: increased interest in their daily work, satisfaction in being teachers, and increased efforts to improve. The documentary film of the whole included interviews with teachers regarding what was significant in their experiences in the league. At the head of the list was their sense of our knowing what they were doing and supporting them in the daily work. This was something they had missed most in their careers: evidence of such knowing, caring, and support in their district contexts.

A very interesting phenomenon emerged early on. Some parents found creative ways to claim residence (without moving) in areas where a league school existed to secure eligibility for their children to attend. Apparently, the word got out that some interesting things were going on there, perhaps from local newspapers. I believe that identification of UCLA with the sought-after school contributed to the interest. Subsequently, I used the "parental satisfaction" criterion on visiting a league school to determine whether I would be comfortable sending our children there. In intensive visits to all eighteen schools toward the end of the fourth year of our initiative, I concluded that I would be uncomfortable with only one.

Our research findings, hypotheses, puzzlements, and recommendations were reported in a clutch of books and papers published in the mid-1970s.[9] The work provided a large part of the conceptual underpinnings of the nationwide school improvement program of |I|D|E|A| known as Individually Guided Education (IGE) that supported thousands of principals and teachers seeking to improve teaching and learning in their schools. This work began to fade when the |I|D|E|A| role as alternative drummer and critical friend was withdrawn in order to free up resources for other endeavors of the Kettering Foundation. There is now plenty of evidence supporting the hypothesis that continuation, not necessarily as the driving force, of the external supportive role that initially accompanied productive school renewal must be to some degree sustained in order to lessen the chances of a relentless downward spiral of decay.

INSIDE AND OUTSIDE OF SCHOOLS

The preceding nine chapters address primarily circumstances in which I was very much involved. I was part of or close to the places where the romances of teaching and learning inside of schools unfold. The forces outside of schools that influence these romances were seldom the stuff of sustained conversation with colleagues.

Purposeful teaching and its management in educational institutions is a human-intensive enterprise. There is little time for educators to think about the larger social and political context of their work. Colleagues and I, now associated with many educators in schools and colleges across the country and in our leadership program sessions back home in Seattle, are aware of how eager they are to come together to discuss both common interests and experiences and the ubiquitous influences of this cultural surround.

When the complexities of learning and teaching inside of schools are juxtaposed with this array of influences on the outside—especially in eras of "reform"—there commonly appears to be a formidable disconnect. It is as though the diverse panoply of local schools scattered across the land and the nation's system of schooling were two different enterprises. The former is a highly personal, social, and essentially moral human endeavor experienced and remembered by almost everyone as "school." The latter is the machine that supposedly serves the local cottage industries—a machine that needs fixing and money even after many people see personal need for it declining. No wonder that polls consistently show far more public support for the local school than for schooling.

The purpose of the local school is to provide all the young with the education not provided elsewhere in the cultural context. The purpose of schooling is to support all the local schools in this endeavor. When the schooling machine takes over the purpose of the local school—as increasingly it has done in recent years—this democracy and its citizens are headed toward deep trouble. The public expectation and visions of public schools accessible to everyone in large measure created the special phase of being human that we refer to as childhood. Turn schooling into a well-oiled machine tool for fashioning children according to visions of economically productive adulthood, and we will lose both childhood and the sense of a public that our local schools sustain.

In the rest of this chapter and the two that follow, I endeavor to add to my narrative of schools on the inside, or close to it, more about the forces influencing schooling from the outside. I also endeavor to address some of the resulting influence of the schooling enterprise on local schools and the people connected to them.

This places a burden on my writing as well as on your reading. Trying to tell a story from the dual perspectives of being part of it while also trying to film, so to speak, concurrent events in the larger context is not easy. The play *I Am a Camera*, from which the later musical *Cabaret* was derived, comes to mind. The brilliant actress Julie Harris played the part of the American expatriate, caught up in the context of Germany's Third Reich in the mid-1930s. She endeavored to square the ongoing commonalities of her daily life in Berlin with the nightly context of the windows of the Jewish shopkeepers' premises being smashed.

The writer F. Scott Fitzgerald apparently struggled with the impossibility of being part of the romance—for instance, to be in the ballroom, dancing—while looking in on the romantic scene through a window. As an adolescent, I thought there was nothing more romantic than a canoe passing across the moon's light on the water. But I realized that, being in the canoe, I would no longer be experiencing what I had seen from the beach.

The way the schooling context is changing currently, the chances of having romances with schools during childhood and looking back on them nostalgically in adulthood appear to me to be declining. I look at some of the roots of this decline in what follows while trying still to recount aspects of my personal odyssey. Unfortunately, the romantic side of my life's work becomes more muted in the process.

SCHOOLING'S FALL FROM GRACE

Events of just one week in early April 1968 still pass through my mind like reruns of a memorable movie. I was, during that period of my life, going to Hamburg, Germany, a couple of times each year as the U.S. representative, appointed by our Department of State, on the board of directors of the UNESCO Institute of Education.

I left Los Angeles on Sunday, March 31, on the overnight flight to London where I would pick up my connection the following morning. The captain was not playing out an April Fool's joke when he woke us up at 5:00 a.m. He apologized for the early awakening but thought we would want to know that President Johnson had just announced his decision not to run for a second term. He was too weary and depressed by continuation of the Vietnam War. Returning to the Los Angeles airport on Friday afternoon, I turned the key in my car, and the radio came on almost simultaneously with the start of the engine. Martin Luther King had been assassinated the evening before.

The nation was being wrenched from within and without. Education and schooling always were close to the surface of public interest during the second half of the twentieth century. And criticism was often in fashion. But these characteristics quickly get pushed aside when epochal events and critical issues threaten the norms of daily life, whatever they might be. War and racial tensions are two of these. They and a couple more ended what I still consider to be the schooling decade and contributed to the decline of public schooling that followed and continued.

My dozen or more visits, each of several days, to the clean and trim city of Hamburg brought home to me the degree to which war is not something declared, ended, and then finished. Nor can the tragedies be measured solely by the killing of soldiers and the economic cost of atrocities. The institute was one of several post–World War II enterprises supported, I believe, in part by private philanthropy to atone for atrocities of the Nazi regime. My days in Hamburg brought home to me sharply, each morning, atrocities committed by the other side.

I usually walked the mile or so to the home of the institute—outward from the business center. Coming toward me each morning from the clean and shining commuter trains were the conservatively well-dressed and well-groomed men and women hurrying to their white-collar jobs. I always was struck by their unsmiling faces, the near absence of laughter, and the occasional muted greetings.

I could think of only one explanation. Hamburg had been handsomely rebuilt since it was systematically bombarded in six huge air raids, four British and two American, between July 24 and August 3, 1943. There probably were few people among the many coming toward me whose mental spaces were not still partially filled by the lasting horrors of those nights when so many of their brothers, sisters, relatives, and friends perished in horrible deaths. About forty thousand people, nearly all civilians, perished in the firestorms. You might want to skip the next paragraph—the report of Anne-Lies Schmidt, who found the bodies of her parents and saw what had happened to others.

> Women and children were so charred as to be unrecognizable; those that had died through lack of oxygen were half charred and recognizable. Their brains tumbled from their burst temples and their insides from the soft parts under their ribs. How terribly these people must have died. The smallest children lay like fried eels on the pavement.[10]

During the first two years of the 1960s, I had spent a considerable amount of time in visits to New York as a member of James B. Conant's team studying teacher education in the United States. Each morning, I took the same route from east to west across the center of Manhattan to offices rented for the time of the project. I was startled early on to meet, coming toward me, people whose faces I now recognized. In that teeming city! Soon, we were greeting one another cheerily, sometimes stopping for brief conversations. The overall tone of these morning encounters contrasted sharply with those of early morning Hamburg. Later, this tone tilted for a time after two airplanes sliced into the twin towers of the World Trade Center on September 11, 2001. The horrors of that morning always will be in the minds of those closest to the tragedy and its victims. For most of us who grew up in Canada or the United States, war has been a far-off military engagement that affects the lives of those most closely associated with it and variously disrupts our daily routines. At the close of the twentieth century, however, the century of unprecedented *scientific* progress, a third of the world's 193 nations were embroiled in conflict.

The dangerous inequalities of schooling between suburbs and inner cities in the United States, particularly those with heavy concentrations of minority families, had been documented years before the much-respected Conant portrayed them as "social dynamite" in his *Slums and Suburbs*, published in 1961. Getting rid of the slums and these inequalities was central to Lyndon B. Johnson's Great Society agenda, addressed by Congress in 1965. Getting better teachers and more educational resources into poverty-area schools was a major part of the proposed strategy. Fostering more integrated school populations was another. But the Coleman Report that startled the president the following year did not tip public support in the intended direction.[11]

James Coleman later softened his devastating conclusion: What children bring to school from their homes and encounter there from other homes, not teachers and their practices, is what contributes most to their academic attainments. Needless to say, this was a downer for educators. What caught public attention was not the revealed need for the conditions of families in poverty to be improved but the possible danger to the education of children from advantaged homes in increasing the percentage of children from disadvantaged homes in their classrooms. The cause of integration received a devastating blow. The social dynamite perceived by Conant was not defused. The potential for making all our public schools commonly good—a potential that had fired the enthusiasm of many educators earlier in the decade—withered. And with it withered the public purpose of schooling.

THE SCHOOLING DECADE

At about the time of my never-to-be-forgotten trip to Hamburg during the first week of April 1968, colleagues and I were a couple of years into the League of Cooperating Schools initiative and its accompanying study. Also, I was writing a piece on contemporary education and schooling for *The Great Ideas Today*, an annual publication of Encyclopaedia Britannica, Inc. In it, I described not only the sweeping attempts nationwide to redesign curricula in all the school subjects—notably and not surprisingly in mathematics and science—but also the efforts, particularly in the big cities, to lessen the inequalities in school-based educational opportunities.

Just a few sentences from this writing juxtapose the scope of the attempted penetration into established practices in that era against the narrow rigidity of the later one that became politically correct early in the present century:

> It was a time of innovation. The programs of local parent-teacher associations featured topics such as nongrading, team teaching, and individualizing instruction. Primary-age children talked glibly of "sets" and "the commutative law." Parents became uneasy when structural English began to replace the age-old grammar they had known. High-school students in Nevada followed a weekly timetable determined by a computer in Palo Alto, California. Elementary-school pupils in Mississippi spent part of their mathematics lessons responding to computer terminals controlled by a computer and instructional staff at Stanford University. The egg-crate school, in at least a few places, began to yield to the concept of malleable, flexible space which could be adapted to the needs of teachers and students.

. . . these changes were not general. But they were and are relatively well known and discussed by both educators and well-informed laymen. Today, it is fair to say, every major city in the United States and most of the outlying schools are trying non-grading, team teaching, flexible scheduling, programmed or computerized instruction, and interesting first departures in school building design. And, of course, new instructional materials are carrying the so-called curriculum-reform movement into most of the schools of the nation. Unfortunately, limited understanding and clumsy implementation often have blunted the thrust of recent educational reform.

But note that last sentence. We see here the common cycle of enthusiasm engendered, ideas introduced, dialogue stimulated, support not sufficient and sustained, and the beginnings of decay I describe in the concluding sentence of the opening paragraph of that essay.

For the United States the years from 1957 to 1967 constituted the Education Decade. There may be education decades again, but it is unlikely that there will be another quite like this one. It began with Sputnik and the charge to education to win the cold war. It ended with a hot war and the growing realization that education is a long-term answer to mankind's problems and must not be confused with social engineering. The danger now is that we are becoming disillusioned with education, without realizing that we are only beginning to try it.[12]

CONTINUING AFFECTION FOR THE LOCAL SCHOOLS?

Policies for local settings of widely varying circumstances determined in far-off places by people whose opinions are not tempered by long-term personal experiences and relevant knowledge tend to suffer from inflated expectations and inadequate, often misguided, strategies. The latter presage failure; the former breed disillusionment. When policies also are tied to an instrumental role in the nation's needs, as is usually the case with politically driven reform of the schooling enterprise, the compassionate attention upon which the local school depends weakens. Discontent is compounded.

While I was writing the piece for *The Great Ideas Today*, my embryonic worries about the future of public education were accelerated by the sudden demise of an enterprise of great promise. I was chairing a commission charged with designing a national center for developing educational programs for all our preschool children. The assistant education commissioner responsible for launching this initiative urged me to come to Washington for a year to get it off the ground before then moving to the chosen site where I would direct its functioning. A few months later, another official brought to me the news that the initial $30 million budgeted for this enterprise had been transferred to the war chest. We would not have made the recommended family moves, but this venture was now off the federal agenda.

The fallout in subsequent years was much more devastating than even the rapid decline in support for strengthening public education might suggest. Yet, the nature and powerful impact of the sea change in public attitudes toward our system of schooling—not the local school—was largely obscured by the rush to blame it for not doing both what it is capable of doing and what it cannot do. The ever-insightful Robert M. Hutchins saw beyond what is more scary for democracy than shortcomings in schools, which, with caring and support, might readily be remedied. In 1972, pondering schooling's sudden fall from grace, he wondered what had happened to the institution that so recently had been "the foundation of our freedom, the guarantee of our future, the cause of our prosperity and power, the bright and shining beacon . . . the source of our enlightenment, the public school."[13] Although Hutchins was blessed with a touch of protective cynicism, I doubt it was sufficient to lead him to believe that the cloud of disillusionment he saw hovering over the schooling landscape would spread to deflate public affection for the local school.

Chapter 11

Tidying the Mind
in an Untidy World

Educational science cannot be constructed simply by borrowing the techniques of experiment and measurement found in physical science. . . . Educational practices provide the data, the subject-matter, which form the problems of inquiry. They are the sole source of the ultimate problems to be investigated. These educational practices are also the final test of value . . . of all researches. To suppose that scientific findings decide the value of educational undertakings is to reverse the real case.

JOHN DEWEY[1]

At the beginning of the twentieth century, philosopher-psychologist William James referred to two contrasting themes running through the character of American life as "the hard and tough" and the "soft and tender." He saw them as needing to be in balance. Although both always are visible, one tends to dominate over the other in cycles of change.

This has been the case, I believe, with schooling. So long as secondary education was only for the few and favored during the early decades of the century, a curriculum of the "hard" subjects was little questioned. That curriculum did not at first change much with the growth in attendance, accelerated by the Great Depression of the 1930s. But it was much questioned for its relevance to a more diverse student body, and the roots of more child-centered schooling at all levels were nourished.

During the later years of the forty-year span from 1910 to 1950, the proportion of subjects classified as academic in the high school curriculum dropped significantly, as did enrollments in them. New courses taking up the balance were justified not only as necessary to increasing the holding power of the schools but also as better preparing youths for responsible citizenship, work, and personal satisfaction.[2] There emerged little middle ground in the ongoing educational debate. The argument of the "progressives" for a democratic, inclusive secondary school said little about the acquisition of knowledge the "classicists" perceived to be essential for wise citizenship and a productive life.

The debate became intense after World War II and led in 1955 to the closing of the doors of the Progressive Education Association, but not to the demise of advocacy for curricula and pedagogy designed to connect with the daily life problems of children and youths. Unfortunately, what subsequently ensued should have been seen by moderates on both sides of the debate as savaging their respective positions.

The "back to basics" movement that surged in the 1950s and has enjoyed successive high tides ever since gave short shrift to the most credible themes of both the classical academic and the progressive educational credos. It reduced the liberating essence of the subject disciplines to a dreary regimen of secondhand content delivered by textbooks and teacher telling. It nourished a system of schooling better suited to the packaging, distribution, and standardization of milk products than the development of thoughtful, responsible, caring members of a social and political democracy.

Climbing out of what we have created, as much by omission as commission, will require a collaboration of the citizenry, educators, policymakers, philanthropists, and, yes, sectors of the business community around a common school mission of a kind not yet experienced in this work in progress we call democracy. And it will take time—far beyond the time we normally allocate for education commissions to do their work. The process of renewing our schools and the educational infrastructure of which they are a part must become a way of life throughout the land.

I ended Chapter 10 with Robert M. Hutchins pondering what had happened to the school we had long regarded as the foundation, source, and beacon for what we deeply valued. I pick up in this chapter and the next a chunk of the odyssey through which colleagues and I set out to inquire deeply into the conduct of schooling and the education of educators for them in the United States. I further describe in the next chapter how the pieces came together in formulation and initial testing of a comprehensive agenda for educating the young in the social and political characteristics of a democratic society and for the wisdom required of its citizens. In effect, the agenda seeks to blend the "hard and tough" and the "soft and tender" in the encompassing fabric of schooling.

Our first purpose was to map the terrain so that the most critical problems and issues, as well as the most promising catch-hold points, for effecting renewal might become apparent. A personal expectation was to tidy my mind regarding the array of hypotheses cluttering up my ecology of educational belief.[3] Hence the title of this chapter.

I shall not burden readers with details regarding the findings, conclusions, and recommendations of the study of school change briefly described in the preceding chapter, the study of schooling introduced in this one, and the study of the education of educators addressed in the next.[4] Even pulling from them the elements most relevant to the educational agenda that emerged provided a challenge to colleagues and me over a period of years. Friend and colleague Ken Sirotnik, with the input of many people who contributed, has done yeoman service in providing a synthesis of work in a report that includes considerable description of the three studies referred to above.[5] In the opening paragraph of Chapter 1, he catches the essence of our later pilot implementation of the resulting agenda in a few words: "an enduring, systematic renewal effort of K–12 schools and the education of educators in accord with a strong agenda of educational principles that we believe are consistent with the purpose and practice of public education in a democratic society." In what follows, I add to his portrait only a few brush strokes that provide a personal perspective.

I want to make clear that this tidying of the mind is not to be likened to the construction of a Frank Lloyd Wright architectural treasure to be carefully preserved by its owners. Nor to a ladder, each step of which one throws aside in climbing to a higher truth. Each rung in one's belief system must be revisited, again and again, to see how well it stands up under careful scrutiny.

THINGS CHANGE

In Chapter 10, I found it necessary to stay with the theme of a great decade for the public school that faded in the late 1960s, largely because of circumstances in its cultural context. I chose to focus on war, race, and growing public awareness of the limitations of schools in fulfilling the American dream. In doing so, I got ahead of the personal and professional story I have been endeavoring to relate. There is an odd parallel in the narratives of context and the trajectory of experiences in the Goodlad family.

We enjoyed the ambience of Malibu. Contrasting with the picture portrayed in movies over the years, Malibu was a great place to raise young children. Our two reveled in it. Not having raised teenagers elsewhere, we assumed only that adolescence brings on its own array of problems to challenge both the young and their parents. We had not counted on the frequent intensity of the sun and Len's susceptibility to its rays. We think that it was the frequent carpooling with the sun coming through the left-side window of her car that contributed significantly to the necessity of her undergoing facial surgery. It was a devastating emotional experience that she handled with characteristic absence of complaint. The inner pain ran deep.

In late November 1966, I returned from an assignment of visiting for a couple of weeks schools in Asia and Europe serving Americans abroad, partially supported by our Department of State. Three weeks later, a colleague observed that I appeared to have weathered well what had been a grueling trip. I had replied, "Today I feel as though I'm coming apart at the seams," and two days later, I was in bed, delirious, striking out in my sleep at horrors I could not stave off. And, when awake, I tried desperately not to go to sleep and bring on the delirium. Dr. Morrison visited me several times before deciding that he had to get me to the

UCLA hospital for care and diagnosis. He was baffled and so were the physicians he called upon there. Failing to get an answer, he had me moved back home again to Len's care. I entered into a nutritional regimen added to the family one we followed soon after coming to California, which, together with the climate, had taken care of Stephen's health problems that had contributed to our decision to leave Chicago.

It was during the early stages of my long climb out of the pit that I twice struggled up from the University Elementary School (UES) to tell Chancellor Murphy that the activities in which I already was engaged were too satisfying to be endangered by adding the deanship of the Graduate School of Education to them. He asked me to write a prospectus on the needs to be addressed in seeking to move it to first-rate status. Clever fellow! On my third such trek, he summarized the staggering array of major commitments he carried in addition to his leadership of UCLA and almost embarrassed me over my reluctance to take on more. Then, tough bargainer that he was, he said that he would allocate the twenty-two additional positions I had said were needed if I would take on the deanship but that he would not renew the offer if he had to re-open the search for a dean. (Dr. Murphy left UCLA a year later to join the Times-Mirror Corporation in Los Angeles. His successor, Charles Young, honored this commitment.)

He quickly sensed my weakening. Pushing it further, he answered two questions I was about to ask: "When you want help with your plan, see Foster (the vice-chancellor). If you want to dream, see me." Still weak from my illness, I was functioning more by instinct than mental alertness; nonetheless, I learned some useful lessons about leadership from our engagements.

I was unaware of a dire pronouncement Dr. Morrison had made to Len during the depths of my illness: "If John survives, he probably will have some permanent disability and might not be able to continue his work." Talking about this months later, we decided to seek a place where we could live more easily and cheaply than where we now were. On vacation the summer before, we had dined one evening with Len's parents in a little café across from Lummi Island in the state of Washington. At dusk, a small fishing boat slipped quietly through the narrows between us and the island. The San Juan Islands, of which Lummi is one, are so close to the border that cruising in a boat to the north or west of them, one never quite knows whether one is in Canada or the United States.

Now, looking to the next summer's vacation, with my physical health still uncertain, was our necessary next move to be, this time, home again, home again, Finnegan, almost in the place where our near-half-century sojourn had begun? During that vacation, we chartered a small cruiser for a week and explored both sides of the border. Available properties with small cottages were close to nonexistent. Nearing the end of our week and feeling discouraged, we pulled into a boat slip of an island marina on the U.S. side of the border to spend some time with a real estate broker who had been trying to assist us. By the time we had turned in the cruiser in Anacortes, the self-proclaimed Gateway to the San Juans, and were driving on Interstate 5 to California, we had signed mortgage papers on island acreage. A second mortgage covered the construction of the cottage that was to be ready by the following summer.

So far as we knew, Dr. Morrison was the only person outside of our family aware of the seriousness of my illness. Indeed, beyond the few people who worked most closely with me, I doubt that colleagues in the Graduate School of Education and the UES knew anything other than that I was away, perhaps with the flu. Ordered to stay in bed, I cheated just as soon as I felt able to walk around a little. Lying on my back on the living room sofa, I used a little dictaphone to respond to the piles of papers and correspondence brought to me several times a week. I am not sure that members of the two faculty groups even knew that I was not in one or the other of my two offices. Perhaps that thought should have worried me more than it did. I was still very pale and weak when I met several times with Chancellor Murphy. He appeared not to notice. Back to work once more, I slowly increased my daily hours and tried to follow orders not to extend them into the evening.

It took a year for my still-undiagnosed illness to give up on me and creep away, leaving no apparent need for us to be full-time island retirees. But events that were to follow made us realize how fortunate we were to have this place of solace that contributed so much to the eventual closing of our long journey's circle. Just two years later, we were struck with two more blows. Shortly before Christmas, we were looking forward to the visit of long-time friends, one of whom had been in our wedding party, and their daughter of Paula's age. At dinner together on Christmas Eve, I faintly heard the truck that was to deliver the hand-wrought table Len had admired but regarded as, for now, out of reach. She did not notice. Ron and I deliberately stayed up after everyone else had gone to bed. Then, quietly, we removed the dining room table and hefted the new arrival from the driveway to replace the other.

We dined on that table by candlelight on the evening of Christmas Day and then adjourned to continue our conversation before the fireplace. An hour or two after retiring for the day, we were awakened by Norma's repeated cries of "Fire." The flames already had climbed from a cushion safely beyond the fireplace screen, we had thought, into books on nearby shelves and upward toward the roof decking. We called the fire department from the bedroom in our end of the house while everyone hurried out through nearby sliding doors. As a friend wryly remarked several days later, we should have delayed a little in calling the fire station so as to let it burn to the ground. The charred remains of the entire center portion of the house that assaulted dawn's arrival was even more dismal and depressing than we had anticipated.

Len's nesting instincts had resulted in an abode that mightily pleased us. In anticipating the arrival of Norma, Karen, and Ron, we had been, we later realized, a little smug in thinking that they would enjoy what she had put together just as much as we had enjoyed the three nests their greater resources had enabled them to create over the shorter time of their marriage. Some biblical cautions of childhood came back to us.

Miraculously, the table was spared for later enjoyment. The mats of our Christmas dining had burned into the wood, which had to be planed down a quarter of an inch to produce an unblemished surface. We will be forever grateful to Wayne Gordon, my associate dean, and the covey of colleagues he quickly recruited and led in packing, labeling, and storing in the garage everything that was salvageable. During the second month of the six required to restore the house for occupancy, Len came to realize that she had to give up her near-daily visits to pick through the ruins in order to put a stop to her tears. Then, just as she was beginning to discipline herself to cease this routine and we were counting our blessings over all of us having escaped the fire safely and for having our island nest, her mother passed away.

We had become very familiar with the sights and convenient stopping places along I-5 from California through Oregon to Washington and British Columbia. We divided our summer vacation between the homes of my mother and Len's parents in Canada. Just before each summer's departure from Los Angeles, I took Paula and Stephen into a couple of bookstores where they could lay claim to any books that caught their interest. With the building of the cottage, they piled up enough to last the whole summer on the island. The agreement with Chancellor Murphy was that my appointment as dean would keep me in residence only for the academic year, although I would still be accountable for the school's well-being during the summer. There is a small airstrip on the island, and so I was able to commute by air through Seattle to Los Angeles for visits of a few days each several times during July and August.

THE DISMAL DECADE

There was not, in the 1970s into the 1980s, just growing discontent with schooling. It was accompanied by lack of confidence in the ability of schooling to change or be changed. I recall a conversation, circa 1975, with fellow officers of the National Society for the Study of Education of possible topics for the society's upcoming yearbooks. We thought that there should be one that analyzed the immediate past and current schooling scene. "But, for goodness sake, don't put 'change' in the title," said a member of the group. "It has become a dirty word."

By about 1973, colleagues and I were wrapping up our support of the League of Cooperating Schools, the clutch of books reporting the work, and studies of early childhood education that culminated in three books addressing practices in the United States, England, Israel, and a couple of Asian countries. Including the one on a mankind school, we produced ten books between 1972 and 1976. Their subsequent existence was scarcely noticed. There was little interest in analyses of proposals for and processes of educational change. But books attacking the schools found their way to readers within and beyond the educational community. Clearly, this was not a promising time for us to remain engaged with educational renewal.

Parents with school-age children do not simply forget about schools during periods of their fall from grace. The mood of the general public from the early 1970s into the early 1980s—years I refer to as the dismal schooling decade—was more one of inattention than criticism. The latter became the playing field of groups with interests other than improving *public* schooling. The more they could make it look bad, the greater the likelihood their proposals for alternatives would gain attention. Part of the strategy was to discredit proposals for change, no matter how solidly informed, coming from any source that could be tied to the self-interests of the so-called educational establishment. Colleges of education and teacher educators were identified as prime suspects.

The irony here is that, even if the charges had been well founded, a substantial body of knowledge relevant to school policies and practices, much of it produced by scholars with no attachment to schools for active participation in the implementation of their work, was discredited or ignored. There was at the time more available knowledge relevant to educational practice than there was to medical practice in 1910 when the Flexner Report provided the impetus for grounding medical education in the research culture of university-based schools of medicine.[6] Such is now characteristic of all our major professions but is ignored for personal, social, vocational, and academic development of this nation's young.

Many factors stilled the lively local debate over educational issues and school practices that had characterized the schooling decade. One of them was the shallow penetration of the outcomes of scholarly inquiry into the public domain. The media preferred to ferret out and highlight bad practices. Parents admitted to being confused and increasingly directed their attention to what schooling should do for them instead of what they should do for their schools. They became more open than they had been before to alternatives: vouchers for private schools of choice, home schooling, choice within their districts, parent-run schools "free" of their district, and more. Charter schools and distance learning via technology were as yet only embryonic.

What now were to be the prospects for public schooling to bind together the people of an America of "multiple communities defined by different interests, races, ethnicities, regions, economic stratifications, religions, and so forth"?[7] Or is this not necessary in a nation to which the people swear common allegiance? Or is contributing to the work-in-progress we call democracy not a role of schooling? Strangely, these questions were little asked or discussed. They were scarcely inferred in the presidential election debates of the 1980s or the decade that followed. The substance of the No Child Left Behind Act that became the educational law of the land by 2002 suggests that we need not worry ourselves locally with such matters. The Department of Education will rewrite the questions, provide us with the answers, and tell us what all schools must do.

Several colleagues and I were made restless by the call of hypotheses that we had not yet explored enough to enlighten our educational beliefs. Our Study of Educational Change and School Improvement conducted with the League of Cooperating Schools had dug deeply into problems and processes of effecting educational change in schools but less into practices needing to be changed. Since no commission reports that would seek to engage the nation's schools in reform were visible on the horizon, it appeared to us that the time was ripe for tidying our minds regarding prevailing educational conditions in our schools. Fortunately, the Kettering Foundation was interested in what we proposed: a broad and deep examination of the conduct of elementary and secondary schools in the United States.

Those of us who planned and conducted a Study of Schooling during the dismal decade were egregiously naive in our expectations that we could provide a kind of global positioning system (GPS) to guide a long-term assault on the deep structure of schooling that had so successfully defied successive eras of school reform. We thought that our efforts would provide wonderful romances with schools for all those who would become engaged in their renewal for at least the decade to follow the conclusions of our inquiry. With continuing renewal then assured, the demeaning concept of school reform would disappear with the practices that deny for so many of our young people the romances that come with joy in learning.

We did not anticipate what would come over the horizon just before we concluded our work. Alas, the word, the concept, and the repeated processes of school reform were reinvigorated in 1983 in a federally commissioned report, *A Nation at Risk*, that perceived the sorry condition of our schools to be something an enemy nation might have imposed upon us.[8] Three major studies, including our own, published during 1983 and 1984 that together provided GPS maps for comprehensive renewal of the nation's policies and practices of schooling were ignored.[9] Instead, the schools were called upon to do more intensively what they already were doing in order to strengthen the nation's position in the global economy to one of unchallenged leadership. Teachers and their young charges were to do it. But the nation neglected to give our schools the tools for the proposed crusade.

Then, when the economy surged in the 1990s, there was, rightly, not a word in the press about the triumph of schooling in the war it was to wage. The young foot soldiers called into battle and entering school had not yet graduated into the workforce. But our public schools remained in the grip of the god of economic utility, nonetheless. And the call for reform did not abate.[10]

The most serious indictment of schooling one might make today is that so many citizens educated by the cottage industry that provided the schools of their romantic memories have had their minds colonized by the rhetoric of a mission that the schools cannot attain. The near silence of parent and educational organizations regarding the current federal agenda of so-called school reform that might well have been imposed upon us by an enemy nation is alarming.

We had put a lot of time into conceptualizing our study of schooling, coming at the task from many perspectives. I remember well the sessions of imagining what visitors dropping in from outer space would want to know about the place we call school. Hovering above one, what might be their guesses about the big yellow bugs lined up one after another with tiny bugs coming out of them? What might we tell them about some of these places if they stayed with us for several days?

We discovered that, after a time, we began to enrich our description of major components of schooling we called "commonplaces"—elements common to all schools. We ran out of commonplaces not previously introduced after identifying a dozen or so: organization, students, teachers, materials, rules, significant others not there every day or even at all, and more. We planned to study them all.

We consulted our superb advisory committee (chaired by Ralph Tyler), requesting early on its help in identifying similar macrostudies of phenomena and people from whom we might get help in designing our methodology. Educational historian Lawrence Cremin could not recall a parallel. We took from sociologist Robert Merton's account of a comprehensive study of World War I the necessity of developing deep, layer-on-layer descriptions.

Down the road quite a bit, one of our senior staff members—probably either Bette Overman or Ken Sirotnik—referred to our having some 20,000 pieces of data (data points) on each school. These did not represent all of our information. The small teams that sat for days in classrooms of each school, systematically following a design of recording what they saw (a process for which they had been carefully trained), learned a great deal in their casual conversations with principals, teachers, and students. In writing the final report, I was still getting additional information from staff members who were visiting every school in the sample and providing feedback regarding our findings. Perhaps the magnitude of the study is best grasped from my dedication in the frontispiece of *A Place Called School*: "To those individuals—more than 27,000 of them in number—who provided the data on which this book is based."

We were picking up along the way impressions about my parallel interest—the prevailing connection between the education of educators and school policies and practices. These rather consistently supported the hypotheses I had brought from earlier experiences and were being strengthened from another initiative three of us were carrying forward simultaneously. There was no way, it turned out, to escape the urge to test these later through disciplined inquiry. I realize now how closely we were following John Dewey's wise counsel regarding "educational *practices* provide the data, the subject-matter, which form the *problems* of inquiry."

I regard careful inquiry as necessary to gaining insights into not only the ongoing practices of human affairs but also the deeply seated assumptions that guide them. These assumptions are rarely brought to a level of consciousness by the parents, students, and teachers closely connected with the local school. Consequently, these groups are not alert to the implications for practice when politically driven reforms based on different assumptions enter into the schooling enterprise. When realization belatedly dawns, it commonly is accompanied by feelings of helplessness. The operational—commonly referred to as conventional—wisdom of the citizenry is seriously shortchanged by the neglect of its education in both formal and informal education. The educational research development community has not well served its educative role in the public arena.

STRENGTHENING THE UNIVERSITY-SCHOOL RELATIONSHIP

One of the most obvious and yet, until very recently, ignored educational needs is to connect sectors of the immense knowledge-production of higher education to elementary and secondary schools and the preservice and in-service education of their teachers. Ironically, the least connected universities are those ranked high for their research productivity; the most connected are rarely among the leading research-oriented institutions but produce the most teachers. Strangely, the top-ranked schools of education prepare few or no teachers. Eliminating preservice teacher education has accompanied their rise to increased prestige. We would think it odd for the top-ranked schools of law and medicine to prepare no lawyers and physicians.

Chancellor Murphy and I had agreed on three overarching priorities for UCLA's Graduate School of Education. The first of these was to bring it into line with the institution's clear ambition to be ranked with the Berkeley campus in the top cluster of the nation's premier universities. Translated, this meant that every professor was to become widely recognized for his or her scholarly work. Second, the school was to become a leader in the profession of education writ large, not just among its own genre of entities nationwide. This meant innovation in ideas relevant to both educational practitioners and the education of the citizenry. Third, the school was to connect with practice. This meant that it was to embrace practitioners not only in the identification and conduct of relevant research but also in the development of initiatives for its use in educational improvement. This further meant outreach into nearby schools and school districts.

These expectations were not new to me. They were close to what I had perceived the role of the University Elementary School to be and what I saw as guiding my responsibilities as its director. I had come at an auspicious time. Clearly, what Chancellor Murphy and I discussed for the Graduate School of Education was in the image of expectations for the campus, which were, in turn, embedded in the master plan for the entire University of California at the time of our arrival in 1960.

The challenge of catching up to the esteemed Berkeley campus was daunting. It asked much of the faculty. There was no shortage of applications from professors in a range of disciplines to conduct research projects in the UES. Many of these might just as readily have been conducted in nearby public schools, but the logistics of gaining access and especially approval to use children as subjects were far more complex. Only rarely did we receive a proposal that might have shed light on a problem we were struggling with or engage our teachers in truly collaborative inquiry. Professors were generous in sharing their research interests and findings, but I can recall only two or three who inquired into what we were about in order to determine the prospects of a shared initiative.

My conclusion after several years was that university-based laboratory schools, to achieve the ends rhetorically espoused for them, must have attached to them a mix of teachers, researchers, developers of instructional programs and materials, research assistants, and facilities characteristic of research and development centers in the social and behavioral sciences. The UES did not come close to having such resources. We would have approached such a structure in the League of Cooperating Schools if members of our staff had held dual appointments with the schools. There may be a place for laboratory schools, but I now believe that they must be part of a close partnership with educator-preparing universities and have far more independence than local public schools enjoy today. I began to envision a structure for UCLA and surrounding school districts in which the UES would perform a unique role.

We made good progress with the first two goals for the School of Education that Chancellor Murphy and I had discussed but fell short of my expectations for the third. The good work of the faculty—built up for the future by most of the new appointees being assistant professors— in advancing their research careers and increasingly taking leadership in their professorial associations contributed significantly to the school's attainment in 1977 of top ranking among those of public universities.[11] A decade later, Clifford and Guthrie completed their study of ten schools of education in public and private universities rising to prominence since the 1950s. They cited the work of the UES in crediting the UCLA Graduate School of Education with leadership in connecting to educational practice.[12] It pains me somewhat to think about what this contribution might have been had colleagues and I achieved what we set out to do while we were simultaneously conducting our study of elementary and secondary schools in the second half of the 1970s.

BUILDING A UNIVERSITY-TO-SCHOOL BRIDGE

Clearly, today's top-ranked schools of education did not gain their recognition by courting close relationships with schools and preparing teachers. Brought from England to conduct an independent study of several, Harry Judge wryly reported that an education dean (actually a composite of several he had interviewed) proudly proclaimed that his faculty did not prepare teachers; it studied them.[13] Faculty members of the school I served as dean quickly realized that not just the interests of UCLA depended on their scholarly productivity; their employment and careers depended on it. Early on, I came to the realization that the only alternative for reducing the outrageously high ratio of students to faculty members was to radically cut the large numbers in our teacher education programs. Some faculty members wanted these to be entirely eliminated.

Few were interested in my proposals for being of greater service to schools by partnering with them for the pursuit of common interests, even though they recognized the potential benefit of gaining easier access in order to conduct their research. Nonetheless, I harbored the belief that, once the possibilities for positive symbiotic relationships became apparent, a gratifying percentage would want to become involved. I also harbored the belief that, unless this vision became widely shared and implemented, schools of education would become an endangered species in higher education. The dominating individual research agendas might suffice for the short haul but were not good investments for the long-term future of education schools. These beliefs have hardened in my mind over the intervening years.

It became obvious that faculty members would not devote significant time in connecting with schools until such work moved much higher in the reward structure. On the assumption that schools of education ultimately would be judged in large part for their contribution to school quality, I concluded that we should create a research and development center committed to such work supported in part by soft money and adjunct personnel.[14] We already had a nucleus in the UES with its line-item funding in the university budget. I proceeded on the assumption that this would be a *laboratory*, since I had the authority to create such. Centers and institutes had to be approved by the Board of Regents.

In looking from the UES across busy Sunset Boulevard to the hedged and treed grounds of a private school sanctuary, it dawned on me that we needed a kind of conceptual bridge by means of which theoretical and practical educational commerce might easily pass back and forth between the university and partner schools. In effect, this would be an extension of the League of Cooperating Schools concept enriched by what we had learned about such collaboration.

On the university side, we needed a research and development entity that would provide what the UES sorely lacked and that would bring together faculty members whose research interests required schools with school-based educators whose work could be enhanced by easy access to and participation in the scholarly activity of the academy. Paul Heckman, Ken Sirotnik, and I, already closely associated in the study of schooling, began to talk about this "bridge facility." The only possible space for it that I could see was on the UES grounds, a space then occupied by a decrepit prefab building used for storage and, occasionally, by a few faculty members in the psychology department.

I began to envision a lovely little building joined to those of the UES by a bridge over the stream bed. A happenstance conversation with a graduate student in the school of architecture brought a famed architect into my embryonic stage of planning. He subsequently guided her in translating my thoughts about the project into a superb architectural concept. Now we needed a substantial amount of money to translate the visual concept into lumber, bricks, and mortar.

From time to time, I shared these embryonic plans with the nine elected members of the school's Educational Policy Committee and reported progress in monthly faculty meetings. Several years earlier, we had created the Laboratory in Teacher Education, and so the Laboratory in School and Community Education was not a novel concept. In retrospect, I think that most faculty members saw it more as meeting the needs of the UES than their own, although several inquired into the potential of the envisioned new building for the conduct of their research. Few saw the need for it as part of a bridge to surrounding schools.

Meanwhile, what became the Southern California School-University Partnership was taking shape. With the help of Assistant Dean Richard Williams and Professor Jay Scribner, both in the field of educational administration, Paul, Ken, and I were able to identify about two dozen school districts led by superintendents believed to be providing good leadership. Most of these accepted our invitation to join us for conversation regarding the relationship we had in mind. Sixteen of these then joined in shaping a partnership of their districts and the university dedicated to working together.

With a substantial grant in hand from the Charles Stewart Mott Foundation, I so informed the executive vice-chancellor, and the new Laboratory in School and Community Education came into being. The challenge now was to put the pieces together so that the educational commerce envisioned would take place. Alas, that lovely little building necessary to the laboratory's research function never took its planned place beside the existing UES.

UCLA was in the process of planning the largest, and what turned out to be the most successful, fund-raising campaign in its history. The deans of its several schools were members of the rather large group assembled by the development office under the direction of Chancellor Young. Our earlier proposal for a campaign to finance the laboratory's building was out of sync and had to await approval for inclusion in the much larger one.

I began to grow uneasy about the search for space on the already-crowded campus for structures being included on the development wish list to be funded by the results of the campaign. Several times, I was called to meetings regarding how nearby changes in the landscape might affect the UES in such daily routines as parents delivering and later picking up their children. There were rumors that the business school was eyeing for its planned expansion the space I was attempting to stake out for the laboratory.

Late in the 1981–82 academic year, I was invited to serve a fourth five-year term as dean. I said that there was no need to confirm such. I would rather proceed a year at a time since I doubted that I would remain in the post for five; I was growing increasingly interested in getting more closely involved in the UES and putting together the pieces of the new laboratory. The higher education side of my hybrid career had dominated for too long; I needed to restore balance.

Subsequently, I began to look at possibilities for creating at the UES temporary space suited to the work of a director of the laboratory until quarters became available in the proposed new building. I found myself walking down there more and more often as planning and then remodeling proceeded. I began to imagine that what had been sorely missing when I became director of the UES might well emerge. Directing the laboratory that would encompass the UES and the new research center and connect with the Southern California Partnership began to appeal to me as providing the ideal hybrid balance in my work.

I shared my thoughts with the executive vice-chancellor—the fourth to whom I had reported over the preceding fifteen years—and told him that 1982–83 would be my last year as dean. Little did I know that it also would be my last year of being directly responsible for the conduct of a school for the young. Years before, I had not realized on the day I drove sadly away from Biscoq that I would not again teach daily a class of children. The hybrid balance that I thought lay just ahead was not to be.

MORE ENDINGS AND BEGINNINGS

It is, I think, correct to say that my romances with schools, as I have tried to portray them, were over. From here on they were to be vicarious. And so, the story I set out to tell might well end here. But richly satisfying years were yet to come. They took me more and more into the incredible gap between the school system we have and visions of what it readily could and should be—visions far removed from the politically driven school reform of the concluding fifteen years of the second millennium into beginnings of the third.

There are few romances to be found in these years. Instead, they involve a struggle for the soul of the American public school. What follows is heavier stuff than what precedes. Change often emerges as a reaction to excess, and clearly today's school reform era is a quintessential model of excess, perhaps the harbinger of better things to come. To quote once more the words on one of Sister Corita's serigraphs, "We harvest the fruit of hope in order to begin again to hope."

Many things did appear to be coming together during my last year as dean of the Graduate School of Education (GSE). Its top ranking, five years before in the Cartter Report, was now paying off in attracting students and faculty members. Most chapters of *A Place Called School*, my report on the study of schooling, were in the hands of my editor at McGraw-Hill, the publisher. I was working on revisions whenever I could find a little time during what had become, almost routinely, seventy- to eighty-hour workweeks. Ken was, among other things, tidying up the data bank of our study, readying it for the use of others. Paul was doing yeoman service with the Southern California School-University Partnership and helping the interim principal of the UES we had recruited from the Beverly Hills school district. Madeline was now teaching in the GSE with more time available for working with schools and school districts nationally and internationally. And the work of recruiting a new dean was under way.

Advice to deans: Do not give a year's notice of your intent to step aside. Chances are that the first search for your successor will fail and a temporary replacement will be required anyway. And the announcement will make you a lame duck, creating a year of uncertainty prior to filling the position. There probably will be several inside candidates, each with a small supporting constituency. Some of these will give outside candidates a rough time in the interviewing process.

Not surprisingly, several very good finalists in our search turned us down or we turned them down, and a second search began. The good colleague who had been my associate dean for the entire sixteen years accepted an interim appointment, and so we were luckier than in most comparable pursuits.

I was to have a year of leave and then, on my return, continue as a professor and director of the UES, with the expectation of encompassing it within the new Laboratory in School and Community Education that I had been heading, *ex officio*. Len and I planned to spend the year in our cottage in the San Juans. This was to be the beginning of "her time." What a daydream that turned out to be! *A Place Called School* was published in late summer, just as most school years were beginning. Education editor Edward (Ted) Fiske's review began on the front page of the *New York Times* and went out to hundreds of newspapers nationwide. Since the preceding spring, when *A Nation at Risk* was published, the media had been hungry for more on schooling, particularly if it was critical. They found us in our island retreat, and we had little personal access to our telephone for several months.

Little did we realize then that the Northwest, the place of summer vacations, would become later the place of our year-long daily lives. Paula and Stephen had been born in a quite different part of the country far away, but they took to the Northwest as their place on earth. Paula was married and had been living there for several years when unanticipated events brought Len and me. Stephen arrived only a few years later. He, who most among us enjoyed warm, dry days in Malibu, is now the one who most enjoys the rainy ones hundreds of miles to the north. Back almost to my place of birth, where I once had imaginary friends in California, it took me several years to quit hunkering down in the rain and instead to embrace it.

What led to our return? Several things, none planned. Yes, we had experienced mudslides, earthquakes, and fire—the sources of sliding, shaking, or burning off the slopes of the Santa Monica hillsides. Yes, illness had led us to our beloved island place. And the year of leave had brought an invitation to give a series of lectures and engage in a few other academic activities at the University of Washington. Perhaps all of these things combined to create easy passage to the Northwest because there was no mind-wrenching decision of the kind that had so enveloped us several times before.

Indeed, there was no rational reason for us to buy, during the year before the one of leave, the lot some thirty-eight feet below the surface of Seattle's Lake Union on which our floating home was later built. We always have enjoyed prowling around the residential areas of cities we visit or in which we lived. On a visit to Seattle, we had seen the development on the lake taking shape and watched, intrigued, the construction of a floating home. Hankering to visit again, I suggested to Len that we spend a weekend in Seattle to see what was going on there.

We were disappointed to learn that all the lots in the location that interested us had been sold; new homes already were floating on the water above most of them. Then, the owner of the house we had watched being constructed months before came out with a newspaper in his hand. He was almost certain that a lot advertised for sale was the one next door to his. Before leaving, we had made all the necessary arrangements for its purchase. Clearly, given the obvious demand, we had nothing to lose. But, with as yet no conscious decision having been made to leave Malibu and UCLA, we had not even begun to add up the pros and cons. Subsequent events—and the lack of them—strengthened the strangely intoxicating pull back to the place that in some ways we had never left.

During the spring of my final year as dean, the name Curtis van Alfen had shown up one afternoon on the daily appointment schedule. He had not stated the purpose of his visit. My incredibly efficient administrative assistant Ann Edwards had blocked in a half hour, noting that he was dean of the College of Education at Brigham Young University and probably was simply paying a visit on his way through Los Angeles—a common occurrence. He and I had hardly begun our conversation when I stepped out to see if Ann could clear my schedule for a couple of hours.

Dean van Alfen had become aware of the promising beginnings of the partnership and my stepping aside as dean, and he wondered if I might consider a visiting professorship at BYU for the following year. He thought that creating such a partnership with neighboring school districts in Utah was precisely the right move for his institution, and he wanted my help. I told him that we had other plans for the year but that a part-time arrangement might be possible. Little did I realize how much the subsequent relationship would contribute to the good work I was to have in what was to become virtually a new career.

Although still employed part time by UCLA, with the closing out of sixteen years as dean and commuting quite regularly between Seattle and Los Angeles, I had that wonderful feeling of freedom experienced when I had resigned many years earlier from my principalship in the Surrey School District of British Columbia. That is, until Ted Fiske's review brought the media calling. We escaped in October to spend two weeks at Sundance, up into the Wasatch range of mountains a short drive from Provo and Brigham Young University. At the university, I engaged in conversations that resulted in creation of the BYU-Public School (five school districts) Partnership the following May—the second of ten partnerships that would constitute formation of the National Network for Educational Renewal early in 1986.

Back on the island, I came across a startling document in a bundle of mail forwarded to me from UCLA. The Educational Policy Committee had voted termination of the Laboratory in School and Community Education! The justification was that it had never been approved. This was, of course, nonsense. Based on the reasoning involved, our Laboratory in Teacher Education created several years earlier had not been approved either. The minutes of faculty meetings showed ample discussion of both. Indeed, we had gone beyond University of California regulations in my keeping the incumbent vice-chancellor informed since the rules reserved final authority of approval to deans.

This was sheer politics, provoked by internal jockeying regarding the ongoing search for the new dean, providing more support for my advice to retiring deans: Giving only ninety days notice is the best way to a smooth transition. Chancellor Young rapped several sets of knuckles in reminding some people he called before him of proper procedures and deans' authority in such matters. But I am not sure that the party or parties most involved were in the group. I recalled then and recall now a remark William Benton—founder of a successful advertising firm, former senator from Connecticut, and later the owner of Encyclopaedia Britannica—had made a year or two after becoming a vice president of the University of Chicago. Referring to academic politics, he said that, in the Senate, at least people played by some rules.

I already was having cautionary thoughts about my future collegial relationships in the GSE. I noted that deans commonly move to other administrative positions within their universities, go immediately into retirement, move elsewhere, or get involved in other interests. One does not spend sixteen years in the post without bailing a few colleagues out of embarrassing situations or failing to reward some who hold over-inflated views of their value to the academic enterprise. How comfortable would I be or how comfortable would such colleagues be in a renewed peer relationship?

I then began to realize that the engine needed to jumpstart what I envisioned for the new—and still alive—laboratory was an unrealistic expectation. Commitments for endowed chairs and other goodies were coming in for the School of Business at a pace not rivaled even by the School of Medicine. A new building on the space where I thought my vision belonged would be a tempting morsel for a corporate CEO to help fund. There would be little point in my waiting around for the bad news Chancellor Young ultimately would have to give me. How much the pending circumstances reminded me of the short letter President Goodrich White had sent regarding my plans for Fernbank Forest! I spared Chuck Young the necessity.

Dean James Doi had been guiding the University of Washington's College of Education into a new organizational structure that put the historical and philosophical foundations, educational administration, and various other pieces into a division of policy and leadership. Dick Andrews, its head, was about to release a notice regarding the recruitment of an assistant professor when he came up with the idea that perhaps it could be upgraded to a professorship in which I might be interested. President William Gerberding countered Dean Doi's request by telling him to keep the existing position open; he would grant the professorship out of his discretionary resources. The full transition of home, place, and work was completed.

Strangely, I do not recall there being any lumpy decisions involved. There was, I think, more of synergy than serendipity in this move. We had just been gone a little longer than anticipated when we first headed up the western slopes of the Cascades thirty-eight years before.

Chapter 12

Toward Schools
Commonly Good

It is in our power to create the kind of society that we want, in the way we want to. . . . Authoritarian solutions are easy to impose, but only those solutions that the stakeholders work out patiently and revisit periodically are likely to survive. . . . Whether in America or elsewhere, we can have a society in which good work is an everyday reality; the only question is whether we have the will to make that happen before it is too late.

HOWARD GARDNER, MIHALY CSIKSZENTMIHALYI, AND
WILLIAM DAMON[1]

During the transition period of bringing some things to conclusion in Los Angeles and beginning others in Seattle, I had a serendipitous conversation in New York with Clark Kerr. Since leaving the presidency of the University of California, he had brought his talents to bear on continuing issues in higher education. He had recently edited the multivolume Carnegie Policy Series that addressed them.

We were attending a regular meeting of a group he chaired, supported by the Mertz-Gilmore Foundation, that had been brought together to advance greater attention to understanding the world in the education of the young. During a break, he expressed to me uncharacteristic exasperation over his recent meeting in California with several education deans. It had become apparent to him that teacher education was a neglected enterprise that required comprehensive overhaul. He thought I should put together a staff to study it as colleagues and I had studied elementary and

303

secondary schooling. He proposed that I talk about it with Robert L. Payton, then president of the Exxon Education Foundation, who would be our guest for lunch.

Needless to say, the idea had crossed my mind before, especially during the years we were studying schooling. But I had kept pushing it aside. I had been in and out of teacher education several times, each of my "outs" being accompanied by giving students my books on the subject and vowing never to get involved again. I knew how bitter Conant's disappointment had been in not being able to arouse public and political concern years before. It appeared to me that the road to renewal in teacher education was strewn with the carcasses of those who had ventured upon it.

Clark arranged for Mr. Payton and me to sit together. We talked of many things, including the education of educators. Flying back to Seattle, I kept thinking about how often the connection between good schooling and teachers of high quality had emerged in our work. I was pulled toward venturing into a major inquiry, but not if I was to experience again the exhausting chase for money that had accompanied our study of schooling.

Back home, I composed a letter to Robert Payton, summarizing both my possible interest and reservations. I do not recall whether or not I had sent it, but it had not reached its destination when Scott Miller, a senior program officer of the Exxon Education Foundation, called to say that he thought *A Place Called School* warranted a sequel on teacher education. I was hooked. Planning grants from that foundation and from the Mertz-Gilmore Foundation produced the design of a nationwide study. Subsequent grants from both eased my concerns over funding, brought into being in 1985 the Center for Educational Renewal (CER) at the University of Washington, and launched years of satisfying work.

The year of transition from Los Angeles to Seattle proved to be both busy and complex. The grants enabled me to recruit Ken Sirotnik, but an attractive offer took the Heckman family to southern Maine and its university there. In casual conversations with Roger Soder in Miller Hall at the University of Washington, I concluded that his considerable talents were at the time underused. And so it came about that he, Ken, and I joined in creating the CER and the National Network (of school-university partnerships) for Educational Renewal (NNER). The ten members listed by *Education Week* in April 1986 included the BYU-Public School Partnership, the Puget Sound Educational Consortium, and the Southern Maine Partnership (directed by Paul). We had been involved in creating all of these. The partnership we had launched in California was in transition following our departure, looking for a university to replace UCLA.

Meanwhile, Ken, Roger, and I were digging into the existing literature on educating teachers as well as literature describing the education of practitioners in a dozen other professions. Abraham Flexner's study of medical education, combined with what we had learned from the study of schooling, provided a good deal of the direct, hands-on methodology we thought would be most productive. Interestingly, the history of problems and issues in professional education, whatever the field, proved to be surprisingly similar, but comparisons surprisingly few. There is much these fields of professional education could learn from one another.

The core of our inquiry consisted of nearly three dozen rather straightforward questions to be answered by studying the descriptions of a representative sample of educator-preparing settings in eight census districts of the United States, from questionnaires to be answered by students near the end of their preparation programs and their teachers, and from interviews with a wide range of people in both the institutions of higher education and neighboring schools and school districts. Our two teams of three members each conducted over 1,800 hours of interviews in addition to engaging in a wide range of informal conversations in all of the participating settings.

Our hosts in the settings did not view us as being on an evaluative junket; they welcomed us and were, in general, rather eager to engage in conversation. We had been very careful to respect the anonymity of the settings involved but most considered themselves "selected," as had the schools in our earlier study. Several managed to track down where we had been before and, thanks to the cooperation of those settings already visited, were looking forward to our visit. The length of the questionnaires was the only complaint we heard, and we readily agreed. Time limitations had prevented us from further refining them before we went on the road, traveling every other week from early September 1987 through most of May 1988. As with schools, we found a remarkable programmatic sameness from very different setting to very different setting—urban, suburban, rural, small colleges and large universities, private and public, historically black, and more. As with schools, we found an absence of clear institutional and programmatic mission, loose connections among the primary stakeholders, personnel overburdened with human-intensive routine and compliance with imposed expectations, and an enterprise geared to longstanding regularities and deep structures. Our conversations about program and institutional renewal were provocative, largely because of its envisioned novelty. Stories of past efforts of renewal cut off by the impositions of new state mandates were, however, not at all novel experiences in our travels from setting to setting.

We were only a couple of years into our work with the ten settings of the NNER when we became acutely aware of collaborative difficulties that we found later to be characteristic of school-university relationships. We did not have the resources to provide the second group of seven partnerships with the support we had given the three we had worked with. We had relied more on their assurance of readiness and interest than evidence gained through close association of the kind we had enjoyed with the initial three.

Individuals representing several of these in our meetings seemed not to have internalized the statement of mission and conditions of the common agenda they had initially agreed to follow. A couple claimed to have renewed their teacher education programs already. Some individuals from universities balked at the idea of "equal" partnership with the school side of the equation. When the question was raised, "Whose agenda is this anyway?" we began to realize that we were not all on the same track, as initially thought.[2]

We kept the network at least breathing through the good work of three able regional coordinators—Dick Clark, Paul Heckman, and Carol Wilson—each serving part time as a "critical friend" of three or four settings, while we intensified our study of the education of educators. We were becoming more and more aware of the fact that partnering is a benign, appealing notion. The partnering of business enterprises with schools was coming into vogue. But our idea of joining the school or college of education and the arts and sciences departments of a university with schools in processes of simultaneous renewal that embraced teacher education clearly is a quite different order of partnering—more like expecting beagles to cuddle up with bunnies. We became acutely aware that education in and commitment to a well-defined common agenda and an infrastructure supporting the interests of all participating parties would be necessary—and perhaps even then not sufficient.

GENESIS OF AN EDUCATIONAL AGENDA

We had come to the study of the education of educators aware of the considerable disconnect between elementary and secondary schools and institutions of higher education. But I do not think we anticipated the degree to which this study would link with our earlier studies of educational change and schooling in revealing and even explaining the consequences—the hold, if you will, of the deep structures of both sets of institutions on their policies and practices.[3]

Ken, Roger, and I certainly carried in our heads some hypotheses about the degree to which both sets of institutions in their conduct reflect the class-oriented values that exist in our society. We certainly had read a good deal of the writing of those revisionists and reconceptualists who view "the common school" as not at all common, serving a selective role in differentiating the educational opportunities of the haves and have-nots. And, of course, there are those wags who tell us that the crown jewels in our system of higher education are our substitute for those of a royal family.

Mission

What did surprise us was the near absence in our deliberately purposeful conversations and interviews of references to the roles of either schools or universities in providing for the young an introduction to the

freedoms and responsibilities of citizens in a democracy. On every college and university campus in our sample, I asked assembled groups of
students who were near the end of their teacher education programs
what they saw their purposes as educators to be. None got even close to
suggesting serving their schools in a democratic mission. Few said anything about purpose beyond attending to their future pupils' classroom
learning. Connecting their school to some larger public good was seen
as the possible responsibility of the principal. Are we, then, to leave
enculturation of the young into a social and political democracy to the
teachings of the marketplace?[4]

Professors thought this process of enculturation to be very important
but admitted that it was not an articulated purpose of their educational
programs. Some said that the idea of educating for civil dispositions and
civic responsibility merited attention but that many of their students
were too young to become versed in the concepts and principles
involved. We found three settings where, clearly, some of these were
being attended to in the so-called historical and philosophical foundations of education courses, but even in these institutions, few students
were able to recall much about those teachings encountered early in
their programs.

We did not find in the descriptive materials published by the institutions in our sample statements of mission that included commitment
to preparing the young for responsible citizenship. Indeed, after a brief
summary of institutional history, most of these documents got quickly
into a listing of administrators, academic and professional divisions, and
programs. Colleges connected to various religious sects did include language of moral and ethical commitment. In general, however, the
absence of articulated educational purpose suggests the assumption that
no justification of worth is necessary. The faith of a public in higher
education is, presumably, taken for granted.

I had walked the halls of each school in our study of schooling with
the principal and, occasionally, with a vice-principal. Always, I brought
our conversation around to expectations of parents. Almost always, I
was told that there was no commonality among them, that there were
no agreed-upon purposes. Some wanted more of this, some more of

that. I encountered no awareness of there being almost unanimous public agreement on personal, social, vocational, and academic development of the young in schools. Without communicating with one another, Ernest Boyer and I both entitled chapters in our books on schooling "We Want It All."

Furthermore, interest in all four of these purposes is so balanced that we complain as parents when one appears to us to be neglected. These principals seemed not to realize that parental demands for one usually mean that they perceive it to be out of balance with the others. Schools could satisfy many parental concerns by developing mission statements articulating all four purposes and providing periodic reports on their continuing attention to them.

A rewarding feature of all three of the major studies earlier described was that gathering the array of data occupied a considerable period of time. Consequently, we were into thinking about problems and issues emerging before we were nearly overwhelmed by data collation and interpretation. Early on, we became intrigued with the paradox presented by lack of clear articulation of and commitment to an educational mission in the institutions we were studying and yet the considerable agreement of parents and teachers on the purposes of schooling.

It appeared to us that most people going about their business each day possess a kind of intuitive awareness of what Ken Sirotnik refers to as "a 'moral ecology' held together by a political democracy and the fundamental values embedded in the system," which I cited in Chapter 11.[5] For many immigrants, especially from countries with despotic regimes, it is the expectation of entering into this ecology, however dimly envisioned, as much as anticipated economic betterment that brought them to the United States of America. Coming from Canada, I had previously experienced much of what I had anticipated. Boning up for the questions in the one-on-one interview that preceded declaration of my now being a citizen presented no great challenge, but for most, it was a mini-apprenticeship in our rights and responsibilities. The tears, cries of joy, and hugging among strangers of the hundred or more people pronounced citizens on that day a half century ago will be in my memory for the rest of my years.

Being born into citizenship does not enculturate one in the concepts and principles of this moral ecology that we refer to as democracy. Nor, of course, does preparation for the award of citizenship. Should not our schools, whether private or public, provide in common the necessary apprenticeship? Ken, Roger, and I built the necessity for such into the mission statement of the agenda we designed for the second and much more rigorously constructed iteration of the National Network for Educational Renewal: Agenda for Education in a Democracy.[6]

Conditions and Strategies

It is not my intent here to provide a detailed description of the agenda, but to address some aspects of why and how it came about. Implicit also is my intent to make clear the fundamental difference between an agenda that emerged out of decades of reflective experience and comprehensive inquiry into the phenomena of schooling, teacher education, and educational change and those many agendas that emerge out of the short-term deliberations of busy people, many of them strangers to the terrain. The sporadic school reform initiatives emerging from the latter almost always single out as targets students and teachers who, with little or no added leverage, are to do better what they already do.

Most of what we found missing were the conditions necessary to creating a potent culture for change and renewal or, for that matter, to implementing the misguided reform agendas imposed upon them. Our fear has been that our agenda would be caught up in the clichés of easy implementation and thus doomed to ignoble failure. A mission is not just a set of "out there" purposes to be attained. The agenda provides a portrait of conditions to be put in place and strategies for doing so. Mission, conditions, and strategies are all guided by the same concepts and principles. In other words, they must all be in accord with the agenda's democratic underpinnings. Achieving democracy by authoritarian means is an oxymoron.

For the most part, we found the educational institutions we studied to be safe, stable places. The people responsible for them were, on the whole, committed to the well-being of their students and, indeed, to their daily work—which took up about a quarter to a third more time each week than does the work of most people. As with most professionals, their commitments are not easily put aside. Teachers are consumed by the labor-intensive enterprise of providing safe daycare for the young, a steady stream of group educational experiences in a small space, and a necessarily controlled environment of myriad interpersonal relationships. Reflection on mission, assessment of progress, and change were seen by some as an unaffordable luxury; by others a wearying burden to be avoided.

Is it any wonder that strategic planning, to use the corporate nomenclature, is virtually a nonevent? Is it any wonder that future teachers, with memories of their years as students in school, focus their preparatory attention on being ready to manage a class and want to gather up acorns for later winter days of teaching? Complaints of teachers are little about being unable to handle the subject matter of the curriculum but much about being unable to deal with diverse groups of students and their parents. Again, most reformers have teachers' needs diagnosed all wrong. It is ironic, with information so accessible, that computers are so infrequently put to work in relieving teachers of the information-giving role they still play, leaving the time for renewal they and their schools so badly need.

We found in the settings we studied, almost uniformly, three or four groups of personnel, each isolated from the others, engaged in delivering teacher education: in the arts and sciences and the departments of education in colleges and universities, in the cooperating schools, and between the two sets of institutions supervising student teachers scattered about.[7] For many, preparing teachers was not their primary work. Planning together ranged from casual to nil. Rarely were several student teachers members of a cohort group, readily conversing together in a school setting; rarely were they participants in schoolwide staff responsibilities—apprentice faculty, so to speak. A major task of the director of teacher education was that of checking curricular offerings against state requirements for teacher licensing and ensuring that there were people to staff them.

Teacher educators caught up in this splintered enterprise, much controlled by outside forces, have good reason to envy and be awed by professional education in other fields such as law, the whole of it embraced by one institutional unit answering primarily to one external requirement, the bar exam, which is significantly influenced by those who provide the instruction. It was to this greater unification of intent, program, and authorization for practice that we addressed our major recommendations: one composite faculty with clearly marked boundaries of responsibility, an overall unifying agenda, "teaching" partner schools similar to the teaching hospitals of medical education, future teachers in cohorts engaged with experienced teachers in the renewal of these schools and the teacher education program, and the whole encompassed within a center of pedagogy, equal in support and autonomy to university-based schools of business, engineering, law, and medicine. As with law and medicine, certification of successful completion of the preparation program would authorize sitting for the external licensing examination required for entry into practice.

We spelled out some five dozen conditions that emerged from our findings in the field and from reflection on them as necessary to robust programs grounded in democratic principles of mission and conduct. Most of these connect the theory and practice of teacher education with the theory and practice of teaching and learning embedded in the substantial knowledge base that has steadily grown over the past several decades. We grouped these into twenty propositions—referred to as postulates—for renewing schooling and the education of educators. We found both to be geared to the preservation of what exists. Indeed, we found significant change to be a novel idea.

Cultural Norms and Institutional Renewal

The tidying of my mind taking place through all of the experiences described in the foregoing brought sharp awareness of the gulf between the path down which our system of public schooling has been heading and the quite different path my learning tells me is essential. This latter path is necessary, I believe, to the well-being of both our children and our nation. Awareness for me began more than thirty years ago when we commenced the slide of our schools away from home and local place.

We began to attach to schools, in the early 1970s, a role in which they cannot succeed, a role made primary in the 1983 report, *A Nation at Risk*. It is one thing to attach education of the young to decency, civility, civic involvement, good work, and making the most of themselves. In this learning, they can find many romances that help them understand who they are and want to be. But to make childhood instrumental primarily to prepare for adulthood in an unknown future is to play God, the height of sacrilege.

Politically driven school reform is often accompanied by still another oxymoron: "It's all for the children." When I ask groups what is for the children, the silence is deafening. The more schools are drawn away from local control and debate, the more public schooling is regarded as not serving the public and failing. The more it is regarded as failing, the more the people are drawn toward divisive privatization.

There is not anywhere in federal and state debate and platform even the beginnings of a plan for what will replace our system of public schooling in providing the apprenticeship in social and political democracy necessary to the nation's health. Political scientist Benjamin Barber warns us of the danger: "If schools are the neglected forges of our future, they are also the abandoned workshops of our democracy. In attacking not just education but *public* education, critics are attacking the very foundation of our democratic civic culture. Public schools are not merely schools *for* the public, but schools of publicness: institutions where we learn what it means to *be* a public and start down the road toward common national and civic identity. . . . We stay afloat only if we recognize that we are all aboard a single ship."[8]

Chapter 7 of this narrative, entitled "Loss of Innocence," is centered on my four years at Biscoq. My experiences there were, in retrospect, the beginnings of useful learnings about the way in which external expectations and internal dynamics combine to inhibit risk taking for institutional change. Change is at best cosmetic in the absence of a culture of risk. Subtleties in the interactions of key players there provided lessons in when and when not to risk and how much, when and what to trust and when not, when to fight and when to save the energy it takes, when to heed and when to ignore the temptation to move on to new adventures, the edification of harboring a little but not too much cynicism, and more. The human-intensive nature of educational institutions and the democratic ethos most endeavor to sustain complicate the risk-taking leadership required for breaking the bounds of internal custom and external expectations and tend to inhibit common agreement around the substance of serious inquiry.

The most disturbing aspect of my loss of innocence at Biscoq was in coming to realize that, lacking a culture of internal renewal, institutions come to sustain as desirable much of what should be discarded. The goal becomes one of keeping things very much as they have been. Intrusions are welcomed when perceived to massage the status quo; rejected or recast when they are seen to threaten it.[9] The awards go to conformity with mediocrity, hailed as excellence. The book-become-movie, *One Flew over the Cuckoo's Nest*—the story of a mental institution frozen in time—provides the quintessential and simultaneously paradoxical model.

Absent the superbly executed risk taking of Hugh Christie, Biscoq would have come close to being the quintessential custodial but little-educational reform school, conforming to both internal and external reinforcing norms of what reform schools are for and should be. Instead, his influence provided fascinating, if somewhat schizophrenic, educative theater. My loss of innocence there focused on the impact of these internal and external forces on my developing assumptions of what good education is and good teachers should do. My later loss and gain embraced a much larger compass and resulted in several major conclusions about constancy and change in schooling.

Wrong Things Become the Norm

First, the things my experiences and inquiries told me had gone wrong in schools had not gone wrong at all. Rather, they neatly fit a pattern of regularities that have not gone wrong but are the longstanding characteristics of a place called school—the deep structure—whether public or private. These wrong things are commonalities of the schools that we attended once upon a time, that gave some of us romances, some of us nightmares, and most of us both. Many of these are wrongs that ill-informed reform eras seek to have schools do better. Many of these are precisely the wrongs many people include when asked to envision the schools they would like to have in the future. Some of these wrongs are those the neo-Confucian philosopher Chu Hsi sought to remove from China's schools more than eight hundred years ago. Some of these wrongs are those our early settlers brought from Europe where the "moral ethic" transmitted from religious leaders of the sixteenth and seventeenth centuries to parents regarding responsibility for the education of their children was accompanied by a caveat: School was to be "an instrument of strict discipline, protected by the law-courts and the police-courts."[10]

Second, however high-sounding the rhetoric of so-called school improvement or reform, the changes sought by external mandate have rarely been grounded in moral principle or effort to change policies or practices judged educationally wrong. We have heard much in recent years about the wrongness of *social* promotion, as if it were some malignant legacy of a few remaining left-overs from the near demise of progressive education. Actually, the practice referred to would more accurately be called *economic* promotion. Late in the nineteenth century, Presidents Eliot and Harper of Harvard and the University of Chicago, respectively, spoke out strongly against the repeated grade retention of students they saw as causing early drop out from school and problems of mental health of students—essentially a moral argument that influenced existing practices not a bit. A decade later, Leonard Ayres did a study that alerted the leaders of large urban school districts to the added costs of retaining pupils in grades and thus increasing the time and costs of their completing elementary schooling. Almost immediately, the call to principals was to keep moving the children along. *Social* promotion?

Third, the experiences of thoughtful educators with the rigidities, regularities, and ineffective educational practices of a school system that hardened into place years ago, together with the supporting evidence of decades of scholarly inquiry, add up to the need and many specifics for sweeping change—a corpus of informed opinions and wisdom not just ignored but commonly rejected as irrelevant to politically driven agendas of reform. There are in this country no mechanisms powerful enough to counter with funded knowledge the educational media campaigns of powerful political figures, most of which offer quick-fix solutions to the entrenched problems they are supposed to address. Ironically, the Republican Party that opposed creation of a federal department of education, rightly in my judgment, is now exceeding the Democratic Party in using it for the very intervention in schooling it not long ago rejected.

Fourth, the net result of these three sets of conditions is that parents, educators, and the general public are caught between a rhetoric of improving the schools they know and one of making changes appearing to connect better with the lives of children. And most want it all: schools that are safe and orderly attending to the personal, social, vocational, and academic development of the young. Parents want it for their children; teachers want it for their students; and almost everybody else wants it because they have to live in this world with other people's children.

What has been missing, however, are mechanisms built into the infrastructures having sufficient legitimacy to introduce into the system powerfully informed proposals for change. This lack caused little immediate harm when the debate and control of schools were local—when supporting the local school had the moral ring to it of doing good for the children. But it did leave schooling mired in its outdated deep structure and bashing it often in fashion.

The vacuum created by the absence of powerful mechanisms for renewal, combined with continued high public interest in education, invited political intrusion beyond the scope of local school boards. High dependence on property tax levies requiring more than simple majorities for approval has elevated the willingness of school districts to comply with federal mandates in exchange for the low dollar returns that, nonetheless, bail out their shamefully low budgets. There is a nasty word for this kind of relationship in human exchanges.

With the rhetoric accompanying federal dollars neatly geared to the conventional wisdom regarding the economic benefits of schooling, there is little local debate over the wisdom of the imposed agenda—these things too shall pass. Unfortunately, they probably will pass into a new era of failed school reform, perhaps mandated this time by leaders of that other political party not now in power. The schools—particularly in the most impoverished sectors of the country—are left each time a little worse off than they were before.

THE THEATER OF ALTERNATIVE
EDUCATIONAL SCENARIOS

The links between the general public (and even teachers) and accumulating knowledge relevant to education and schooling are weak. There are no research breakthroughs reported by the media comparable to those in the health arena. Knowledge about topics as central as cognition has minimal entry into the conventional wisdom. There are some advantages to this. As my former colleague Sherman Melinkoff, long-term dean of the UCLA School of Medicine, once said, "When a quack cure for cancer gets out into the public arena, there is no bringing it back."

This omission probably contributes to sustaining a kind of theater of alternative educational scenarios that audiences with attachments to schooling find both plausible and entertaining. This is not theater of the absurd but, rather, theater of the near impossible. Like other educators I know, I have made my share of appearances on this stage. Years ago, the education editor of the *Christian Science Monitor* wrote somewhat as follows: "Teachers listen attentively to what John Goodlad has to say and then go back to their classrooms to do precisely what they did before." Having listened many times to visitors at the UES saying that there was no structure in their schools even for discussing what they had seen and would like to do, her observation did not surprise me. Nor would it have surprised me if she had written the same thing about my appearances on the stage at conferences of school board members.

But the reaction of members of an audience at the annual meeting of the Education Commission of the States (ECS) in 1999 both surprised me and contributed significantly to my thinking about material change in schooling. Having worked closely with James B. Conant and having discussed with him his proposal to create the ECS as a substitute for the ministry of education in many nations, I was delighted to be receiving the award created in his honor.

I was a little uneasy about the obligatory speech. I planned to include educational alternatives to the politically driven, high-stakes testing reform movement getting under way, and I was a guest of the organization created to assist chief state school officers and governors in their policy making. The reception had been long and the dinner one of several substantial courses. Perhaps it was because bright lights were in my eyes that I viewed the audience as surprisingly attentive. And apparently it really was.

I do not think the standing ovation was entirely due to my having stayed within the allocated fifteen minutes. I was later told that the conversations that ensued spread out into the restrooms and elevators. The following week, I read in the *Chronicle of Higher Education* the report of a writer who had been part of the elevator discourse that raised and answered a question. It went something like the following: "Why is it that we applaud John Goodlad's proposals but do nothing about them?" The answer: "Because nobody has the power." The same conversation might well have occurred about others who, over the years, have been applauded for their educational proposals. Many names come to mind.

Has the long run of educational theater blurred the distinction between what is real and what is not? Or does the infrastructure of schooling not include mechanisms for significant change? I believe the inertia to be the result of both.

Of course, the blockage is due also to other factors discussed in the foregoing: the deep structure that can be broken loose only with a commitment of resources and time we resist; reform policies directed to strengthening what exists; teacher education geared largely to the status quo; a variety of risks perceived to be contained in giving up the known for the unknown; and more. There is, for example, a kind of cultural unease about changes intended to embrace everybody for fear that equity is finite—inclusiveness reduces my share. Consequently, even though proposals appear reasonably sensible and well informed, it is best to keep them at bay as theater.

Perhaps it is the ubiquitous character of education that causes parents who are lucky enough to find themselves with innovative schools that are highly satisfying to them and their children to look back over their shoulders and worry about what they might be losing that conventional schools provide. The reader may recall my report of those UES parents who were thrilled with their own and their children's satisfaction there but sought tutoring in the curriculum of the schools they were pleased to be avoiding. I might well have referred also to those who urged us to return to conventional school practices during our concluding year. Why? They wanted their children prepared for the not-wanted regularities they expected would characterize the schools soon to be attended.

The alternative scenarios of the script I now follow in educational theater are directed to universal schooling of the young, to schools commonly good for everyone. On the assumption that good is infinite, they are intended to raise the level of the tide for all of them. The script is not copyrighted. Most of it is the work of many people who have contributed to it. Most of it has been brought to the attention of policymakers. Several of the scenarios are crafted below.

Needed: A Comprehensive Narrative for Schooling

The rhetoric linking education and democracy has had a long run since this nation's founding—from Thomas Jefferson through many advocates to the present. Our Agenda for Education in a Democracy has enjoyed considerable attention and acclaim. Since that day of infamy, September 11, 2001, we have been frequently told that our agenda is more important than ever, that it is essential for our young to have deep appreciation and understanding of what it means to live in and sustain a free society.

But the goal of such an agenda's becoming a guiding narrative of schooling struggles for time and attention even among the settings committed to it in the National Network for Educational Renewal. There is widespread belief in the land that high test scores signal good schools in which the traditional educational purposes of personal, social, vocational, and academic development of the young flourish. But, alas, those scores predict little of this. Indeed, they correlate scarcely at all with any virtue one might wish for, whether in the rational or the divine idiom of the moral ecology necessary to the guidance of the ship we are all aboard.

The mandates of the federal No Child Left Behind Act squeeze out the time necessary to the renewal of schooling and teacher education called for in the agenda. It is difficult for teachers and teacher educators to be enthusiastic about a law that an Assistant Secretary of Elementary and Secondary Education contended will, "if implemented the right way, put an end to creative and experimental teaching methods in the nation's classrooms."[11]

Given the present state of the economy, philanthropic support for ventures outside of mainstream public support is hard to come by. Fortunately, there are some admirable exceptions. Boundary-breaking innovative initiatives that flourished in some schools just a few years ago have either disappeared or are of low profile. The e-mail denial of our request to a foundation that had previously supported implementation of the agenda was straightforward: "We're not interested in supporting democratic schools but in improving test scores."

Leaving No Children Behind

Those responsible for the No Child Left Behind Act had either forgotten the Coleman Report of 1966 or were unaware of its implications for leaving no child behind at the starting gate of schooling. James Coleman's conclusions about the impact of social and economic capital on children's learning apply to the early years of life in spades. There has been no refutation but plenty of added evidence to support Benjamin Bloom's stunning report of 1964. His was no single study but a collation of hundreds.[12] He noted that the impact of environment on children's cognitive development is particularly powerful during the first four years, in which about half of the development attained by the late teens is gained. Add up to 30 percent more by the age of eight, and the importance of leaving no children behind because of a deprived early environment shouts out at us. Are we listening? I see little sign of such in federal policy and action.

Listening and acting imply doing what many countries in Western Europe and beyond have been doing for years: providing all young families with a safety net of health, education, and other human services.[13] This means, of course, differentiating the allocation of resources in order to provide a good safety net for all. This will be resisted, as I already have noted, by those who see goodness as finite, resulting in their thinking that they must give up some of the space they now occupy in the net in order to accommodate others. There is nothing new in this obstacle. The essence of our binding moral ecology demands that we remove it.

With many others, I have been advocating for years an adjustment in schooling that would increase access to learning for *all* our children. It has to do with access to the starting gate of schooling. The half or more of four-year-olds now in programs of early education are predominantly from the more affluent half of the population—the half also most able to provide an educative home environment. Both halves should have equal access to early public schooling at the age of four—by the children's fourth birthday, not by the arbitrary late summer date set once a year in today's schools.[14]

When I propose this to audiences of parents of young children, policymakers such as members of state senate committees, school board members, and others, there is a considerable nodding of heads. One would expect this adjustment in school admission dates to have occurred long ago, whatever the entrance age. But the stupid, discriminatory policy of once-a-year admission remains encased in the traditional block of concrete.

In visiting schools, I hear again and again from teachers that many children arrive not ready for school. Noting that they have a legal right to attend on meeting the age requirement, I ask instead why the school is not ready for all the children. I then suggest that the entering children come on their birthdays to be greeted with a brief celebration.

This causes considerable consternation, and so I modify the suggestion by proposing that a day be announced each month when all turning four in, say, February would become eligible to begin and to share the party. This would be a beginning move to break down the graded lock-step of school structure and to ensure entry into a stable classroom culture. Today's initial entry policies are essentially what I encountered on my first day at North Star School more than seven decades ago. To those among us who contend that teachers need only preparation in subject matter, I offer the opportunity to welcome in September and to be alone responsible for a class of twenty five-year-olds during its first three weeks in school.

Retrofitting School Structure

In recommending the availability of schooling for all children by their fourth birthday, I am not recommending lengthening schooling by a year. Rather, I think it should be shortened a year by cutting off two—the last two years of the current high school. We now have a rather sloppy system of schooling—in organization, curriculum, and pedagogy—made compulsory up to the age of sixteen in large measure to keep the older adolescents off the streets and out of the labor market. To keep attendance palatable for as long as possible, we added an array of goodies to the stark and spare institution that came into the Great Depression of the 1930s unchanged for its much more inclusive role. Today, we have a high school that struggles to be academic in a student culture where to be good looking, athletic, or both ranks far above being academically smart in the pecking order of popularity. In some schools, gang members rank higher.

A critical question to be answered is why we continue to include seventeen- and eighteen-year-olds—and even older young adults—in this anachronistic setting. I say "young adults" because virtually everything once almost completely cordoned off as the privilege of working adults is now available to them. Indulgence in alcohol, drugs, and sex is far from absent among younger teens, but the incidence of participation steps up sharply in the culture of the older. Are they best suited to remain as role models for their younger schoolmates?

But, leaving this anomaly aside, what about the academic fit? Increasingly, sharp attention is turning to the misfit between the senior year of high school and what many students aspire to. Common among parents of high school seniors is conversation about graduation requirements having already been met and not much of interest being available. Then there is the surprisingly heavy use of advanced placement in college courses, dual credit for courses in high school that are taken in community colleges, and other arrangements to accommodate academically the young adults referred to above.

Let's just cut into the concrete of schooling's deep structure and retrofit it into an updated, age-four-to-sixteen model better suited to the developmental characteristics of the young and their twenty-first century circumstances. My plan is for there to be three small four-year units, each with differentiated educational functions. These would be somewhat aligned with philosopher Whitehead's stages of learning, briefly mentioned in Chapter 2: the early unit devoted to romantic exploration of children's close-at-hand world, extended through stories of other times and places; the middle unit of greater precision, connecting with the larger human and natural environment; and the third emphasizing generalization and application. Of course, this cycle should characterize the learning environment within each unit beyond its primary emphasis.

Each unit would be staffed by teams chosen to encompass the demands on teaching seen to be embedded in its designated functions and the developmental stage of the students. The three units would stretch over twelve years of general education, no more, no less. Students would neither begin nor end in the same place. Uniformity is the dreary goal most nearly attained when the path is narrow and creativity discouraged. Romances with learning are rare when such is the mantra of schooling.

Since the school I envision is to be an apprenticeship in living together and sustaining our human and natural habitat, the organizing centers for learning are to be largely common, each providing ample opportunity for pursuing individual interests and special talents.[15] Since the teaching staffs of small units are likewise small, schools must be closely aligned with educational resources beyond, if these special interests and talents are to be cultivated. We now have the reality and potential of technology—especially that of multimedia—to effect some of these connections, especially for schools in geographically isolated communities. Inventories of these resources—local and beyond—reveal an incredible pool of potentially voluntary teaching talent.

Curriculum and Pedagogy

There are, lying around unused, more good ideas in the domains of curriculum and pedagogy than in any other area of schooling. The gap between what exists in practice and what should and could be productively used is enormous. The curriculum of elementary schools is organized largely around the roots of academic disciplines torn from the soil that nourished them, dead before their arrival in textbooks. No wonder several professors at the University of Chicago told me that they would prefer that college freshmen come to their classes with their virginity intact in such fields as mathematics and the natural sciences. There would then be little damage to remedy. Even pupils with high test scores in these fields fail to recognize in problems of daily life the relevance of the very concepts and principles tested. Transfer from classroom to workplace is low. As I have written in preceding pages, if learnings are to be part of one's functional repertoire, they must find use there soon and often.

Then why not start with present knowledge hospitable to accretions that explain and enrich rather than with knowledge devoid of experiential context? Better a hungry learner searching for intellectual nourishment than savory educational food in search of a diner. But these are not polarized choices. The pedagogical challenge is to help the two find one another.

As others have tried in years past, I have endeavored to gain support for a proposal that would structure at least part of the school curriculum around scenarios that start with characteristics of the world we live in rather than the disciplines developed to interpret them. The pedagogical intent would be to help the young develop the intellectual tools necessary to addressing the problems and issues arising out of inquiry into these scenarios. The academic disciplines would become the tools rather than the subjects of inquiry. These scenarios would be for the purpose of guiding teachers to begin with children's experiences and beliefs regarding their world. There is plenty of evidence to support the proposition that, once perceived to be relevant to a larger context of interest, the academic disciplines often then become valued in their own right. This in part explains, I think, why those lovers of their disciplines at the University of Chicago were distressed with what they perceived to be abuse of them in the lower schools.

A proposal, absent suitors, that rests in my files would draw educational implications from a clutch of scholars who have transcended their disciplines in addressing the characteristics, problems, and issues in the domains of the transforming world these fields of inquiry are intended to help us understand. Collectively, their disciplines would include the major ones constituting Kenneth Boulding's classification of the world's systems of learning embedded in the human conversation: the human species; the global village (social, political, and economic); and the world as a physical, biological, evaluative, belief, communicative, and expressive system.[16]

The major questions to be asked of these wise people in interviews would be these two: What experiences in your life most influenced your choice of the discipline you chose to study in depth? What turned your interest to inquiry into the larger domains of the human conversation? Over an extended period of time, we would ask them to draw out what would be most important for the rest of us to learn. Scholars and practitioners in the field of education would then engage each of these in determining implications for educating the young. The next step would be the construction of multimedia curricular scenarios designed not for replication but for stimulating the creativity of teachers in fulfilling the educational expectations of the three units of the redesigned school proposed above.

THESE THINGS TOO SHALL PASS

The clock for measuring the passage of time for beginning the overhaul of our system of public schooling has tolled its bell for many years. It has tolled with little effect in more favorable times. The high-stakes risks for local schools in seeking to break out of the current nationwide mold of reform mandates promotes a hunkering down. When reform eras fade or come to a rather sudden halt—as with a change in political party leadership—the urge of schools' stewards is usually to recover lost, not to explore new, ground. When they begin to listen again to the bell tolling, another era of mandates looms on the horizon.

The work in which colleagues and I have been engaged over a large chunk of time powerfully supports the potential for a closely linked partnering of schools, universities, and their communities committed to a common agenda to sustain renewal. There is a clutch of other initiatives with agendas that connect closely with ours. It takes a powerful coordinated effort to sustain renewal—a process of keeping institutions on a steady course while shedding old regularities and taking on the new. When some of the energy required is being siphoned off to cope with what the federal laws mandate, it is the rare renewal effort that is not slowed down or stifled. When leadership is not widely shared, designated positional leaders are sorely tried.

Our initiative of advancing the Agenda for Education in a Democracy is better positioned than some others not aligned with what currently is politically correct. Our studies of change confirmed those of others: When the positional leaders who champion boundary-breaking initiatives leave, support for their causes commonly evaporates. Consequently, with the second iteration of the NNER taking shape, we created in 1992 the independent, nonprofit Institute for Educational Inquiry (IEI), with the initial purpose of ensuring cadres of well-prepared leaders in each setting.

Several of us moved quickly to design the IEI Leadership Program that brought to Seattle over successive years key personnel from every NNER setting. We largely succeeded in getting in each cohort a mix representing the university arts and sciences departments and colleges of education and K–12 schools participating in teacher education. Each cohort participated throughout a year in four sessions of four and one-half days each in reading, seminars, and conducting projects focused on problems and issues arising out of endeavoring to implement the agenda in their own settings. Most of these representative teams later took responsibility for conducting adaptations of the IEI program in their own settings. Ken Sirotnik's report on the NNER showed very clearly that settings devoting most attention to developing a strong leadership group suffered least loss of momentum with the retirement or departure of designated positional leaders such as deans and school administrators.

However, the present era of simplistic, one-size-fits-all reform has spread across the nation like kudzu, squeezing out almost everything but preparation for tests. With their time and energy so consumed, even the most committed and enlightened educators have difficulty hanging on to the better practices that not long ago they were trying to replace.

I trust that this era of school reform mandate, too, will pass. But, as I have noted, the study of several reform eras of the past half-century reveals a disturbing cycle. Each leaves behind it a flat weariness, an "eduvirus" of inertia. Next time, as the era stalls and begins to fall, we must hasten with the implementation of two initiatives we should be planning now. The first is to develop a script for aligning our schools with the best informed lore of knowledge and belief that exists—a plan for bringing our schools into the twenty-first century. The second is a script for creating an infrastructure that simultaneously supports renewal and protects the nation from the monkeying around that so far has characterized school reform. To repeat, we must begin these things now; otherwise we will spend our time and energy in repeating the aftermath of the reform cycle—getting back to where we were before it spread its mantle over the nation's schools.

A few years ago, I received a short document and then a visit from a Canadian sociologist of extensive international experiences, David Wolsk. He expected a great deal of me: the coordination of an effort much like what I have just described but for the world, not just the United States. The concern stated in his written proposal was that there is no infrastructure for dealing in an orderly way with the world's present circumstances. As earlier noted, we entered the present millennium with a third of the world's 193 nations embroiled in conflict. David saw powerful education as our only hope. Of course, there are many treatises on our dilemma, most of which cite education as the solution. But these, too, have been the stuff of theater.

David's plan sounded grandiose, but he quickly demonstrated the reasonableness of its considerable cost when contrasted with the many times greater cost of the plethora of less comprehensive efforts that failed to slow acceleration of worldwide problems. In brief, his plan was to identify a hundred of the most thoughtful thinkers of the world, recruit a fund-raiser for each, and set them individually to work, full time, in preparing a comprehensive educational plan and the infrastructure of its implementation. My small job was to monitor the whole and bring the pieces together collaboratively into an appealing quilt.

Not persuaded, I suggested to David that he cut the number of wise people to twenty-five, carefully chosen to represent each of the major pieces that ultimately would be integrated. My second suggestion was that the initiative be coordinated by an individual widely known and respected worldwide.

At about the same time, I was writing a much less ambitious proposal of two parts. The first called for the president of the United States entering office in 2005 to take action on a massive study, completed the previous year, conducted by a team of scholars selected by the National Academy of Education. The study had delved into the deep malaise of early twenty-first century schooling out of sync with its context. The president was passionately delivering the charge to his newly appointed commission, its members selected in conformance with criteria of independent judgment and integrity, which would for a considerable period devote its attention to educational solutions directed to the elimination of this malaise.

The above account is, of course, fictitious. The second proposal is one that addresses only a piece of the necessary quilt—that of effecting curricular and pedagogical change described a few pages back. Neither is sufficient.

The documents setting forth conditions necessary to the social and political functioning of the Republic omitted specific reference to responsibility for the conduct of education. But there was much said and written then and since regarding the relationship of education to a robust, renewing democracy. Although there is much to be said for this omission, it left the nation with a vacuum that has drawn eduviruses into it.

Do we not need more clarification of what is appropriate and inappropriate federal involvement in schooling? Do we not need a clear mission for schooling grounded in the same moral and ethical principles of democracy itself? Do we not need mechanisms for change as free from political intervention as our wisdom can create and our integrity protect?

Colleagues and I have found education to be as complex a concept and endeavor as democracy itself. The nation has tinkered with its conduct in schools in era after era of expensive, simplistic reform that has succeeded only in depriving many young people of the romances with learning that should be their and their children's heritage.

The need now is for a Bill of Educational Rights and an Educational Constitution intended to ensure and renew this educational heritage. But it is not, however, *only* for the children. This legacy is also the strongest guarantee people could have that the moral ecology now holding us together will be strong enough to ensure the freedoms, responsibilities, and justice embedded in its democratic principles.

Afterword

We do not—or should not—want merely . . . to be content with maintaining or recovering the status quo, holding frozen in amber a now-distant past.

ROGER SODER[1]

One does not casually cast from memory a place that was home and filled with good work for a quarter of a century. Especially if it was once a distant place of imaginary friends and chimeric destiny. Perhaps that is why I do not recall our deciding to leave southern California or saying goodbye to friends and colleagues there.[2]

Actually, the geographic transition spread out over several years; the mental one is not over. The gravitational pull toward the Northwest began, I believe, not long after our leaving Chicago and coming to Los Angeles. Paula and Stephen had been with their grandparents from their early years, but only occasionally. They regarded them as adults with special connection to their parents. Then, Interstate 5 introduced them to the concept of membership in an extended family. The homes of my mother and Len's mother and father in British Columbia became their homes, too, oases to be in for a while each summer.

In Chapter 11, I noted that a strong sense of place in the Northwest was being added during summers on the island. Most days, Paula and Stephen explored the shoreline in our little boat. There were coves lined with seaweed where they caught rockfish, cleaned them, and then cooked them for the supper table. It is the rare author writing about romances with boats who fails to quote Kenneth Graham (in *The Wind in the Willows*): "There is *nothing*—absolutely nothing—half so much worth doing as simply messing about in boats."

We come close, I think, to gaining a sense of the preciousness of the world in which we live and our responsibility to it when we walk for a time on its soil and rocks and live with its trees and water, instead of only on concrete and around the things human beings make from these. A good many summers passed before it became apparent that Paula and Stephen were losing enthusiasm for the usual return to Los Angeles. Another place was beginning to colonize their minds, although we knew that, in just a few days, they would once more become absorbed with friends and activities. There was much of interest and much to learn in both places.

I will not try to guess what was entering Len's mind. She had her own reasons to welcome the gravitational pull. However, she has never anguished over wanting to be elsewhere than where she was nor envied someone else's nest. The existence of our just-built island house had eased a little the pain brought about by the fire that swept through the one in Malibu. After reconstruction, the smell of smoke lived on, anything but a nostalgic reminder. Some years later, she spent most of a year alone in her father's house, visiting with him twice daily during the long hospitalization that preceded his death. To break the loneliness, she sought occasional sanctuary in the familiar setting of our island home, a two-hour drive and a ferry ride away.

I sometimes wonder if humankind ever will manage—or want—to get along without a caste system. Its virulent presence implies that democracy is likely always to be a daunting work in progress. For several years after settling into what a colleague at UCLA, educational philosopher George Kneller, later referred to as Smart Seattle and feeling very much at home, I often felt looked upon as a visitor or transient. A question asked of me, in a rather circumspect and cautious way, appeared to imply the speaker's view of my being on a long sabbatical leave from southern California and UCLA. There seemed to be more embedded in it than "How do you like Seattle?" And my answer seemed less than satisfying, "I'm living where I want to be, doing what I want to do."

The implications of my having stepped down in the educational caste system were more explicit in formal introductions: I was the former dean of the Graduate School of Education at UCLA; my relationship with the University of Washington was obscure. I thought that being a professor there represented a clear affiliation. A year or so after my appointment, Dean Doi laughingly reported that several of my colleagues asked him if he wasn't worried about my possible interest in replacing him. His answer was that his security in the post would be increased with the appointment of seven or eight former deans.

I was beginning to realize that, in the transition into the hybrid career described in the last several chapters, I was steadily giving up major sources of romances with schools: teaching the young or their teachers. Yes, there was a great deal of teaching in the various initiatives in which colleagues and I were engaged. But much of it had more to do with strategies for promoting the moral conduct of schooling than engaging in the moral pedagogy of teaching. Our studies resulted in recommendations for an agenda that includes both. I guess that, at the time of moving to the Northwest, I was lusting to be more player than strategist and coach. Interestingly, in the world of professional sports, it is the players who are paid the most. When some say that they would play for little or no money, they often mean it but are glad that their words are ignored.

For me, becoming dean of a university's professional school was the end of the road in the administration of higher education. The prospect of more money and a house (and more power) in several presidencies to which I was invited was of no interest. Moving up in the caste system would separate me too much from why I became an educator in the first place. There is no better evidence of this observation than the increasing frequency of including corporate executives and military leaders in the candidate pool for university presidencies and school superintendencies.

During my last two years as dean, I stopped formal teaching. I did this not because I wanted to but because I was cheating the students. I had hung on for a couple of years before by co-teaching with Louise Tyler. But I cheated both her and those in our class. I simply was not getting into their lives; I was addressing the "stuff" of the course. Administration and strategies became my full-time thing.

Other deans who made similar decisions before their years were up have mentioned to me what I subsequently experienced: a wonderful lightness of being. They were back to teaching. It is not that we regretted our deaning. Rather, it was the sense of being home again. And hence my answer: I'm living where I want to be, doing what I want to do.

There had been a long gap between my most memorable romances with schools and coming fully home. These had come with the Woodward's Hill one-room school, my class in the little church, and Biscoq. The Englewood School and the UES had provided deeply satisfying learning and collegial experiences, but, I realize now, they did not include the close connections with the young people that schools are for. What I further have come to realize is the incredible similarity of the moral principles of teaching the young and those of teaching their elders. There are similar romances to be had. These are what I had the good fortune to experience again after throwing off the administrative shackles and entering into virtually a new career.

Perhaps this is why I grew impatient with the frequent references to my former place in the academic hierarchy. I was to have two episodes of teaching as satisfying as the three referred to above, this time with adults. The memories of those early years came flooding back, rejuvenating me. I came to realize that not the loneliness of Woodward's Hill School, not the lower status of the White Rock Elementary School in the caste system of schooling, and not the culture of incarceration at Biscoq had robbed me of romances with all three. Nor could my depression over schooling's fall from grace and the dominance of the economic narrative in its current conduct take away from me the romances to be had in the symbiotic joining of teaching and learning.

If learning is, above all else, what it means to be human, and learning with others is what sustains a renewing culture, then it is necessarily lifelong. It does not end when schooling ends. And the romances of the young with learning must not be endangered by making schooling instrumental to adults' predictions of their future. Nobody has come back from the future to tell us what it is like. This perversity has been so excessive that school learning in the present era of reform scarcely connects with the lives of the young in *today's* world.

It is one thing to pay attention to one's students; it is quite another to pay attention to one's teaching. Both are necessary, I think, to experiencing the romantic flow of teaching. Fortunately, for most learning, the self is both teacher and learner, especially in adulthood. Otherwise, I would feel even more guilty than I do for letting my teaching get rusty during the period described in the preceding three chapters. I think I still managed to pay attention to my students. But continuing to teach was more for my mental health than their education.

Although teacher education was the central focus of our study of the education of educators, we picked up a good deal of information about the preparation of school principals. We were not happy with what we found and decided to do something about it at the University of Washington. We found Dick Andrews, head of the College of Education division offering degree programs in educational administration (of which I was now a part), to be concerned about similar issues. He assembled a group representing the Puget Sound Educational Consortium and put us to work.

Within a few months, we had designed a program quite different from those we had found in our research and recruited a cohort of teachers into it. Released from their teaching duties, they were to spend a full year essentially as novice assistant principals in schools, spending a weekday and each Saturday at the university in reflective seminars and sessions for the development of some essential knowledge and skills the job requires. Uniquely, this was not a degree program, although some credits could be used to satisfy requirements for a master's degree. Some of those chosen already had earned that credential.

Candidates did not self-select. They were chosen by a committee representing both the university and the participating school districts. The criteria were many and comprehensive. A very able cohort of experienced teachers has been selected each year over the fifteen years this program has been in existence, and graduates are eagerly sought for positions that become available.

Five themes constituted the original design of the curriculum, not broken down into courses. We had decided that, since education (and therefore teaching) is a moral endeavor, so must be educational leadership. I had the good fortune to take on teaching responsibility for one of the five themes, a role that provided deep satisfaction over the next six years. Joining me for each of these were, I recall, about seventeen or eighteen experienced teachers, ranging in age from the late twenties into the fifties, whose experiences in teaching the young were much fresher than mine.

We read and we talked for the first several sessions. For each session, they brought me a "Dear John" letter, telling me about and reflecting on the readings, experiences in their new posts, and whatever else they wished. I returned these at our next session with my comments and questions on each and reactions to what they had written. Meanwhile, they were looking into their school settings for what we referred to as moral dilemmas—situations about which more data might be useful but which were grounded essentially in moral principles, and particularly conflicting moral principles.

During the second half of our sessions together, each presented a dilemma, explained why it was in essence moral, and took a stand on its clarification or resolution. Needless to say, our conversations were intense. I recall almost every participant over the years admitting to wrenching changes in educational belief. Especially gratifying to me was the degree to which they saw as critical to their school's functioning and to their new learning and that of the students the kind of ethical and moral culture that lay within the power of all the stakeholders to create.

I always will remember the words of a member of one group, spoken as the confessional that so often characterized our concluding evaluative session: "I now see the immorality in many practices I simply assumed to be norms of schooling. The fact that I am only becoming aware of these after a dozen years of teaching pains me. Surely I should have been aware and doing something about them a long time ago." But teacher education is a neglected enterprise, rarely granted the time and resources required for grounding teachers in the education required for developing democratic character in the young.

The second series of teaching experiences with adults, still ongoing, that ranks in satisfaction with those of decades ago with children and youths began in the summer of 1992. I wrote earlier of the Leadership Program colleagues and I created in the Institute for Educational Inquiry to ensure in each setting of the National Network for Educational Renewal cadres of people deeply immersed in our Agenda for Education in a Democracy. We began the planning in February, and a group of eighteen delegated participants joined us six months later.

Although they were selected, we required that each provide a written statement of interest in coming and commitment to attending all four sessions, one in each quarter of the 1992–93 year. The readings sent out before the first and in between the other sessions were many and comprehensive, drawn from fields such as sociology, political science, philosophy, history, and psychology, and included novels. All participants had graduate degrees, nearly half doctorates, in a diverse array of fields. This initial group was not as evenly balanced in professional affiliations—elementary and secondary schools, colleges of education, and departments in the arts and sciences—as we had sought to obtain. Nor was it sufficiently diverse in race and ethnicity. The balance improved with each successive group until all three affiliations were nearly equally represented. We could have, later, built the entire membership with people of differing races and ethnicities. And the number holding doctoral degrees increased to 75 or 80 percent.

We knew at the outset that this was to be a challenging series of teaching experiences. I do not think we quite anticipated that it also would be a series of incredible learning experiences. Participants were our colleagues in every way, constituting as a group a rich array of life experiences—from their places of origin and present abodes, travel, reading, teaching, management, and administration. We established close personal bonds early on, bonds that promise to be lifelong. A visitor to the annual meeting of the Leadership Program's graduates, referred to as Associates (of the institute and the agenda), commented: "I have never before seen so much hugging among people coming together at a conference."

My big learning has been about learning. Because so much of one's cognitive functioning is established by the age of eight, we tend to underestimate the rest of life's learning trajectory. And we tend to underestimate the changes in belief that come from encounters with contrary ideas. In evaluative sessions and informal gatherings, many of the Associates have spoken about the degree to which deep reflection during our sessions together precipitated profound changes not only in their thinking but in their teaching.

Over the past decade, I probably have participated in a hundred and fifty of these intensive days—and perhaps that many more short formal and informal sessions stimulated by the larger core of the Leadership Program's curriculum. In all of these, I have learned a great deal about the activities of the Associates in their home settings. What emerges above all from these interactions is overwhelming awe of the commitment and dedication represented in the daily work of the teachers and administrators with whom I have had the good fortune to be associated in the nationwide settings of the NNER.

But this is not a new learning. It is, rather, confirmation of learning from earlier associations. Is there something about educational work that brings out the best in those who choose it? Or is it those who choose it that make good educational work? I assume that it is both; that positive symbioses are at work. Years ago, I was somewhat amused by the wry comment of Jerry Brown when he was governor of California and an *ex officio* member of the University of California Board of Regents. It was to the effect that professors should be less concerned about their salaries since the work in which they are involved is so good.

But I am not at all amused by the high incidence of trashing our public schools, those who work in and for them, and those who teach their teachers. A fury arises in me. This, too, is nothing new. Philosopher Alfred North Whitehead stated this matter better many years ago: "When one considers in its length and breadth the importance . . . of the education of a nation's young, the broken lives, the defeated hopes, the national failures, which result from the frivolous inertia with which it is treated, it is difficult to restrain within oneself a savage rage."[3]

The land and air routes between Los Angeles and Seattle are heavily traveled, much like those between Boston and Washington, D.C. Most of my excursions to California are connected to present and past work. Almost always, I encounter educators once associated with the League of Cooperating Schools or the Southern California Partnership. Invariably, these are lodged in their whorls of memory like lush islands in life's stream. They recall people with whom they were closely associated and what was accomplished together, and they often refer to some residue that still remains. There is nearly always wistfulness in remembering, coupled with gratification for learnings gained. They speak also of educational freedoms lost and new requirements imposed. Is this to be the future of school-based work: a period of renewal followed by one of reform and the cycle repeated?

Len and I have visited together several times the California place of past cycles in our lives. Malibu residents may have appeared to be joking when they quipped, "If you don't slide off, you'll burn off or shake off or wash off." But they mirrored reality. At about the time we were readying to leave, the young man negotiating the sale of our house was trying to save his cottage on the beach below from washing away with the highest tides and waves in many years. During the twenty-two years of living in Malibu, several wicked brush fires had licked along the edges of our property; one of the region's biggest earthquakes brought us out of our beds early one morning; and the biggest mudslide in years forced a long detour around our access road for several years. Many residents were not this lucky. Those whose houses suffered slides and earthquakes rarely rebuilt. Those who suffered fires usually did as we had done.

But I do not think we would have rebuilt a second time, as some people we knew of did. Several years after our departure, a raging fire swept away the area that had been spared before. On a later visit, we drove in from the north on Pacific Coast Highway. We began to encounter charred hills not far south of Oxnard. Then the hillside terrain began to look like one of those World War I battlefields in black-and-white movies. Past the landmark pier in Malibu, we turned into the road that would take us up the lower slopes to the scarily narrow detour winding its way around the hills to the better one leading downward to our former home.

We began to realize that, this time, the sheriff's order to evacuate would have had to come very early because the only escape route would have been toward the oncoming fire. We were shocked and saddened by what we found and did not find. There was no house. Only ashes and part of the fireplace. The surrounding terrain was like one of those battlefields. We shuddered to think of what might have been but for the gravitational pull to the Northwest—a miracle of serendipity. The cycles of schooling appear to be not unlike the cycles of human life.[4]

On one of our visits, we were able to gather for dinner at our little hotel four of the five members of a family that had become very close to us. During our years in Malibu, keeping the hillside brush away from our home had been too much for me. We were lucky to have Roberto assigned to the task by one of the nurseries that tended to such needs. Len had noticed that he was a kind of leader among the workers, picking them up in his truck each morning and dropping them off at the various residences in the area to which each was assigned for the day. But he was paid little. She asked him why he did not take on this work as his own business. He said that he had not thought of it. But he then became an independent contractor, delivering and picking up not only men who worked outside, but also women who worked inside the houses scattered about in the hills and on the beaches.

Anita, Roberto's wife, came to our house. And so began our relationship. As their children came along—Roberto Jr., Antonia, and David—Len saw to it that they got good medical care. She picked up a little Spanish, which aided the body language and various exclamations with which she and Anita communicated quite well right from the beginning. The family never failed to pay a visit on Christmas morning.

At dinner, Anita, now a citizen and driving on her own, sat like a queen with her oldest son Roberto, a lawyer, and her youngest child David. Antonia had not been able to join us. She was occupied with her studies at UCLA. Years before, I had helped Roberto Jr. steer his way through the processes of getting admitted there. The assistant dean for student affairs of the Graduate School of Education and I had learned that we had to follow up minority students who had encountered problems in the standard admission processes. White candidates who had difficulty quickly sought explanations. The Latino and Latina candidates simply disappeared.

When Roberto came out of the admissions counselor's office to say that he had been accepted as a freshman, there were three students waiting for him. They were in their sophomore or junior years. I was assured that they would take care of him. UCLA did a fine job of supporting these networks of minority students that were largely self-generating. The campus moved quickly from a heavily dominant white student body to one of considerable diversity. Roberto went on to law school. Antonia soon followed him as an undergraduate and then prepared to teach.

Four years ago, Anita, Roberto Sr., and David spent several days with us on the island. It was a wonderful visit. Roberto looked up in awe at the Douglas fir trees. "Some of them must be more than a hundred feet tall," he said. "Yes," I replied, "some are." Anita would not let Len get up to do anything. David stayed in his room most of the time, reading. A few months later, he received word of being admitted to Harvard with a tuition scholarship. Anita and Roberto, immigrant parents from Mexico, had good reason to be proud. They spoke proudly, too, of Antonia's becoming a teacher.

I have been fortunate to have had romances in teaching along the full range of our formal educational system. The most satisfying have been at the lowermost and uppermost ends. Those of the latter almost invariably lead to lifelong friendships. Some of my former students have become virtually family. Zhixin Su and Jianping Shen are two of these.

Zhixin was the interpreter assigned by the education ministry of the People's Republic of China to eight of us from the United States who visited schools and universities there a couple of decades ago. We became a close-knit group during the three weeks we were together. Zhixin had cried at the fence that separated us as we left her and boarded the train for the last short leg of our trip into Hong Kong. A couple of years later, our grants for the study of teacher education supported her master's and doctoral studies and then a postgraduate research assistantship at the University of Washington.

Jianping came from East China Normal University to join us in our work and pursue doctoral studies at about the time Zhixin was finishing.

Today, Zhixin is a professor at California State University, Northridge, and Jianping at Western Michigan University. Both have been successful in securing funds to support students in their studies.

We hear from them quite frequently and occasionally get together. Jianping never misses calling on Thanksgiving Day, Zhixin on Christmas. This past Thanksgiving, Jianping told me about the research he and some of his students are conducting on different kinds of teacher education programs. Zhixin was unable to reach us this past Christmas, but did so the day after. She and her mother had on the previous day cooked dinner for thirty people, some Zhixin's students, some visitors to the center she directs that, among other things, connects with scholars in China.

I am reminded of a brief conversation more than four decades ago in the lobby of the Hilton Hotel in downtown Chicago. The American Educational Research Association was meeting there. One of my mentors, Virgil Herrick, and I were chatting when Elliot Eisner, a leading arts educator today, joined us. I had chaired his master's and doctoral committees at the University of Chicago. This was the first time we had seen one another since he completed his dissertation. His comment to Virgil about not knowing how to thank me was virtually a query. Virgil's answer was quick and unequivocal: "Go thou and do likewise."

I think I sometimes have replied similarly when student colleagues such as Zhixin, Jianping, and others have struggled with this quandary. But Virgil's response scarcely needs articulation. It is embedded in the moral sinew of the teaching occupation and the moral language—spoken and muted—that guides its conduct.

Zhixin had been unable to reach us during the time she was free from cooking on Christmas Day because we were engaged in a telephone ritual that has taken place on that day ever since we left California. The initial greeting is invariably from Roberto Sr. When Len turned the receiver over to me, David greeted me. He would be on his way back to Harvard soon to complete the final semester of his baccalaureate. He had majored in political science. What would he do following graduation? Join the staff of a candidate for the next presidential election.

Len called out to me to get Anita on the line, but a younger voice of quite different nuances came on. It was that of Antonia—the one member of the family we had not seen or spoken with in a long time. She wanted to talk school. I learned that she hoped to begin work on her master's degree at UCLA in the fall but would try elsewhere if she could not arrange to do that and continue with her teaching.

Many of the best and most experienced teachers were quitting or intending to soon, she told me, some looking for other jobs and some taking early retirement. "Why?" I asked. "It is so discouraging," she said, "all those tests and regulations. There is no time for doing the kinds of things that would be interesting for the children, no room for creativity. But I am going to stay on. I like teaching, and the children need me."

Yes, the children need her. But both have a fundamental right to romances with the learning our schools must provide. Education is for the long term. Parents and teachers, however, view the education of the young within a short span of time. The necessary romances are contemporary. Never before have I seen teachers and teacher educators with such dismal perceptions of contemporary, politically driven expectations for schooling. Many perceive little prospect for student romances with learning or their own with teaching arising out of preparing for and taking tests. Presumably, today's disturbing excesses of the hard and tough ultimately will be blended with the soft and tender. But when?

What teachers working with the young, especially those in harsh environments, need above all else is hope—hope that their teaching will contribute significantly to their students' living good lives of learning. Then teachers will know that they do good work. To quote Samuel Johnson (from *The Idler*), "It is necessary to hope . . . for hope itself is happiness, and its frustrations, however frequent, are yet less dreadful than its extinction."[5]

That polls consistently report high-level public, especially parent, satisfaction with their *local* schools is a tribute to teachers like Antonia. What she expressed to me that Christmas morning is what most of the many aspiring teachers in our study gave as their reason for going into teaching. They are a precious resource we do shamefully little to preserve. What they represent is nicely captured in the words of James G. March, distinguished professor emeritus of four academic departments at Stanford University: "The fundamentals of being a teacher lie in a set of actions and a view of one's self that are not conditional on their consequences but on their consistency with the essential nature of being a teacher as exemplified by generations of predecessors and a thoughtful contemplation of teaching."[6]

Staying on as a teacher under daunting circumstances probably means always being able to answer "yes" to a very old question: "Thou that teachest another teaches thou not thyself?"[7]

Notes

CHAPTER 1

1. Annie Dillard introduces a major theme of my story. See her "To Fashion a Text," in William Zinnsser (ed.), *Inventing the Truth: The Art and Craft of Memoir* (Boston: Houghton Mifflin, 1987). This epigraph is from p. 57.

2. Martin views schools, as designed, more to satisfy the interests and needs of adults than of children. See Jane Roland Martin, *The Schoolhome* (Cambridge: Harvard University Press, 1992).

3. These books are classics in the field of education: Dan C. Lortie, *Schoolteacher* (Chicago: University of Chicago Press, 1975); and Philip W. Jackson, *Life in Classrooms* (New York: Holt, Rinehart and Winston, 1968).

4. For elaboration on the concept of flow, see Mihaly Csikszentmihaly, *Flow* (New York: HarperCollins, 1990).

5. Benjamin S. Bloom's book, *Stability and Change in Human Characteristics* (New York: Wiley, 1964), considered to be one of the most significant books on education of the 1960s, has stood the test of time.

CHAPTER 2

1. The epigraph is taken from Laurent A. Parks Daloz, Cheryl H. Keen, James P. Keen, and Sharon Daloz Parks, *Common Man* (Boston: Beacon, 1996), p. 31.

2. These views are taken from Neil Postman's *Building a Bridge to the Eighteenth Century: How the Past Can Improve Our Future* (New York: Knopf, 1999).

3. For more on boundary breaking in schooling, see Neil Postman and Charles Weingartner, *Teaching as a Subversive Activity* (New York: Delacorte Press, 1969). The quotation is from p. xiv.

4. I refer later to this deep structure of schooling. See Barbara Benham Tye, *Hard Truths: The Deep Structure of Schooling* (New York: Teachers College Press, 2000).

5. Among classics in education is Alfred North Whitehead, *The Aims of Education* (New York: Macmillan, 1949). The quotation is from p. 29.

6. For more data from our observations of classrooms, see John I. Goodlad, M. Frances Klein, and Associates, *Behind the Classroom Door* (Worthington, Ohio: Charles A. Jones, 1970). See particularly Chapter Three.

7. Sizer envisions the places secondary schools should be, not what most are. See Theodore R. Sizer, *Places for Learning, Places for Joy* (Cambridge: Harvard University Press, 1973).

CHAPTER 3

1. Harold Reid and Don Reid, "The Class of '57" (1972), found on the album entitled *The Best of the Statler Brothers* (New York: Phonogram, Inc., PolyGram Records, Inc., 1975).
2. The apt description, "shopping mall high school," was introduced in the book by Arthur G. Powell, Eleanor Farrar, and David K. Cohen, *The Shopping Mall High School* (New York: Macmillan, 1984).

CHAPTER 4

1. Ralph W. Tyler was mentor to thousands of people in all walks of life. The citations are from interviews conducted just before his death by Diana Buell Hiatt, "No Limit to the Possibilities: An Interview with Ralph Tyler," *Phi Delta Kappan* 75 (June 1994): 786, 788; and Louis J. Rubin, "Ralph W. Tyler: A Remembrance," *Phi Delta Kappan* 75(June 1994): 789.
2. For more on Jayber's life at Pigeonville College, see Wendell Berry, *Jayber Crow* (Washington, D.C.: Counterpoint, 2000), pp. 46–54.
3. Most of the leaders in the ongoing debate to which I refer come to life in the book by Ellen Condliffe Lagemann, *An Elusive Science* (Chicago: University of Chicago Press, 2000).
4. For a fascinating, comprehensive history of this intellectualism of the working class, see Jonathan Rose, *The Intellectual Life of the British Working Class* (New Haven, Conn.: Yale University Press, 2001).
5. These categories of systems of knowledge and knowing of the human conversation are adopted from Kenneth E. Boulding, *The World as a Total System* (Newbury Park, Calif.: Sage, 1985).

CHAPTER 5

1. Sir Ernest Barker, *Age and Youth* (London: Oxford University Press, 1953), p. 292.
2. For a more detailed account of my foray into progressive education, see John I. Goodlad, "Coping with Curriculum," in Philip W. Jackson (ed.), *Contributing to Educational Change* (Berkeley, Calif.: McCutchan, 1988), pp. 180–181.

CHAPTER 6

1. Alfred North Whitehead, *The Aims of Education* (New York: Macmillan, 1929), p. 29.
2. There is now a large and comprehensive body of literature on guiding the learning of individual children in class situations. A useful primer for parents

and teachers is provided by Benjamin S. Bloom, *All Our Children Learning* (New York: McGraw-Hill, 1981). See especially Chapter 8.

CHAPTER 7

1. William Glasser, *Schools without Failure* (New York: Harper & Row, 1969), p. 26.
2. The common use of standardized achievement tests tends to obscure rather than highlight these critically important individual differences. See John I. Goodlad and Robert H. Anderson, *The Nongraded Elementary School*, rev. ed. (New York: Teachers College Press, 1987); and Robert H. Anderson and Barbara Nelson Pavan, *Nongradedness: Helping It to Happen* (Lancaster, Penn.: Technomics, 1993).

CHAPTER 8

1. Wendell Berry, *Jayber Crow* (Washington, D.C.: Counterpoint, 2001), p. 69.
2. Nobody has captured better the phenomena of rain in the coastal Northwest than David Laskin, *Rains All the Time* (Seattle: Sasquatch Books, 1997).
3. John Dewey, *The Sources of a Science of Education* (New York: Horace Liveright, 1929), p. 33.
4. For further information on the AATES, see John I. Goodlad and Floyd Jordan, "When School and College Cooperate," *Educational Leadership* 7 (April 1950): 461–465; and John I. Goodlad and Floyd Jordan, "The Atlanta Area Teacher Education Service," *Educational Administration and Supervision* 37 (October 1951): 329–336.
5. For a full report on findings, conclusions, and recommendations, see John I. Goodlad, "Some Effects of Promotion and Nonpromotion Upon the Personal and Social Adjustment of Children," *Journal of Experimental Education* 22 (June 1954): 301–328.
6. Regarding the concept of nongrading, see John I. Goodlad and Robert H. Anderson, *The Nongraded Elementary School* (New York: Harcourt Brace, 1959); reissued with a new introduction (New York: Teachers College Press, 1987). See also, Robert H. Anderson and Barbara Nelson Pavan, *Nongradedness: Helping It to Happen* (Lancaster, Penn.: Technomic, 1993).
7. Prescott's considerable role in the book he used as a resource is not clear: Commission on Teacher Education, *Helping Teachers Understand Children* (Washington, D.C.: American Council on Education, 1945).
8. See Chapters 6 and 7, by Caroline Tryon and Jesse W. Lilienthal III, on the concept of developmental tasks in Association for Supervision and Curriculum Development, *Fostering Mental Health in Our Schools*, ASCD Yearbook (Washington, D.C.: The Association, 1950).
9. These persistent life situations of children are detailed in Florence Stratemeyer et al., *Developing a Curriculum for Modern Living* (New York: Bureau of Publications, Teachers College, Columbia University, 1947); and 2nd edition (New York: Teachers College, Columbia University, 1957).

10. Prescott's views on the centrality of childhood become clear in Daniel A. Prescott, *The Child in the Educative Process* (New York: McGraw-Hill, 1957).

11. The quotation is from James B. Conant, *Two Modes of Thought* (New York: Trident Press, 1964), p. 30.

CHAPTER 9

1. The epigraph on educational change with which this chapter opens grew out of our work with the League of Cooperating Schools referred to near the end of this chapter and discussed in more detail in Chapter 10. The book by Mary M. Bentzen (published by McGraw-Hill in 1974) is one of a half-dozen reporting this project.

2. For a short but informative description of the Englewood Project, see M. Frances Klein and John M. Bahner, "Curriculum Change in Concert: The Englewood School Project," in Kenneth A. Sirotnik and Roger Soder, *The Beat of a Different Drummer* (New York: Peter Lang, 1999), pp. 29–44.

3. An underlying assumption of "the workshop way of learning" that came into full bloom in the 1950s and is virtually a convention of in-service education in many fields today is one of building on the assets of participants. They bring both practical and theoretical knowledge that adds to whatever is brought by those convening the workshops and "experts" brought in as consultants. Nonetheless, this assumption has not eliminated the popularity of the lecture.

4. I deliberately chose not to be in Englewood when Lee Zimmerman and, later, John Bahner began their first years as principals of the Englewood School. Teachers and parents knew me and would have, to a degree, turned to me for leadership. Lee and John were best served by clearly being the designated leaders and not yielding to me.

5. For descriptions of schools struggling to be "good enough," as Sara Lawrence-Lightfoot puts it, for their circumstances, see her *The Good High School* (New York: Basic Books, 1983).

6. For more information, please see Note 6 of Chapter 8.

7. John Bahner's doctoral program was the last I chaired at the University of Chicago. He worked on revisions of the dissertation almost up to the time of my departure for California late in the summer of 1960. The material quoted is from pages 99 and 100 of his "An Analysis of an Elementary School Faculty at Work: A Case Study," unpublished doctoral dissertation, University of Chicago, 1960.

8. The remarkable rise of the University of California during these years is recounted by Clark Kerr in a highly readable two-volume memoir, *The Gold and the Blue* (Berkeley: University of California Press, 2001 and 2003).

9. Other than for beginning and ending the day, there were no schoolwide scheduled times at the UES. Teachers decided when to take breaks for their classes. In addition, they were not interrupted by announcements piped into classrooms electronically at intervals throughout the day.

10. In her book, *Cultural Miseducation* (New York: Teachers College Press, 2002), Jane Roland Martin addresses the critically important question of what cultural liabilities should be dropped and what assets sustained through education in a democratic society.

11. See John I. Goodlad, M. Frances Klein, and Associates, *Behind the Classroom Door* (Worthington, Ohio: Charles A. Jones Publishing Co., 1970) for this report on schooling as we observed it during what was then regarded as a period of robust change.

CHAPTER 10

1. In *Education Lost: Reflections on Contemporary Pedagogical Practice* (Toronto, Ont.: OISE Press, 1989), David Solway describes the emptiness of mechanical teaching "methods" devoid of grounding in deep reflection regarding the necessary nature and mission of the entire educative context. The epigraph is from p. ix.

2. Wendell Berry, *Life Is a Miracle* (Washington, D.C.: Counterpoint, 2000), p. 152. Berry concludes his book with further thoughts on this powerful human continuity: "This living procession through time in a place *is* the record by which such knowledge survives and is conveyed. When the procession ends, so does the knowledge," (p. 153).

3. My paraphrasing of Howard Gardner comes from his "The Quality and Quantities of Educational Research," *Education Week* 4 (September 2002): 49, 72.

4. I am grateful to those many, many people—far too many to list here—who have been partners and colleagues, some long-term, in the educational journey I have tried to describe. Without them, there would be little to recount. The names of several of the many are included simply because they played major roles in episodes deeply embedded in my whorls of memory.

5. I am indebted to Naomi Klein for her concept of the "colonization of mental space," as she elegantly states it, that often transpires from the teaching of this cultural surround. See Jane Slaughter's interview of Klein in *The Progressive* 66 (October 2002): 33–37.

6. Ulich's *Education and the Idea of Mankind* (New York: Harcourt, Brace & World, 1964) was one of three books on the idea of mankind we managed to produce before the council's finances ran out.

7. Much of what we did and learned in the conduct of this work is described in our book: John I. Goodlad, M. Frances Klein, Jerrold M. Novotney, Kenneth A. Tye, and Associates, *Toward a Mankind School: An Adventure in Humanistic Education* (New York: McGraw-Hill, 1974). I was fortunate in being able to bring to it what I was learning from an international initiative I had launched that, like the council's experience with funding, was not carried very far because of the lack of needed resources.

8. The agreement effected in 1966 and a revised version confirmed by all parties three years later constitute Appendixes B and C in my 1975 report on the

conduct and accompanying study of the league, *The Dynamics of Educational Change* (New York: McGraw-Hill). Part of the revised agreement reads as follows: "The League seeks to implement a strategy for change based upon the assumption that the single school is a viable agent for change, *given certain supportive conditions*" (emphasis added).

9. The books in chronological order of their appearance as the McGraw-Hill Series on Educational Change are as follows: Carmen M. Culver and Gary J. Hoban (eds.), *The Power to Change* (1973); David A. Shiman, Carmen M. Culver, and Ann Lieberman (eds.), *Teachers on Individualization* (1974); Richard C. Williams, Charles C. Wall, W. Michael Martin, and Arthur Berchin, *Effecting Organizational Renewal in Schools* (1974); Mary M. Bentzen and Associates, *Changing Schools* (1974); Kenneth A. Tye and Jerrold M. Novotney, *Schools in Transition* (1975); and John I. Goodlad, *The Dynamics of Educational Change* (1975).

10. Backed by world opinion, the warring parties avoided civilian targets during the early phase of World War II. But that subsequently changed. One American estimate of the later phases places the death toll of the area bombings of Germany at 305,000 noncombatants. The report of Anne-Lies Schmidt appears on page 78 of Jonathan Glover's moral history of the twentieth century, *Humanity* (New Haven: Yale University Press, 2000).

11. Coleman's federally commissioned report so shook the people in the office of U.S. Commissioner of Education Harold Howe (and, indeed the commissioner himself) that its presentation to President Johnson was delayed for a couple of weeks. See James S. Coleman, *Equality of Educational Opportunity* (Washington, D.C.: Government Printing Office, 1966).

12. The reference here is to John I. Goodlad, "Schooling and Education," in Robert M. Hutchins and Mortimer J. Adler (eds.), *The Great Ideas Today 1969* (Chicago: Encyclopaedia Britannica, Inc., 1969), pp. 101–145. The quotes are, in order, from pages 125–126 and 101.

13. The quoted words of Robert M. Hutchins are taken from his "The Great Anti-School Campaign," in Robert M. Hutchins and Mortimer J. Adler (eds.), *The Great Ideas Today 1972* (Chicago: Encyclopaedia Britannica, Inc., 1972), p. 54.

CHAPTER 11

1. John Dewey's *The Sources of a Science of Education* (New York: Horace Liveright, 1929) is frequently cited in the scholarly literature but has been largely ignored in educational research. The quotation is found on pp. 26, 33.

2. Historian Richard Hofstadter grouped the several themes of the proposals to broaden the curriculum of the secondary school to be more inclusive of and connected with the interests of an increasingly diverse student body under the rubric "life adjustment" education. He was more evenhanded in his criticism than were many other critics in that he recognized the challenge of making a school for the few into a school for the many. But he was deeply disturbed by

what he saw as writing off the intellectual potential of the many by moving them along through flaccid, nonchallenging programs. See especially Chapter 13, "The Road to Life Adjustment" in his *Anti-Intellectualism in American Life* (New York: Knopf, 1964).

3. My thanks to friend and colleague Mary M. "Maxie" Bentzen who referred to our work with the League of Cooperating Schools as seeking to tidy our minds in an untidy world.

4. There is for each of these studies a single volume reporting findings, conclusions, and recommendations. In chronological order, see my *The Dynamics of Educational Change* (New York: McGraw-Hill, 1975); *A Place Called School* (New York: McGraw-Hill, 1984; reissued 2004); and *Teachers for Our Nation's Schools* (San Francisco: Jossey-Bass, 1990).

5. Kenneth A. Sirotnik and Associates, *Renewing Schools and Teacher Education* (Washington, D.C.: American Association of Colleges for Teacher Education, 2001).

6. Abraham Flexner, *Medical Education in the United States and Canada* (New York: Carnegie Foundation for the Advancement of Teaching, 1910).

7. The quotation regarding America as a collection of multiple communities is from Kenneth A. Sirotnik. He goes on to argue for the role of public education in contributing to a moral ecology that binds these communities together. See his "Society, Schooling, Teaching, and Preparing to Teach," in John I. Goodlad, Roger Soder, and Kenneth A. Sirotnik (eds.), *The Moral Dimensions of Teaching* (San Francisco: Jossey-Bass, 1990), p. 307.

8. See National Commission on Excellence in Education, *A Nation at Risk* (Washington, D.C.: Government Printing Office, 1983).

9. The three books referred to are Ernest L. Boyer, *High School* (New York: Harper & Row, 1983); Theodore R. Sizer, *Horace's Compromise: Redesigning the American High School* (Boston: Houghton Mifflin, 1984); and John I. Goodlad, *A Place Called School* (New York: McGraw-Hill, 1984; reissued 2004).

10. Neil Postman succinctly portrays the accompanying distortion of the aims of education and its potential consequences when economic utility becomes the guiding narrative of schooling. See his book, *The End of Education* (New York: Knopf, 1995).

11. For the report ranking schools of education, see Allan Cartter, "The Cartter Report on the Leading Schools of Education, Law, and Business," *Change* 9 (February 1977): 44–48.

12. For the history of these ten leading schools of education, see Geraldine J. Clifford and James W. Guthrie, *Ed School* (Chicago: University of Chicago Press, 1988).

13. See Harry Judge, *American Graduate Schools of Education* (New York: Ford Foundation, 1982).

14. My thinking had been very much influenced by the writing of sociologist Paul F. Lazarsfeld who saw the need for organized arrangements to advance neglected, inadequately recognized, or currently important areas of human interest or

concern. See his *Organizing Educational Research* (Englewood Cliffs, N.J.: Prentice-Hall, 1964). In his later book, *The Creation of Settings and the Future Societies* (San Francisco: Jossey-Bass, 1972), Seymour B. Sarason saw the necessity of such new settings being staffed with a core group of "worriers" joined in common purpose.

CHAPTER 12

1. Howard Gardner and his colleagues note that, in the "flow experiences" of good work, "we feel totally involved, lost in seemingly effortless performance." *Good Work: When Excellence and Ethics Meet* (New York: Basic Books, 2001), p. 5.

2. For a report on the early beginnings of this first iteration of the National Network for Educational Renewal, see Kenneth A. Sirotnik and John I. Goodlad (eds.), *School-University Partnerships in Action* (New York: Teachers College Press, 1988).

3. I have referred several times to this deep structure and am indebted to Barbara Benham Tye for her analysis of it in her *Hard Truths: The Deep Structure of Schooling* (New York: Teachers College Press, 2000).

4. For the nature of this good and the role of education in contributing to it, see John I. Goodlad and Timothy J. McMannon (eds.), *The Public Purpose of Education and Schooling* (San Francisco: Jossey-Bass, 1997).

5. This concept of a moral ecology links especially to the writing of Robert N. Bellah and others, *Habits of the Heart: Individualism and Commitment in American Life* (New York: Harper & Row, 1985). See especially pages 284 and 335.

6. This revised agenda has guided the NNER without challenge and with only minor revisions since the early 1990s. Components and its ethical and moral grounding have been presented in more than a dozen books and a clutch of journal articles and other publications. Its basic features and much of the reasoning behind them are summarized in a book entitled simply *Education for Everyone: Agenda for Education in a Democracy* (San Francisco: Jossey-Bass, 2004).

7. We viewed staff members in these teaching partner schools to be members of the teacher education faculty brought together in centers of pedagogy as equals. See Richard W. Clark, *Effective Professional Development Schools* (San Francisco: Jossey-Bass, 1999); and Robert S. Patterson, Nicholas M. Michelli, and Arturo Pacheco, *Centers of Pedagogy* (San Francisco: Jossey-Bass, 1999).

8. Benjamin R. Barber, "Public Schooling: Education for Democracy," in Goodlad and McMannon (eds.), *The Public Purpose of Education and Schooling*, p. 22.

9. The teacher of many of us regarding change and the culture of educational and other types of institutions is Seymour B. Sarason. See his *The Culture of the School and the Problem of Change*, 2nd ed. (Boston: Allyn & Bacon, 1982).

10. The book from which the quotation is taken regarding the apprenticeship in adulthood to be provided by schools provides an interesting but controversial history of the status of children over a considerable period of time. See Philippe Ariès, *Centuries of Childhood*, trans. R. Baldwin (New York: Vintage Books, 1962). The quotation is from page 413.

11. The quote attributed to former Assistant Secretary Susan Neuman was reported in the October 25, 2002, edition of *The Record*, Stockton, California.

12. Benjamin S. Bloom, *Stability and Change in Human Characteristics* (New York: Wiley, 1964).

13. I have not seen a better portrait of what this safety net would look like here in the United States than the one developed years ago by a California task force, *Early Childhood Education* (Sacramento: California State Department of Education, 1972).

14. The Economic Policy Institute has published a superb, research-based report on the preschool factors that result in many children having been left behind before they reach the starting gate of schooling. See Valerie E. Lee and David T. Burkam, *Inequality at the Starting Gate* (Washington, D.C.: Economic Policy Institute, 2002). Please note that the entrance age factor is one I have added to the authors' analysis of social background differences among children entering school.

15. I see here the productive joining of Jane Roland Martin's concept of *The Schoolhome* referred to in Chapter 1 and the highly refined attention to individual interest and talent represented in Eliot Levine's *One Kid at a Time: Big Lessons from a Small School* (New York: Teachers College Press, 2002).

16. I have adapted these from Boulding's *The World as a Total System* (Newbury Park, Calif.: Sage, 1985) in a proposed curriculum grounding for the general education of all teachers. See my "The Learner at the World's Center," *Social Education* 50 (October 1986): 424–436.

AFTERWORD

1. Roger Soder, "Education for Democracy," in John I. Goodlad, Roger Soder, and Timothy J. McMannon (eds.), *Developing Democratic Character in the Young* (San Francisco: Jossey-Bass, 2001), p. 188.

2. I remember clearly, however, the tearful, yet also celebratory, gathering attended by hundreds of educators in the Southern California Partnership to extend best wishes to Paul, just before the Heckman family left for Maine. I think they sensed not only that they were losing the caring attention he had given them but also that the partnership itself was entering a period of uncertainty, just as it was becoming important in their lives.

3. Alfred North Whitehead, *The Aims of Education* (New York: Mentor Books, 1949), p. 26.

4. Interestingly, there have been since our coming to Seattle a major earthquake, mudslides that have pushed houses into Puget Sound, and fires not far distant that have destroyed both houses and thousands of acres of spectacular trees like those that so fascinated Roberto, referred to later.

5. Thanks, Roger, for leading me to Samuel Johnson. The quotation is from Samuel Johnson, *The Idler*, edited by W. J. Bate, John M. Bullitt, and L. F. Powell, vol. 2 of *The Yale Edition of the Works of Samuel Johnson* (New Haven, Conn.: Yale University Press, 1963), p. 182.

6. James G. March, "Yo sé quien soy" ("I know who I am"), in Kenneth A. Sirotnik and Roger Soder (eds.), *The Beat of a Different Drummer* (New York: Peter Lang, 1999), pp. 281–282.

7. I found this concluding question on the cloth cover of a little book written by George Ricks of London, England, published in the How to Teach series by D.C. Heath & Co, Boston, 1893.